FIXED-INCOME ARBITRAGE

WILEY FINANCE EDITIONS

FINANCIAL STATEMENT ANALYSIS
Martin S. Fridson

DYNAMIC ASSET ALLOCATION
David A. Hammer

INTERMARKET TECHNICAL ANALYSIS
John J. Murphy

INVESTING IN INTANGIBLE ASSETS
Russell L. Parr

FORECASTING FINANCIAL MARKETS
Tony Plummer

PORTFOLIO MANAGEMENT FORMULAS
Ralph Vince

TRADING AND INVESTING IN BOND OPTIONS
M. Anthony Wong

THE COMPLETE GUIDE TO CONVERTIBLE SECURITIES WORLDWIDE
Laura A. Zubulake

MANAGED FUTURES IN THE INSTITUTIONAL PORTFOLIO
Charles B. Epstein, Editor

ANALYZING AND FORECASTING FUTURES PRICES
Anthony F. Herbst

CHAOS AND ORDER IN THE CAPITAL MARKETS
Edgar E. Peters

INSIDE THE FINANCIAL FUTURES MARKETS, 3RD EDITION
Mark J. Powers and Mark G. Castelino

RELATIVE DIVIDEND YIELD
Anthony E. Spare

SELLING SHORT
Joseph A. Walker

TREASURY OPERATIONS AND THE FOREIGN EXCHANGE CHALLENGE
Dimitris N. Chorafas

THE FOREIGN EXCHANGE AND MONEY MARKETS GUIDE
Julian Walmsley

CORPORATE FINANCIAL RISK MANAGEMENT
Diane B. Wunnicke, David R. Wilson, and Brooke Wunnicke

MONEY MANAGEMENT STRATEGIES FOR FUTURES TRADERS
Nauzer J. Balsara

THE MATHEMATICS OF MONEY MANAGEMENT
Ralph Vince

THE NEW TECHNOLOGY OF FINANCIAL MANAGEMENT
Dimitris N. Chorafas

THE DAY TRADER'S MANUAL
William F. Eng

OPTION MARKET MAKING
Allen J. Baird

TRADER VIC II: PRINCIPLES OF MARKET ANALYSIS AND FORECASTING
Victor Sperandeo with T. Sullivan Brown

TRADING FOR A LIVING
Dr. Alexander Elder

FIXED-INCOME ARBITRAGE
Analytical Techniques and Strategies

M. Anthony Wong

in collaboration with
Robert High

Wiley Finance Edition
JOHN WILEY & SONS, INC.
New York • Chichester • Brisbane • Toronto • Singapore

Copyright © 1993 by John Wiley & Sons, Inc.

Library of Congress Cataloging-in-Publication Data

Wong, M. Anthony
　　Fixed-income arbitrage : analytical techniques and strategies / M. Anthony Wong, in collaboration with Robert High.
　　　　p.　　cm. – (Wiley finance editions)
　　Includes index.
　　ISBN 0-471-55552-5 (cloth)
　　1. Fixed-income securities.　2. Program trading (Securities)
　　I. High, Robert.　II. Title.　III. Series.
　　HG4651.W64　1993
　　332.63′2044—dc20　　　　　　　　　　　　　　　　　　　　　92-45088

Printed in the United States of America

10 9 8 7 6 5 4 3 2 1

Dedicated to my mother, Kam-so,
my wife, Alice,
and my daughter, Frances

Foreword

Few advances in modern finance have produced as profound an effect as arbitrage.

This investment activity, which identifies and then acts on the price and value disparities between securities or markets, has become the force that links otherwise disparate financial instruments together.

Through arbitrage techniques, sophisticated traders can enhance portfolio investment returns, hedge away unwanted inventory price risk, and pursue speculative profits. In each task, investors must demonstrate a high degree of market knowledge before they can even begin to seek out the relative value disparities at the root of all successful fixed-income arbitrage programs.

But this is easier said than done. Although there are certainly different approaches, a comprehensive arbitrage program involves the decomposition, analysis, and ultimate reconstruction of a financial instrument into its component parts. Through this exercise, sophisticated investors can more clearly see the mechanics and, ultimately, the specific price and value disparities at any point in a financial instrument's design and pricing.

Although arbitrage is sometimes criticized as a disruptive investment activity because of the effects it is said to have on seemingly unrelated markets or instruments, this stigma is unearned. Arbitrage practices in modern finance seek to identify statistically-proven relationships that exist not only between market instruments, but also between markets themselves. In many cases, this has not only produced better hedging, risk management, and inventory control practices, but also led to the development of new investment products that are better suited to modern financial practices.

In this book, *Fixed-Income Arbitrage: Analytical Techniques and Strategies*, M. Anthony Wong, in collaboration with Robert High, has advanced the literature in fixed-income arbitrage by offering a solid foundation for a better understanding of this important new area.

This book presents the rationale, foundation, and basic tools needed to analyze fixed-income instruments, including those found in the cash and derivatives markets. To illustrate many points further, the book also includes specific case histories.

The scope of this book is impressive because it includes current areas of opportunity in the cash and derivatives markets, including options and futures. The book also devotes a section to fixed-income arbitrage technology, in the form of fixed-income analytics, decision support, and trading systems, which has helped make new applications in arbitrage accessible to a larger audience. This section is especially attractive because few investment books discuss the role of technology, which has probably done more to advance modern finance than any other single factor.

At the tactical and strategic levels, the book includes mathematical models and algorithms useful for studying the yield curve and for pricing option-like securities, including profitable opportunities in options arbitrage and yield-curve arbitrage.

This book is inclusive in content and impressive in scope, but it is also an important work in advancing the critical role of arbitrage in the global fixed-income markets. There has been much rhetoric about the importance of a global fixed-income marketplace, but few proponents have done anything to explain how this market actually works. This book is a welcome exception. It will increase the level of understanding about current global fixed-income market mechanics and open new opportunities for innovative instruments and risk management practices. Few books can hope to accomplish more.

Michael Moss
President, Index Futures
Chicago, Illinois

Preface

"Bond Arbitrage Trader Was Paid Over $20 Million in 1990!"

From this and other similar headlines, readers of the financial press, including Wall Street practitioners and Main Street observers, cannot help wondering how arbitrage traders and hedge fund operators consistently generate significant profits for their employers and investors. Most outsiders perceive arbitrage trading as a highly sophisticated computer game played by "rocket scientists" equipped with technologically advanced "black boxes." This book is written to unveil part of the myth often associated with *fixed-income arbitrage*.

Fixed-income securities trading can be viewed as a multiple-person game whose players include issuers, dealers, brokers, nonleveraged institutional investors, and the highly leveraged speculators and arbitrageurs. Profit opportunities exist because different participants have different objectives, constraints, market outlooks, and skill levels. Riskless arbitrage opportunities occur infrequently, if at all, in the secondary market. Arbitrage traders instead make money by consistently identifying relatively mispriced securities and executing relative-value spread trades with attractive risk/reward ratios. Successful fixed-income arbitrageurs are actually masters in **relative-value trading** who have perfected their skills through experience, hard work, and continual self-improvement.

Relative-value trading involves the simultaneous buying of a relatively cheap security and selling short of a relatively rich security. For example, two U.S.

Treasury issues with similar investment characteristics (coupon and maturity, or duration and convexity) are expected to have similar prices; otherwise, there would be low-risk profit opportunities because the two prices must eventually become very similar. To dealership traders, relative-value analysis provides an important tool for hedging away unwanted inventory risks, whereas sophisticated portfolio managers use relative-value trades to enhance their portfolios' investment returns. This book is written for financial professionals who are interested in acquiring an in-depth knowledge of relative-value trading. These professionals include (1) dealership traders and their sales forces, (2) proprietary traders in banks, securities firms, and hedge funds, and (3) investment managers of insurance, mutual, and pension funds. This book is also intended for finance students and other newcomers to the fixed-income securities markets; it attempts to provide a systematic introduction to the various aspects of securities trading in the debt market.

This book assumes that you have some basic background in financial markets, but mathematical sophistication is not a prerequisite. It aims to provide a detailed and practical treatment of relative-value analysis and its applications in the fixed-income securities market. This is not a treatise on fixed-income financial theory, but two chapters are included that describe in detail most of the widely used analytics and some of the more advanced mathematical models and algorithms. A related chapter is devoted to the use of analytics and computer technology on the fixed-income trading floor. For each arbitrage strategy presented in this book, the underlying thought process, the associated risk/reward analysis, and the relevant money management discipline will be illustrated using specific examples.

HOW THIS BOOK IS STRUCTURED

This book is focused on fixed-income arbitrage. Chapter 1 presents a set of arbitrage scenarios to illustrate the variety and complexity of the arbitrageur's activities. Chapter 2 provides some background information on the U.S. fixed-income securities markets, with a section devoted to the rapidly growing bond markets in Europe and Asia.

The basic tools that are routinely and extensively used in analyzing fixed-income instruments are provided in Chapter 3. Advanced mathematical models and computational algorithms, useful for studying the yield curve and for pricing option-like securities, are discussed in Chapter 4; also included is a section on models that have been specifically developed to evaluate mortgage-backed and other asset-backed securities. Chapter 5 presents three approaches to the implementation of quantitative analytics on the computerized trading floor. A case study in the development of a trading system is provided in the Appendix to that chapter.

Consistently profitable opportunities that frequently arise in the short-maturity sector of the U.S. debt markets are presented in Chapter 6. "Squeeze play" is the most important risk factor for most short-maturity arbitrage trades, and its adverse impact is demonstrated by a detailed case study of the infamous 1991 two-year note squeeze. Classic relative-value trades in the intermediate- to long-maturity sector, including yield-curve spreads, basis trades, and cross-market plays, are given in Chapter 7; their applications in foreign bond markets are also discussed. In Chapter 8, option arbitrage strategies and relative-volatility trades are illustrated with examples. The important role played by options in all relative-value trading is also specified.

Arbitrage trading is a business whose success is critically dependent on many factors, including capital commitment, degree of leverage, and quality of infrastructure and personnel. Ultimate success, however, depends on excellent teamwork, including strong management support, excellent strategies, and top-notch execution. These points are addressed in Chapter 9.

M. Anthony Wong
Scarsdale, New York

Acknowledgments

I would like to thank Karl Weber of John Wiley & Sons for convincing me to write this book, especially because most of my colleagues and friends working in the arbitrage business discouraged me from finishing it. I was fortunate to have Bob High's help in writing this book. He wrote most of Chapter 4, and was also responsible for organizing the materials in Chapters 2, 3, and 5. Special thanks go to Alice Au, Gerald Chan, David Lambert, Laura Lomurno, and Michael Yip for reading early drafts of the manuscript. I have benefited from numerous discussions with many current and former colleagues, but their desire to remain anonymous will be honored; I am grateful to all of them.

Contents

1

A Repertoire of Arbitrage Techniques

Making money in securities dealing and/or proprietary trading with little or no risk fits most pragmatists' definition of arbitrage. This chapter presents a set of arbitrage scenarios to illustrate the variety and complexity of arbitrageurs' activities. Examples of primary market arbitrage via innovative financial engineering are presented first. Esoteric products, including mortgage and options derivatives, structured and distributed by pioneering bond dealers and other market makers (mostly banks), have brought significant profits to these firms, which enjoy substantial technological and knowledge-based advantages. Although riskless arbitrage opportunities seldom arise in the secondary markets, a few classic examples are included to illustrate the basic principle and the practical complexities. Relative-value traders generally take on significantly higher risks while trying to profit from mispriced yield or price spreads; equipped with "statistical arbitrage" strategies, these traders aim to be consistently profitable by repeatedly exploiting significant price or yield discrepancies among related financial instruments.

"'Yield Curve Arbitrage' Rewards the Skillful" was the headline of a *Wall Street Journal* article that appeared on July 27, 1989. The reporter, Craig Torres, described how traders at Bear, Stearns & Company made a "$20 million pot of gold through a little understood and often lucrative strategy that bond professionals call *yield curve arbitrage*." This chapter presents a set of arbitrage

1

scenarios, including yield-curve arbitrage, that are often referred to as **fixed-income arbitrage**. As the reader will soon realize, however, some of the activities conducted by so-called fixed-income arbitrageurs do not deserve to be termed *arbitrage* at all. (For an excellent description of the meaning and history of the term *arbitrage*, see Weisweiller, 1986.)

PRIMARY MARKET ARBITRAGE VIA INNOVATIVE FINANCIAL ENGINEERING

In financial economics, a market is said to be relatively "complete" when there is enough variety of liquid assets that virtually any eventuality can be either bet upon or protected against with a selected subset of these assets. The introduction of options, for example, makes the financial markets more complete because of the unique timing and risk/reward characteristics of options. Similarly, financial innovations, including stripped securities, swaps, index-linked debts, and collateralized mortgage obligations (CMOs), enhance the market's completeness. The pioneering firms that structured and distributed these innovative products made handsome profits via **primary market arbitrage**, at least during the early stage of each product's life cycle. Although price competition is certain to reduce the profit margin over time, firms that can also provide efficient execution will make up much of the margin decline through increased volume.

Stripped Treasuries

Securities stripping is an important tool for financial engineers. Traditional securities including stocks, Treasury bonds, and mortgage-backed securities, have all been stripped to create derivative securities that cater to the demand of certain institutional and individual investors. A steady supply of issuers, who are always looking for tax/accounting, credit spread, and riskless arbitrage opportunities, is also necessary for these financial innovations ultimately to become successful.

The market for zero-coupon Treasuries has grown significantly since 1981. The process in which a Treasury security's principal amount due at maturity is separated from its semiannual coupon payments is termed "Treasury stripping." Each of the separated coupon payments, as well as the principal amount, becomes a new zero-coupon security that makes a single payment on its own maturity date.

Unlike a Treasury issue whose coupon interests have to be reinvested at the prevailing interest rates on the future coupon dates, zero-coupon bonds offer investors an opportunity to lock in the market yield at the eventual rate of return without having to worry about reinvestment risks. Strong demand for the high-credit stripped Treasuries has come from domestic pension fund managers, insurance companies' asset/liability managers, and individuals investing for their retirement or their children's educations. Because foreign bonds have a maximum maturity of 10 years or less, foreign investors, especially Japanese insurance companies and pension sponsors, have also become steady buyers of zero-coupon Treasuries.

Banks were the main issuers of stripped Treasuries in the 1970s. For tax purposes, the prevailing cost basis for Treasury bonds was allocated entirely to the bond's principal portion. To execute a tax/accounting arbitrage, a bank would strip Treasury securities in its portfolio and, depending on the circumstance, either accelerate income by booking the profits obtained from selling off the coupon strips (taxable gain was equal to the net present value of the strips sold) and retaining the principal or, conversely, book a tax loss by selling only the bond's principal portion. By the late 1980s, bond dealers became the major issuer of stripped Treasuries. The pioneering dealers realized in the early 1980s that they could sell the stripped components at a combined price much higher than the underlying bond's market price; attractive profits were made even after deducting significant transaction costs related to inventory hedging, administration (legal and accounting), and distribution. (For a detailed description of the zero-coupon Treasuries market, see Kluber and Stauffacher, 1986.)

Stripping is an example of market innovation via financial engineering. Its ultimate success depends on two critical factors. First, the new product has to meet some previously unfilled niche and complete the market. In this case, the zero-coupon bond's lack of reinvestment risk appeals to both domestic and foreign pension fund and insurance portfolio managers; the introduction of stripped Treasuries also enhanced the value of the underlying bonds as increasing numbers of bonds were bought to be stripped. Second, there has to be a strong financial incentive for issuers to continue supplying the new product. In this instance, commercial banks became the issuers when they wanted to take advantage of the tax/accounting arbitrage opportunity that existed in the 1970s, and bond dealers have since been stripping Treasuries as part of their primary market arbitrage activities.

Collateralized Mortgage Obligations

The phenomenal success of collateralized mortgage obligations (CMOs) indicates that their introduction represented a truly significant innovation and that they satisfied some previously unmet investor demands. First introduced by the Federal Home Loan Mortgage Corporation (FHLMC) with the sale of a $1 billion issue in June 1983, hundreds of billions of CMOs have been sold by a variety of other issuers, including government agencies, thrifts, homebuilders, insurance companies, mortgage banks, and arbitrage corporations. Because of their popularity, CMOs have effectively revolutionized the sources and methods by which homes are financed.

A CMO's "collaterals" are residential mortgage pools, guaranteed either by FHLMC, Federal National Mortgage Association (FNMA or "Fannie Mae"), or Government National Mortgage Association (GNMA or "Ginnie Mae"). Because homeowners have the right to prepay at any time, a mortgage pool's cash-flow timing is uncertain, unlike a Treasury bond's, and is subject to educated guesswork. Investors in mortgage-backed securities are therefore exposed to the risk that homeowners will prepay at the most inopportune time—when re-investment rates are much lower than the original mortgage rates.

The cash inflows received by the CMO issuer from the mortgage collaterals are divided according to some pre-specified rules and allocated to several "tranches" of bonds. Consider a classic CMO with four tranches. The first tranche bond pays a stated interest on its quarterly coupon dates; if the underlying mortgage pool prepays, holders of the first tranche bonds will also receive prepayments that reduce the tranche's outstanding principal amount. Meanwhile, the second and third tranche bonds also pay their stated coupon interests at regular intervals. No principal prepayment, however, will be made to holders of these tranches until the first tranche ceases to exist; when that happens, all subsequent prepayments are then allocated to the second tranche holders only. In successive fashion, holders of each tranche will receive prepayments as its immediate predecessor tranche retires. The last tranche of a typical CMO is an accrual bond, or Z-bond, which pays no interest or principal until *all* the early tranches have ceased to exist.

To protect against bond default, the AAA-rated CMOs are always over-collateralized to ensure that all the promised tranche payments will be covered under the "worst case combination" of future prepayment patterns and interest rate paths. The difference between the underlying collaterals' cash flows and the eventual tranche payments is the CMO's **residual**. Because the worst case scenario never occurs, the residual's internal rate of return represents the issuer's financial incentive to undertake the risk and expense of initiating a CMO.

Few debt investors would consider residential mortgage pools as ideal portfolio assets; these pools' *expected* maturities belong in the intermediate sector, but they could become short-term investments via unexpectedly fast prepayment. However, CMOs are derivatives of their underlying mortgage pools, composed of several tranches with different coupons, maturities, and prepayment risks, that are targeted to specific short-, intermediate-, and long-end debt investors. The Z-bond, with its expected long maturity, appeals to pension fund managers, and the first tranche, with its qualification as a liquidity investment, has attracted thrift and bank portfolio managers. Insurance companies, on the other hand, are steady buyers of the middle tranches. Again, CMOs represent a successful innovation because they provide a combination of risk and reward that is impossible to replicate via investment in other existing debt securities.

Government housing agencies, homebuilders, mortgage securities dealers, insurance companies, banks, and thrifts are regular CMO issuers. For example, CMOs were important financing vehicles for homebuilders in the middle 1980s because of the prevailing tax and accounting rules. A CMO issuer in this case was the homebuilder's finance subsidiary, which supplied mortgages to buyers of their homes. For accounting purposes, the homebuilder could record a gain on the sale of a home financed by the subsidiary, but could recognize that income over the mortgage loan's lifetime for tax purposes. CMO (primary market) arbitrage, meanwhile, was extremely profitable for the innovative dealers who created the original structures; CMO residuals were generating internal rates of return well over 20 percent during the first few years of CMOs' existence. (Because of over-collateralization, CMO arbitrage's profitability is measured by its residual's internal rate of return; a high return indicates a much stronger demand for the CMO tranches than for the underlying mortgage collaterals.) CMO arbitrageurs began peddling residuals to institutional investors when years of fierce competition eventually drove down the residuals' return to unattractive (to the dealers, but not to some low tax-bracket investors) levels. Finally, because the underlying collaterals for CMOs can be eliminated from the issuer's financial statement, by current accounting standards, CMO issuance is an efficient and effective way for banks, thrifts, and insurance companies to move massive amounts of mortgage assets off their balance sheets. With financial institutions, especially banks and insurance companies, looking to strengthen their financial ratios in the past years, there has been a steady proliferation of asset-backed securities, including instruments backed by receivables such as credit card and car loan payments.

Remarks

1. In primary markets where innovative products such as mortgage derivatives are initiated and distributed, well-capitalized dealers, who have invested the time and effort to develop the infrastructure and technology needed to create, evaluate, and hedge such complex instruments, consistently generate handsome profits because of their substantial technological and knowledge-based advantages.

2. A by-product of market innovation is that it provides new profit opportunities for secondary market arbitrageurs. With the introduction of zero-coupon bonds and CMOs, for example, arbitrage traders could start monitoring the relative value of the Treasury strips and the CMO tranches with respect to other related instruments, including similar-duration Treasuries and their derivatives.

SECONDARY MARKET ARBITRAGE: CLASSIC EXAMPLES

Arbitrage traders make their money on excessively mispriced interest-rate spreads; they borrow money at the risk-free rate, if possible, and lend money at rates much higher than their borrowing rate. To accomplish this, arbitrageurs are constantly looking for lucrative interest-rate differentials embedded in the relationships among financial instruments and their derivatives (including futures and options), usually with the aid of advanced analytics and computer technology. Stock index arbitrage, options arbitrage, and credit spread arbitrage are classic examples in which embedded interest-rate differentials are routinely exploited by arbitrageurs.

Basis Trading

The price of a Treasury bill (T-bill) future contract and that of the only cash Treasury bill deliverable against the contract will always converge on the last trading day of the future contract (contract date). A profit opportunity arises when a significant price (or yield) difference exists between a future contract and its underlying cash bill, after adjusting for the cash bill's carrying cost (the difference between its market yield and its repo rate–based financing cost) from today's settlement date to the contract date. If a trader *goes long the bill basis* by simultaneously selling short a T-bill contract and buying long the deliverable bill, the resulting trade is mathematically equivalent to being **long the cash bill's implied (or embedded) repo rate from today's settlement date to the contract date**. Consequently, this basis trade is an arbitrage if the cash bill's **actual repo rate** for the same time period is *lower than* the cash bill's **implied repo rate** embedded in the trade. Conversely, an arbitrageur will *go short the bill basis* by simultaneously buying long a T-bill contract and selling short the deliverable bill if it is determined that the contract is excessively cheap *relative* to its deliverable cash bill, which happens when the cash bill's actual repo rate from today's settlement date to the contract date is *higher than* the cash bill's implied repo rate for the same period. If the future contract is fairly priced against its deliverable cash bill, then going short (or long) the bill basis is mathematically equivalent to betting that the cash bill's implied repo rate, which is a measure of short-term interest rate, is going up (or down). The bill basis trade can therefore be viewed as a synthetic money market instrument.

Although a handful of Treasury notes are deliverable against each two-year note future contract, the cheapest-to-deliver issue for short-sellers of the future contract can be readily identified by an arbitrageur's proprietary relative-value analytics. The distinctive feature of the two-year note basis trade is that the cheapest-to-deliver issue usually remains unchanged throughout a future contract's active trading life, even if the market prices (or yields) and volatilities of the deliverable Treasury notes change drastically. Consequently, as in bill-basis trading, a profit opportunity exists when a significant price (or yield) difference exists between the future contract and its cheapest-to-deliver issue, after adjusting for the issue's carrying costs to the expected delivery date in the contract month. Again, the arbitrageur will buy long the excessively cheap instrument (a future contract, for example) and simultaneously sell short the relatively rich instrument (the cheapest-to-deliver note, for example). Similar to the bill basis, the two-year note basis trade can be used as a synthetic money market instrument to make a directional bet on short-term interest rates.

It is difficult to spot a riskless bill-basis arbitrage, and a two-year note basis arbitrage is tricky to execute even when the opportunity exists. However, through continuous monitoring of a combination of these two basis trades and other short-term interest rate investments, executable arbitrage trades can often be identified.

The cheapest-to-deliver issue for short-sellers of a Treasury bond (T-bond) future contract often changes in identity as the yields of, and the yield spreads among, the deliverable issues change over time. A T-bond basis trade, therefore, consists of four component bets: (1) bond yield level, (2) local yield-curve configuration, (3) forthcoming bond market volatility, and (4) the costs of carrying the deliverable issues to the expected delivery date in the contract month. Profit opportunities arise when any one or more of these components are excessively mispriced. An arbitrageur will buy a deliverable issue's basis (that is, buy the cash issue and sell a weighted amount of the future contract), if it is determined that this basis is underpriced, after adjusting for the prevailing market volatility level and for the issue's carrying cost to the expected delivery date in the contract month. If the market volatility component of the bond basis is mispriced, the arbitrageur will also use bond options to exploit this profit potential. Opportunities in the five-year and ten-year note basis trades are similarly identified, using the arbitrageur's proprietary model for evaluating the various interest rate options embedded in the delivery process of the future contracts. Basis trading was one of the bread-and-butter strategies for U.S. fixed-income arbitrageurs in the early 1980s, when few market participants knew how to properly evaluate the future contract's various embedded options.

Options Arbitrage

By combining (1) the sale of a call option, (2) the purchase of a put option with the same strike price and expiration date, and (3) the purchase of the underlying cash or future instrument for the options, a trader is said to have executed a **conversion** trade. A **reverse conversion** trade, on the other hand, involves (1) the purchase of a call, (2) the sale of a put with the same strike and expiration date, and (3) the sale of the underlying cash or future instrument for the options. These simple arbitrage strategies require little arithmetic skill; they occur when an option position (for example, long a call) and its synthetic equivalent (for example, short a put and short the underlying instrument) are trading at different prices, after adjusting for any difference in interest costs.

Suppose that a T-bond contract can be sold at a price of $103^{60}/_{64}$. Calls, with a strike price of 102, expiring in three months, are offered at $3^{16}/_{64}$; puts with the same strike and expiration date have a $1^{23}/_{64}$ bid. With these prices, a reverse conversion trade can be executed by selling the future contract, buying a call, and also selling a put. The combined position has a riskless profit of about $2/_{64}$, calculated as follows:

The three-month interest cost of the trade's initial $1^{57}/_{64}$ cash payout, based on a 3.25 percent risk-free rate, is about $1/_{64}$. The reverse conversion position, excluding interest cost, gives a payout of $3/_{64}$ no matter what the T-bond contract price is at the close of trading on the option's expiration date. For example, if the contract's settlement price is 102 on the option's expiration date, then (1) the short T-bond position will bring a $1^{60}/_{64}$ gain, (2) the call option will expire worthless and bring a $3^{16}/_{64}$ loss, (3) the put option will also expire worthless and bring a $1^{23}/_{64}$ gain. The net gain is therefore $3/_{64}$ and the result is the same no matter what the T-bond contract's settlement price is on the option's expiration date. Stated in another way, the reverse conversion position effectively earns a riskless $3/_{64}$ interest in three months, while the financing cost of the trade's initial cash outlay of $1^{57}/_{64}$ is only $1/_{64}$.

In the United States, several hedge funds and securities firms made handsome profits in the early 1980s by consistently executing this type of simple-minded "black box" arbitrage in the equity option markets, and in the fixed-income markets, dealers and options market makers have also successfully employed these strategies. Opportunities in mispriced conversions and reverse conversions, when they occur, are not readily exploitable by most off-the-exchange or non-dealer traders. Proprietary arbitrageurs, equipped with advanced computers and telecommunication equipment, continuously monitor, identify, and profit by eliminating such opportunities.

Other Classics

Stock Index Arbitrage. Stock index arbitrage is equity's version of basis trading. Price discrepancies between a stock index future contract and a market basket of securities that have high market value correlation to the underlying index are exploited by arbitrageurs who will *sell a stock index contract and buy the cash stock basket* if the future contract is excessively *overpriced* relative to the underlying cash market index. Conversely, arbitrageurs will buy a stock index and sell the cash stock basket if the future contract is relatively underpriced.

Credit Spread Arbitrage. Treasury bills are regarded as riskless investments because they are backed by the full faith and credit of the U.S. government, whereas the London Inter-Bank Offered Rate ("LIBOR rate") reflects interbank credit risks. Consequently, the LIBOR rate is always higher than the yields of Treasury issues with the same maturity; otherwise a credit spread arbitrage would exist. Similarly, the yield of a Japanese government bond (JGB) should always be lower than that of a debt instrument issued by a Japanese corporation. But in the early fall of 1988, for example, the 10-year JGB future contracts actually traded at a yield almost 50 basis points *higher* than the fixed-side yield of a 10-year Japanese yen-based interest rate swap. Because JGB future contracts have much better credit than the financial institutions or corporations paying the swap's fixed-side interest, such an interest rate discrepancy presented a clear *credit spread arbitrage* opportunity for alert traders. In fact, by November 1988, the JGB future contract's yield settled back to levels far below those of the corresponding swap yield, after the various arbitrage firms had collected their profits.

Remarks

Quantitatively oriented arbitrageurs have also reaped significant profits in the past decade from trading convertible bonds and warrants in the U.S. and Japanese markets. More recently, profit opportunities existed in the creation and market making of exotic and/or long-dated options. Finally, closed-end fund arbitrage, in which an excessively mispriced publicly listed fund is traded against the fund's own portfolio holdings, also proved fruitful to the resourceful arbitrageurs.

STATISTICAL ARBITRAGE BASED ON RELATIVE-VALUE ANALYSIS

In the mature, highly liquid, technologically sophisticated U.S. fixed-income markets, classic arbitrage opportunities are practically nonexistent, yet fixed-income arbitrage continues to generate consistent profits. Instead of waiting for the infrequent riskless opportunities, the pragmatic arbitrageur (also known as a "relative-value trader") would take on some risks while still trying to profit consistently from mispriced yield or price spreads among related financial instruments. In effect, the risk arbitrageur, or relative-value trader, looks for risk that is itself mispriced by the market. Relative-value traders would put on a spread trade when the yield discrepancy is determined to be statistically significant, whereas the "purist" arbitrageur would wait for the mispriced spread to get so excessive that a riskless scenario arose before taking any action. By repeatedly spotting statistically significant price or yield spreads and executing the corresponding relative-value trades with attractive risk/reward characteristics, the relative-value trader expects to be consistently profitable because the odds are generally in the trader's favor. The risk-averse purist, on the other hand, is content to forgo the profits (and losses) generated by statistical arbitrage opportunities that frequently exist.

Intermarket Yield Spreads

Consider the credit-spread arbitrage examples described in the last section. Suppose that the 10-year JGB future/swap yield spread had historically traded within the 5 to 45 basis points range. A relative-value trader would have bought the spread when it first traded below 5 basis points, whereas a purist would have waited and bought this spread only after it became negative. Although both traders would make money eventually (the purist's profit would be larger), the relative-value trader obviously took on a bigger risk. On the other hand, if the spread never became negative and instead traded back to its historical median of 20 basis points, the purist would have missed a good risk/reward trade.

For another example of statistical arbitrage based on intermarket spreads, consider the yield difference between a Treasury note and a similar-duration Treasury bill in the 9-to-12-month maturity sector. The Treasury note usually trades at a higher yield than the comparable bill because of the Treasury bill's greater liquidity; this yield spread has a historical normal trading range of zero to 28 basis points. For the relative-value trader, a statistical arbitrage opportunity arises when this spread trades below 3 basis points or above 25 basis points. For example, on January 3, 1989, the 10-month bill and note both traded at the same 9.08 yield, and two months later, the then 8-month bill traded at a yield 20 basis points lower than that of the then 8-month Treasury note.

In addition to the yield curve for Treasury bills and notes, short-end relative-value traders also monitor the "Eurodollar strip" yield curve, which can be constructed mathematically from the prices of the strip of Eurodollar future contracts. Eurodollar future contracts are the most liquid financial instruments in the world, and a contract's ending value on its last trading day (contract date) is the same as the prevailing 90-day LIBOR rate. Since LIBOR rates reflect interbank credit risks and therefore contain some risk premium, the Eurodollar strip curve has yields consistently higher than the corresponding yields on the Treasury coupon curve. A statistical arbitrage opportunity arises when the credit spreads trade beyond their normal trading range. For example, during the first two weeks of March 1989, the strip consisting of the front three Eurodollar contracts traded excessively cheap to the Treasury coupon curve. This discrepancy was caused primarily by a series of economic indicators suggesting that the U.S. economy might be facing significant inflationary pressure. There were also a few large leveraged buyout deals, including the RJR Nabisco transaction, to be financed during that month, adding upward pressure on short-term interest rates. The highly liquid Eurodollar contracts, especially the front strip, went down much faster than other money market instruments, creating the profit opportunity.

In the intermediate maturity sector, since the mid-1980s, statistical arbitrageurs have been paying a lot of attention to the yield spreads between the current coupon GNMA securities and the 7- and 10-year Treasury notes. Because of GNMA's prepayment risk, the level of this cross-market spread depends on many factors, including (1) interest-rate levels (and the spreads among them) along the yield curve, (2) supply and demand of GNMA securities, and (3) yield volatility levels. In late 1986 and early 1987, for example, when GNMA securities were outrageously underpriced because of excessive prepayment fear, innovative arbitrageurs made huge profits by buying long current coupon GNMAs, selling short weighted amounts of 7- and/or 10-year Treasury notes, and hedging them with relatively cheap long option positions.

Yield-Curve Arbitrage

Instead of betting on intermarket interest-rate spreads, yield-curve arbitrageurs focus their attention on the yield spreads among Treasury issues with maturities ranging from three months to 30 years. For example, on October 22, 1990, anticipating that the Federal Reserve Bank would start aggressively easing monetary policy, a trader expected that the yield spread between the 30-year Treasury bond and the 2-year note would increase from the prevailing 93 basis points level. To bet on and profit from the anticipated yield-curve movement, the trader could **buy the yield curve** by, say, buying $100 million 2-year notes and simultaneously selling short $16.8 million 30-year bonds.

If the yield of the 2-year note moved up (or down) 1 basis point, a $1 million long position would lose (or gain) about $177.00; in other words, the 2-year note's *value-of-a-basis-point* was $177.00 per million. Similarly, the 30-year bond's value-of-a-basis-point was $1,053.40 per million. By weighing the trade with $0.168 million (equal to $177/$1,053.40) of the 30-year bond against $1 million of 2-year notes, the yield curve trader made sure that the combined position was a bet *only* on the yield spread between the two issues; the trade would break even if the yields of both issues went up (or down) by the same amount. It should be noted, however, that the difference between the two issues' carrying costs is a critically important component of a yield-curve trade. In our example, this yield spread traded at 105 points on November 17, 1990, 12 basis points higher than the October 22, 1990, level. The trader would have made, excluding carrying costs, approximately $212,400, which is equal to $100 million (2-year-note) × 12 basis points (profit) × $177 (2-year note's value-of-a-basis-point), or equivalently, $16.8 million (30-year bond) × 12 basis points (profit) × $1,053.4 (30-year bond's value-of-a-basis-point).

This type of yield-curve trading can never be considered a mathematical arbitrage. The two component securities of the trade are only marginally related to one another, and neither provides an effective hedge of the other. The shapes of the yield curve and the yield spreads among Treasury issues with very different maturities are often significantly affected by specific political/economic events, including (1) actual and perceived monetary policy change executed or to be executed by the central bank, (2) political events such as an "energy crisis" that may affect inflationary expectations, (3) supply and demand imbalance of Treasury issues, and (4) extraordinary investment behavior of influential market participants. Risk managers are arguably prudent in considering yield-curve arbitrage trades as speculative bets; indeed, many yield-curve traders use technical charts, standard tools for speculators, to support their trading decisions. Successful yield-curve arbitrage traders (and there are quite a few) are usually experienced and knowledgeable about market irregularities and seasonalities, perceptive and/or well informed about the prospective behavior of major institutions, and extremely disciplined.

Statistical arbitrageurs operating *within* the short- and intermediate-maturity sectors of the yield curve often employ **rolling-down-the-yield-curve** strategies to exploit irregularities in *local* yield curve. The risk and reward characteristics of this type of local yield-curve arbitrage are discussed in Chapter 6 and Chapter 7. Unlike the "big picture" yield-curve arbitrage described above, the excessively mispriced yield spreads identified by the local strategy have much better defined boundaries.

Relative Volatility Analysis in Options Trading

The only unobservable input to an option-pricing model is the underlying financial instrument's volatility between the current and expiration dates. For a selected model, and with the values of all other input parameters completely specified, the price of an option can be computed given the underlying instrument's volatility; inversely, the instrument's *implied volatility* can be found given the option's price. The forthcoming volatility of a financial instrument, and hence the fair value of its options, is unknown and can only be estimated. Options traders often track a security's past volatilities, but historical volatility is normally not a good estimate of forthcoming volatility because a security's volatility varies erratically over time. Relative-value traders focus their attention on implied volatilities, not because these volatilities provide accurate estimates of future volatility, but because they can be used to judge the *relative* cheapness or richness of an option, either against other options on the same underlying instrument or against options on other related securities.

Options versus Underlying Futures.   Every naked, or unhedged, option position has exposure to delta (market direction), gamma (actual market volatility), theta (time decay), and vega (implied volatility) risks. The relative-value trader continuously monitors the various options markets, seeking to identify options that are trading at implied volatilities significantly higher or lower than the expected forthcoming volatility of the underlying instrument. To take advantage of an underpriced option, the trader will buy long that option and simultaneously sell short a "delta-weighted" amount of the underlying instrument. The resulting "delta-neutral" position will have no market directional risk (delta = 0), relatively small time decay (theta is slightly negative), and little exposure to the risk of lower implied volatilities (vega is slightly positive). Because of its positive gamma, this trade may generate significant profits if the underlying instrument's price fluctuates widely in its remaining trading life. Conversely, the trader will sell short an overpriced option and simultaneously buy long a "delta-weighted" amount of the underlying contract.

Options versus Other Options on Same Underlying Contract.   To take advantage of an underpriced call option, the relative-value trader may also buy a delta-weighted amount of the correspondingly underpriced put option on the same underlying instrument. In effect, the trader will be buying a cheap and hedged "straddle" (or "strangle," if the call and put options have different strike prices) to take advantage of the call and put options' low implied volatilities. Moreover, if call (or put) options with different strike prices on the same financial instrument trade at drastically different implied volatilities, the trader may buy or sell a "ratio call (or put) spread" by buying the cheaper option (with the lower implied volatility) and selling a weighted amount of the richer option to capture the mispriced volatility spreads.

Relative-value option traders, as illustrated in Chapter 8, want to take advantage of relatively mispriced options. They do not want any unnecessary market risk in their trade positions. The best approach to hedging an option's position is to use other options that are most similar to it. This way, the trader can eliminate most, if not all, of the other risks and can wait to make a profit when the relatively mispriced options eventually become fairly priced. Moreover, if the identified option is relatively overpriced, it should be hedged with options that are relatively underpriced; if no underpriced options can be found, then some fairly priced ones should be used.

Importance of Options in Fixed-Income Arbitrage. As discussed in Chapter 7, optionality is an unavoidable component of many of the classic relative-value trades. For example, because of the delivery options embedded in the T-bond and T-note contracts, cash-versus-futures basis trading in Treasury notes and bonds combines the components of local yield-curve arbitrage, repo trading, interest rate directional bet, and volatility analysis. Another example is mortgage-backed securities, with their cash-flow characteristics largely dependent on the behavior of the homeowners who hold the prepayment options. The lesser-known implicit optionality of some of the standard arbitrage strategies is presented in Chapter 8.

Remarks

Arbitrage affects the debt markets in a number of ways. Most notably, it helps make the markets more *efficient* because by definition it detects relative mispricings and, by increasing demand for "cheap" securities relative to "rich" ones, acts to bring them into equilibrium. Arbitrage also acts to keep the markets efficient by putting competitive pressure on firms and traders less able to accurately price and/or hedge certain securities, who will find themselves on the losing end of a series of arbitrage trades until they learn the market's lessons or are driven out of it. Less evident, perhaps, are the pressures exerted by arbitrageurs, along with other hedges, to *complete* the market, by introducing or demanding new instruments and combinations of instruments designed to detect and reflect more subtle market features and distortions. Future contracts, options, asset-backed securities, interest-rate swaps, caps and floors, and other derivatives have become essential tools of the arbitrageur, and the markets in such securities have benefited from the vigorous development of fixed-income arbitrage activities.

Arbitrage analysis and risk management are similar in that they both require successful "reverse financial engineering." A risk manager must know how to break down a portfolio into its risk components and evaluate the individual risks. Similarly, arbitrageurs must determine explicitly the risks embedded in each trade's various components. In fixed-income securities trading, the major risk categories are: (1) interest rate level, (2) shape of the yield curve, (3) carrying costs when borrowing or lending securities, (4) volatility level, for options and securities with embedded options, and (5) specific spread risk (for example, credit spread). The presentation of fixed-income arbitrage strategies in the later chapters includes discussions relating to the identification and evaluation of risk components. A guide to the marketplace and to the relevant analytics needed for performing the appropriate risk analysis is provided in the immediately following chapters.

REFERENCES

Relatively little has been written on fixed-income arbitrage and relative-value trading. A collection of articles on arbitrage can be found in Weisweiller (1986). A detailed description of yield-curve arbitrage can be found in Breaks (1986).

Breaks, Jackson D. (1986). "Yield Curve Arbitrage and Trading," in *The Handbook of Treasury Securities* (F. J. Fabozzi, ed.), Chicago: Probus, pp. 183–214.

Kluber, T. J., and Stauffacher, T. (1986). "Zero Coupon Treasury Securities," in *The Handbook of Treasury Securities* (F. J. Fabozzi, ed.), Chicago: Probus, pp. 267–296.

Weisweiller, Rudi (1986). *Arbitrage,* New York: John Wiley & Sons.

2

The Global Fixed-Income Securities Markets

To understand fixed-income securities trading, the trader should first be familiar with the fixed-income markets, their structures, participants, and idiosyncracies. This chapter analyzes the fixed-income securities markets of relevance to arbitrage trading, beginning with the various U.S. Treasury securities, which include Treasury bills, notes, bonds, and their corresponding futures contracts and options thereon. Asset-backed securities are surveyed next, together with their derivatives, followed by an overview of the foreign bond markets. Finally, a description of the principal market participants, their roles, and goals is presented.

STRUCTURE OF THE U.S. TREASURY SECURITIES MARKET

The U.S. Treasury issues marketable securities, including Treasury bills, notes, and bonds, on a regular schedule to finance government spending and debt (budget deficits). These securities ("Treasuries") are backed by the full tax powers of the U.S. government. The Treasury issues short-term debt instruments (bills) in maturities from 30 days to a year on a regular basis. Issuing maturities for notes and bonds range from 2 to 30 years. All these securities are actively traded in the secondary market.

Treasury securities are widely held as investments because of the high credit of the U.S. government, the liquidity of their secondary market, their large outstanding volume, and the broad range of maturities. As of January 1991, the total volume of marketable U.S. government securities outstanding was about $2.2 trillion (Mayer, 1991). Interest income from these instruments is not subject to state and local taxation, although it is subject to full taxation as ordinary income by the federal government. All these factors, and the fact that these securities represent a dollar-denominated stake in the U.S. economy, make Treasuries extraordinarily attractive to many foreign and domestic institutional investors. Holders of these securities include foreign governments and agencies, domestic and foreign banks and other non-banking financial institutions, industrial corporations, and pension and mutual funds.

U.S. Treasury Securities: The Primary Market

The U.S. Treasury market is one of the biggest and most active financial markets in the world. Daily trading volume exceeds $100 billion, with over $2.3 trillion in total securities outstanding. The most important participants in the Treasury market are the elite club of 39 firms that have been granted "primary dealer" status by the Federal Reserve Bank of New York. The Treasury Department, via regularly scheduled auctions, sold new debt directly to primary dealers, who entered bids either on their own account or on behalf of institutional customers (other banks and securities houses). In October 1991, as a result of admitted violations of auction procedures by a handful of Salomon Brothers traders, the Treasury announced that it would open the auction process up to a wider range of bidders, but in practice it is expected that the primary dealers will continue to be the major direct buyers of government debt.

Primary dealers are required to participate in every auction and to maintain a certain average level of participation, typically bidding for about 3 percent of each issue. The primary dealers then resell the securities they have purchased — whether at a profit or at a loss — in the secondary market, to non-primary dealers and institutional investors. Again, primary dealers must maintain a certain level of activity in the secondary market (1 percent market share) to guarantee their dealership status. Primary dealers are required to report the status of their operations to the Federal Reserve Bank of New York each business day, and are subject to regular audits by the National Association of Securities Dealers (NASD).

The U.S. Treasury, through the Federal Reserve System, has established several regular *auction cycles,* thus guaranteeing a certain stability in the timing of issuance of new debt of various maturities. Occasionally, the government will also issue *cash management bills,* with maturities up to six months. Maturity dates are set to coincide with those of existing T-bills to facilitate the trading of such securities in the secondary market. Details of the auction process, and of the different classes of U.S Treasury securities, are given below.

The Auction Process.   Treasury *bills* (T-bills) are discount securities, with no coupon payments, issued by the Treasury with maturities of no more than one year. Securities with issuing maturities greater than one year are *coupon* securities, making semiannual coupon payments. The annual coupon (as a percent of face value) is specified before the issue, and an amount equal to half the annual coupon is paid to the investor every six months. Treasury *notes* are coupon securities that are issued with a maturity of ten years or less, while Treasury *bonds* are issued with a maturity of more than ten years.

The marketable Treasury securities are issued regularly on an auction basis with the assistance of the Federal Reserve System. For example, every Monday the Treasury auctions 91-day and 182-day T-bills and issues them by the following Thursday, and every fourth Thursday it auctions a 52-week T-bill, making it available the following Thursday. Since 1983, T-bills have been auctioned on a bank discount basis, where the bids for the bills are ordered from lowest to highest until the total issue is filled. Non-competitive bids, or *tenders*, may also be entered, specifying a quantity but no discount level. Such bids are filled at the average price of the successful competitive bids.

Bonds and notes are auctioned on a yield basis. Bids are ranked lowest to highest and then filled, starting from the lowest. The average yield of the successful bids is used to determine the coupon of the new bond; the annual coupon is set just below this average yield bid (the next lowest round $\frac{1}{8}$ percent), so new bonds are issued at a slight discount to par. Occasionally, the Treasury will also *reopen* an existing note or bond issue currently trading close to par; such issues are auctioned on a price basis, as their coupon has already been set.

Treasury Bills.   With over $200 billion brought to market annually, T-bills represent about 40 percent of the total marketable securities issued by the Treasury. They are negotiable, noninterest-bearing securities with an original maturity of either 13, 26, or 52 weeks. Bills are offered in denominations of $10,000, $15,000, $100,000, $500,000, and $1 million, in book-entry form only.

Bills are always issued at a discount price, and this price is determined in auctions conducted by the Federal Reserve Bank. Investors in T-bills pay a discount price, but receive the full face value of the bill at maturity. This gain is treated as interest income for federal tax purposes, but is exempt from state and local taxation.

T-bill prices are quoted in *discount yields* to their maturity dates. Suppose a bill with N days to maturity is currently priced at P percent of its face value, that is, at $\$P$ per $\$100$ face value. That bill has a discount yield D defined as

$$D = \frac{360}{N} \times \frac{100 - P}{100} \tag{2.1}$$

To compute the actual price P in percent of the face value, use the formula

$$P = 100 \times \left(1 - \frac{N \times D}{360}\right) \tag{2.2}$$

Note that bill calculations always use a *360-day year*.

The return on a bill held to maturity is also often stated in terms of its bond equivalent yield Y. For bills with less than six months to maturity, this is just the *simple interest* on the bill:

$$Y = \frac{365}{N} \times \frac{(100 - P)}{P} \tag{2.3}$$

or, equivalently:

$$Y = \frac{365}{(360 - N \times D)} \times D \tag{2.4}$$

For bills with more than six months to maturity ($N > 182$), a different formula is used to determine the bond equivalent yield. Bond equivalent means semiannual compounding. So, one solves for the rate Y that, for a starting principal of P, would yield 100 at the end of N days if a coupon of $P \times Y/2$ were paid after six months and reinvested to maturity along with the principal at the rate Y. The equation to be solved is

$$100 = P \times \left(1 + \frac{Y}{2}\right) \times \left(1 + \frac{Y}{2}\left(\frac{2N}{365} - 1\right)\right) \tag{2.5}$$

Expanding, one gets a quadratic equation in Y, which can be solved to give

$$Y = \frac{-\dfrac{2N}{365} + 2\sqrt{\left(\dfrac{N^2}{365}\right) - \left(\dfrac{2N}{365} - 1\right)\left(1 - \dfrac{100}{P}\right)}}{\dfrac{2N}{365} - 1} \tag{2.6}$$

Example 2.1

Consider an 84-day $100,000 face value T-bill with a discount yield of 8.16 percent with $N = 84$ days, $D = 0.0816$, and the price P in percent of the face value computed using Equation (2.2):

$$P = 100 \times \left(1 - \frac{84 \times 0.0816}{360}\right) = 98.096$$

The actual price of the bill will be $98,096. If the bill is held to maturity, its bond equivalent yield, from Equation (2.3), is

$$Y = \frac{365}{84} \times \frac{100 - 98.096}{98.096} = 0.0843 = 8.43\%$$

■

Treasury Bonds and Notes. Treasury notes are coupon-bearing securities with original maturity of not less than one year and not more than 10 years, while bonds have an original maturity of more than 10 years. Both are issued in bearer, registered, and book-entry form, and usually come in denominations of $1,000, $5,000, $10,000, $100,000, and $1 million. Some outstanding bonds are *callable*—redeemable at the issuer's will—five years before maturity, but no notes are callable. The regular issue of four-year notes was terminated in 1991. Currently, the Treasury issues two-year and five-year notes on a regular monthly cycle, while other maturities are issued periodically depending on Treasury needs. For example, in the second week of February 1989, the Treasury issued $10.22 billion in three-year notes, $9.7 billion in 10-year notes, and $9.5 billion in 30-year bonds in its regular refunding auction. Because Congress has imposed a 4.25 percent lid on the rate the Treasury may pay on bonds, and has recently granted only minor exemptions from this lid, the Treasury has not been issuing many new bonds; however, some bonds are typically offered at quarterly refunding dates, often by reopening an old issue. Because of past bond sales, there is a large volume of bonds outstanding, and the secondary markets for both bonds and notes are very liquid.

Bonds and notes are issued through auctions on a yield basis. The bids are ranked lowest to highest and then filled, starting from the lowest. The coupon rates of new notes and bonds are, therefore, determined by the interest-rate market. Investors in these issues are entitled to a regular sequence of semi-annual coupon payments, and to the face value of the issue at maturity. The ratio of the value of the coupon payments made in a year to the face value of the issue is called its *coupon rate*. The future income stream from an issue is determined by its principal value, coupon rate, and maturity date, so these instruments are known as *fixed-income* securities. For example, the owner of

$1 million worth of the U.S. Treasury (UST) 9.125 percent coupon issue that matures on May 15, 2018 will receive $45,625 every May 15 and November 15 up through May 15, 2018; on that date, the owner will also receive the $1 million face value of the issue.

Treasury notes and bonds are quoted in secondary-market trading on a price basis in a special form. A quotation of [100.02] means that the price is $100\,{}^{2}/_{32}$ percent, or 100.0625 percent of the face value. The actual purchase price, or *invoice price* (sometimes also called the *dirty price*) of the bond is the quoted price plus the *accrued interest* since the last coupon payment. Accrued interest for Treasury notes and bonds is determined by the formula

$$\text{Accrued} = \frac{\text{Coupon} \times \text{Actual days}}{2 \times \text{Days in coupon period}} \tag{2.7}$$

For example, the accrued interest on the 9.125 percent issue of 2018 mentioned above on July 4, 1989, would be

$$\text{Accrued} = \frac{9.125 \times 50}{2 \times 184} = 1.24$$

The *yield-to-maturity* of a bond or note is often quoted along with the market price; this yield is defined as the semiannually compounded discounting interest rate that makes the net present value of an issue's future income stream equal to its current market price. The formula connecting price and yield is

$$\text{IP} = \frac{100}{[1 + (y/2)]^{N-1+(d/D)}} + \sum_{k=1}^{N} \frac{C/2}{[1 + (y/2)]^{k-1+(d/D)}} \tag{2.8}$$

where IP = invoice price (including accrued interest)
  N = number of remaining coupon payments
  C = annual coupon in percent terms
  d = actual number of days to the next coupon payment
  D = number of days in the current coupon period
  y = annual yield in decimal terms

If this calculation is performed on a coupon date, it simplifies to

$$\text{IP} = \frac{100}{[1 + (y/2)]^{N}} + \sum_{k=1}^{N} \frac{C/2}{[1 + (y/2)]^{k}} \tag{2.9}$$

In the terminology of financial theory, this yield is the bond's "internal rate of return."

Note that unlike bill calculations, calculations for notes and bonds use a 365-day year and take into account variations in the actual length of coupon periods, which can be from 181 to 184 days, in computing fractional parts.

Zero-Coupon Bonds.   A zero-coupon bond (ZCB) is, as the name suggests, one that makes *no* coupon payments; its cash flows consist of a single "balloon" payment of the face value at maturity. ZCBs are priced at issue at a deep discount from par. Since they have only one cash flow, their bond equivalent (semiannually compounded) yield to maturity can easily be calculated from the issue price P. If the ZCB matures in N years, its yield is calculated by solving

$$\frac{100}{P} = \left(1 + \frac{Y}{2}\right)^{2N} \tag{2.10}$$

Zero-coupon bonds were introduced in the early 1980s, in a climate of very high (up to 16 percent) prevailing interest rates. They were attractive to investors for several reasons. First, for *some* investors they present significant tax advantages. Second, because there is only one payment, at maturity, they *lock in reinvestment rate;* the conventional yield-to-maturity of a coupon security assumes that coupon payments can be reinvested throughout the life of the instrument at the same rate, a generally unrealistic assumption; yield on coupon instruments is therefore exposed to *reinvestment risk* that does not exist for ZCBs. Third, again because their payment is concentrated at maturity, ZCB prices are highly sensitive to fluctuations in interest rates. (In terms of the analytical tools discussed in Chapter 3, ZCBs have a *duration* equal to their maturity—the longest possible duration short of a "negative coupon bond!") For investors expecting rates to fall, this makes ZCBs a very attractive investment. Finally, ZCBs allow one to capture the true term yield for a given term in a fashion difficult to achieve with coupon instruments. This feature enables investors to match exactly a stream of future liabilities at guaranteed term rates. State governments typically fund state lotteries in this manner, for example.

In the high interest-rate climate of the early 1980s, corporate issuers found that they could realize pretax savings of 50–150 basis points by financing their debts with ZCBs. A market soon emerged for "stripped" U.S. Treasury securities, in which coupon and principal payments were separated out, such as TIGRs (Treasury Investment Growth Receipts) and CATS (Certificates of Accrual on Treasury Securities). In 1985, the Federal Reserve introduced STRIPS (Separate Trading of Registered Interest and Principal of Securities), giving the federal government's official imprimatur to such zero-coupon instruments. The first Treasury issues to be stripped were the 11 1/4 percent of February 1995 and the 11 1/4 percent of February 2015. The unit size was set by the Treasury at $1,000. The zero-coupon market has continued to evolve, with the introduction of such variants as stripped municipal bonds and strips combined with other features, such as LYONS (Liquid Yield Options Notes), zero-coupon *convertible* bonds. During the past few years, various kinds of zero-coupon bonds have also been issued abroad, in pounds sterling, deutsche marks, and other currencies.

The Secondary Market and the Inter-Dealer Brokers

The U.S. Treasury issues its debt instruments at auctions, usually to the primary dealers. In the secondary market, primary dealers are active market makers of most outstanding Treasuries. Their counterparties include a wide range of registered dealers (about 2000 of them) and institutional investors in the secondary market. They also trade among themselves through a unique system of six *interdealer brokers*, firms that provide customized electronic screens indicating bid and asked prices and "size" for all the active issues. The interdealer brokers include Cantor Fitzgerald Securities Corp., Chapdelaine & Company Government Securities, Fundamental Brokers Inc. (FBI), Garban Ltd., Liberty Brokers Inc., and RMJ Securities Corp. Only the primary dealers have access to these screens, which display the market levels, bid/offer sizes, and trading activities of the UST market—this is the single greatest advantage held by the primary dealers.

The interdealer brokers provide not one, but *six separate markets* for UST trading. The primary dealers choose the best bid or offer from among the interdealer broker services their firm uses (they probably will not use all six). The dealers usually do not know who is on the other side of the trades they execute, although through parallel phone contact and the industry grapevine they may sometimes have an idea. The interdealer brokers themselves do not "take positions" in the UST market. They do not trade for their own accounts; they are strictly brokers. The interdealer brokers are paid a commission by only one side of every trade (currently $39 per $1 million); buyers receive the bonds, and sellers the cash, through clearing banks and the Federal Reserve without either ever passing through the hands of the brokers.

Dealers may enter bids either for their own accounts, or for those of their customers—the banks, pension funds, and money-market mutuals that make up the bulk of the secondary market. They make (or lose) their money through the bid/ask spread in their market-making activity; through appreciation (or depreciation) of inventories held long or short; and through *positive or negative carry*: the net excess or shortfall in interest income over the cost of financing inventory position.

The Repo Market

Most dealers and proprietary traders do not own outright all the securities in their inventory. Standard practice is to finance holdings by borrowing in the repo (repurchase agreement) market. Treasury securities serve as collateral for loans, with the commitment that they will be "repurchased" at the end of term for the principal plus any agreed-to interest. Maturities of repo agreements are typically very short-term, often overnight. Longer repo agreements are usually distinguished as "term repos."

The tremendous growth in the market for U.S. Treasuries during the 1980s has led to an explosion in the repo market as well, with volume in the overnight repo market exceeding $200 billion and another $200–300 billion in term repos (Trachtenberg, 1987).

Understanding repo and reverse repo agreements is essential to fixed-income securities trading. For example, in an overnight repo agreement, an investor lends a dealer $950,000, secured by U.S. Treasury securities worth $1 million held by the dealer. The sum is to be returned, with agreed-upon interest, the next morning, in exchange for the return of the securities used as collateral. A reserve repo is the mirror image of such a deal: a dealer *lends* funds in exchange for securities provided by the investor as collateral.

While the term "repo" and the language of repurchase agreements make them look like actual sales and repurchases, they are functionally secured loans, and the lending party maintains all beneficial interest in the securities used as collateral, including coupon interest payments. This is important, since the major reason for borrowing is to finance the purchase of other securities, and the interest paid on a repo will rarely coincide with the coupon income from the securities thus financed; the difference between coupon income and the cost of financing the loan is the *cost of carry*: the *net* cost to the holder of financing the purchase of a security. In our example above, if the overnight repo rate were 6 percent and the $950,000 borrowed were used to partially finance the purchase of a security with a coupon of 8 percent, the accrual per $1 million would be:

$$\$1,000,000 \times 0.04 \times \frac{1}{182} = \$219.78$$

(assuming 182 days in the current coupon period). The interest at repo rate 6 percent on $1 million would be:

$$\$1,000,000 \times 0.06 \times \frac{1}{360} = \$166.67$$

and the positive carry per $1 million per day would thus be $219.78 − $166.67 = $53.11, or about one-half of a basis point per day.

Carry may be positive or negative; because repo rates are generally for the very short term, whereas the securities financed have longer maturities, carry will usually be *positive* when the yield curve is *upward-sloping* (usually considered the normal regime for interest rates), and *negative* when the yield curve is *downward-sloping*. Typical overnight repo rates will be slightly lower than overnight Federal Funds rates, but rates can vary based on the "tightness" of money and, especially, on supply and demand for the particular security in question. When demand for a particular issue is high, for example when dealers have taken large short positions in that issue, it may go "special," attracting very low reverse repo rates, since desperate dealers will be willing to lend at especially low rates in order to borrow enough of the security to cover their short positions.

In regimes with steeply sloping yield curves, the cost of carry can be a significant factor in any transaction, and may make or break an apparently profitable trade. Relative value traders cannot afford to ignore the effects of carry.

Debt Futures Markets

The cash markets provide investors with opportunities to trade Treasuries for same or next-day delivery and payment. The Treasury futures market exists so that T-bills, notes, and bonds can be traded for deferred delivery and payment. In practice, however, as little as 5 percent of futures contracts end up in actual delivery. The futures contracts in Treasuries include the three-month T-bill, the two-, five-, and ten-year T-note, and the T-bond future contracts. The bill contract has a face value of $1 million per contract, and the others have a par value of $100,000.

Uses of Futures Contracts. Interest-rate futures markets allow institutions that know their future funding needs or lending capabilities to lock in attractive interest rates when they become available. Futures contracts provide fixed-income portfolio managers with a hedge against unfavorable interest rate movements. They also provide speculators with an easy, leveraged way to bet on future interest rate movements. The financial futures market has grown dramatically since its introduction in 1976.

Futures and the corresponding cash price movements are closely related. However, because participants in the cash and futures markets may have different objectives, there are times when the cash bond and futures contracts trade at prices contrary to their expected relationship. Fixed-income arbitrageurs often seek out these situations and establish trading positions from which they will profit when the expected relationship between the cash and futures prices is reestablished.

T-Bill Futures.   The standard T-bill futures contract traded on the International Monetary Market (IMM) of the Chicago Mercantile Exchange (CME) is $1 million face value of 90- to 92-day bills. The delivery months are March, June, September, and December, with the next eight delivery months traded at any time. Settlement occurs in the third week of the delivery month, usually on a Thursday.

Cash bills are traded on a discount basis, but the IMM quotes bill future prices according to the IMM index, which is

$$\text{IMM index} = 100 - \text{Discount yield in } \% \qquad (2.11)$$

The bill future price P in percent of the face value, using Equation (2.2), is therefore

$$P = 100 \times \left(1 - \frac{N \times (100 - \text{IMM index})}{360 \times 100}\right) \qquad (2.12)$$

Example 2.2

Suppose the IMM index for delivery of a 90-day bill in six months is 91.72. Its market price P, in percent, can be computed from Equation (2.12) as

$$P = 100 \times \left(1 - \frac{90 \times (100 - 91.72)}{360 \times 100}\right) = 97.93$$

The futures price will be $979,300 because the face value is $1 million. If this contract is bought or sold, a margin of $2,000 will be required, and the bill contract will be marked to market daily. Price fluctuations on a bill contract are in multiples of a basis point, or 0.01 percent, which has a value of $(0.01\%) \times (90/360) \times (\$1 \text{ million}) = \$25$. ∎

Hedging with T-Bill Futures.   Suppose that the T-bill yield curve has a positive slope. An investor who has funds to invest for three months has several alternatives. In addition to simply buying the three-month bill and holding it until maturity, the investor can "ride down the yield curve" by buying, for example, the six-month bill and selling it three months later. The latter strategy may give superior results if the yield curve stays the same after three months, but if the yield curve shifts upward, the simple buy-and-hold strategy will give better returns. In order to hedge against possible upward shifts in yields, the investor can buy the six-month bill and sell a T-bill futures contract that settles in three months.

Example 2.3

A three-month (91-day) bill is trading at 8.395 percent. From Equation (2.2) its price is

$$100 \times \left(1 - \frac{91 \times 0.08395}{360}\right) = 97.878$$

Buying and holding it will provide a return of

$$\frac{100.00 - 97.878}{97.878} = 2.168\%$$

A six-month (181-day) T-bill trades at a discount yield of 8.48 percent. From Equation (2.2), the price of this bill is

$$100 \times \left(1 - \frac{181 \times 0.0848}{360}\right) = 95.736$$

If we assume no change in the yield curve, the six-month bill will become a three-month (90-day) bill at our horizon date, and will then be worth

$$100 \times \left(1 - \frac{90 \times 0.08395}{360}\right) = 97.90$$

so riding the yield curve would bring a return of

$$\frac{97.90 - 95.736}{95.736} = 2.2604\%$$

which is better than the buy-and-hold strategy.

If yields rose by 40 basis points, however, the value of the three-month bill on the horizon date would be

$$100 \times \left(1 - \frac{90 \times 0.08795}{360}\right) = 97.80$$

and the return for riding the yield curve would be

$$\frac{97.80 - 95.736}{95.736} = 2.156\%$$

which is slightly worse than the buy-and-hold strategy.

If the three-month T-bill future is trading at an IMM index of 91.72, the delivery price calculated from Equation (2.12) will be

$$100 \times \left(1 - \frac{90 \times (100 - 91.72)}{360 \times 100}\right) = 97.93$$

The three-month return obtained by buying the six-month bill and three months later delivering against this contract is

$$\frac{97.93 - 95.736}{95.736} = 2.292\%$$

which outperforms the buy-and-hold strategy without exposing the investor to the market level risk of riding the yield curve.

■

T-Note and T-Bond Futures.   Treasury note and bond futures contracts are traded with a face value of $100,000 and settlement dates in the months of March, June, September, and December. Ten-year note futures, which are traded on the Chicago Board of Trade (CBT), call for delivery of T-notes with maturities between $6\frac{1}{2}$ and 10 years from delivery date. Contracts can be traded for up to the next eight delivery months, but contracts beyond the nearest three are typically very illiquid. Prices are quoted in 32nds, or *ticks;* one tick is worth $100,000 \times .0003125 = $31.25. Five-year note futures are also traded on the CBT. Deliverable securities are T-notes with $4\frac{1}{2}$ to $5\frac{1}{2}$ years original maturity and at least $4\frac{1}{4}$ years remaining maturity on delivery date. Prices are quoted in 64ths, with the value of one tick equal to $15.625. Two-year notes, which began trading in 1989, call for delivery of T-notes with remaining maturity between 21 months and 25 months. Like the five-year note future, they are quoted in 64ths. Treasury bond futures call for delivery of T-bonds with maturities or call dates no less than 15 years from delivery date. Other features are similar to the 10-year note future contract. There are always several issues deliverable against a given contract.

Contract Short-seller's Advantages on Delivery.   A bond future contract holder taking delivery does not know in advance which bond will be delivered, and therefore how much he or she will have to pay, until just before delivery. Moreover, although there is no trading in the futures contracts during the last seven business days of the month, delivery can take place until the last business day of the month, at the discretion of the party delivering against the futures contract. Because the seller determines which issue is delivered, and on what day delivery occurs, he or she has significant advantages over the contract holder.

Another advantage enjoyed by the futures contract seller is the so-called "afternoon option." This refers to the fact that the bond contract stops trading at 2:00 P.M. Chicago time, but sellers have until 8:00 P.M. to tell the CBT what they will deliver. (Most clearing firms require indications by 6:00 or 7:00 P.M.) Bond future contract sellers can take advantage of any drop in the price of the most deliverable issue after 2:00 P.M. to improve their position, since they will in any case be delivering against the 2:00 P.M. future settlement price. This advantage exists even after the contract stops trading in the delivery month.

The Conversion Factor.   The full invoice price actually paid on delivery is determined by the futures settlement price (FSP) times the contract size, adjusted by a *conversion factor* determined by the coupon and maturity characteristics of the particular bond being delivered, plus any accrued interest:

$$IP = FSP \times \$100{,}000.00 \times CF + Accrued \qquad (2.13)$$

The futures price times the conversion factor, without the accrued, is also known as the *converted price* or *delivery-equivalent price*.

As shown in Example 2.4, the conversion factor is the bond price that on a particular date would provide an effective yield of eight percent divided by 100.

Example 2.4

On August 9, 1988 the September T-bond future contract closed at $86\,7/32$. The UST 10.75 percent of August 15, 2005 was one of the bonds deliverable against this contract. To calculate the conversion factor for this bond, for example, against the September 1988 T-bond futures contract, one takes the next *quarterly* date in the bond's coupon cycle falling in or after the delivery month of the future contract—in this case, 11/15/88—and calculates the bond price corresponding to a yield of 8 percent on that date, which for this bond is $125\,3/32+$ or 125.11 in decimal. The conversion factor for this deliverable bond is therefore 1.2511, and the delivery-equivalent price (DEP) for this bond, in decimal, is

$$DEP = 86.22 \times 1.2511 = 107.87$$

Note that the conversion factor is always *relative to a particular futures contract*. For details on the precise formulas used in the calculation of conversion factors, see (Schwarz et al., 1986). The CBT publishes tables of conversion factors based on these formulas, which are generally used for invoicing purposes.

■

The Cheapest-to-Deliver Bond. The difference between the cash bond price (BP) and the delivery equivalent price (DEP, the future settle price multiplied by the conversion factor) is known as the *bond basis:*

$$\text{BASIS} = \text{BP} - \text{DEP} = \text{BP} - (\text{FSP} \times \text{CF}) \tag{2.14}$$

When it is necessary to deliver against a bond futures contract, the party delivering (the seller of the futures contract) will seek to deliver the bond that has the *highest invoice price* relative to the cash bond price, that is, the issue with the *smallest basis*. This is known as the *cheapest-to-deliver* issue. Consider a bond futures contract seller who decides to make delivery on the last trading day of that contract. Ideally, the short seller would like to deliver a bond that would cost *less* in the market than the invoice price he or she will receive upon delivery; that is, he or she would like to deliver a bond issue with *negative* basis. This is not likely to be possible, however, as arbitrage activity would quickly drive up the price of such a bond. Failing this, the short party will seek that bond with the smallest basis, because it is, literally, the cheapest to deliver *relative to the delivery-equivalent price* the long party (the buyer of the futures contract) is obligated to pay. Familiarity with basis, and the ability to identify the cheapest-to-deliver issue, are essential to any futures trader, as they are the key to the relationship between the cash and futures markets.

Prior to the delivery month, many issues will be potentially deliverable against a given futures contract. If a trader wants to buy a cash bond and carry it to delivery date, "locking up" the trade, which bond should he or she buy and carry? Here, coupon accrual and financing costs become a very real issue. The most desirable issue will generally be the one with the smallest *net basis* = basis − carry, as this will be the issue that will cost the trader the least (or bring the greatest return) *based on current prices.*

Example 2.5

As noted in Example 2.4, the September 1988 T-bond future contract closed at a price of $86\,^7/_{32}$. Bonds with maturities ranging from August 2005 to May 2018 were deliverable against this contract. For some of the deliverable issues, Table 2.1 shows (1) coupon rate, (2) maturity or call date, (3) August 9, 1988 closing price, (4) conversion factor to the September 1988 T-bond future

Table 2.1 Issues Deliverable Against September 1988 Bond Future Contract

Coupon Rate (in %)	Maturity or Call (mo/yr)	Market Price	Conversion Factor	Delivery Equivalent Price	Bond Basis (32nds)	Repo Rate (in %)	Carry (32nds)	Net Basis (32nds)
10.750	08/05	[111.14]	1.2511	[107.28]	114.23	7.250	10.97	103.25
12.000	08/08C	[122.13+]	1.3935	[120.04+]	72.84	7.000	14.29	58.54
9.250	02/16	[98.29+]	1.1376	[98.02+]	26.88	7.000	9.57	17.31
7.250	05/16	[79.11]	0.9171	[79.02]	8.74	7.180	5.77	2.97
9.125	05/18	[99.08]	1.1267	[97.04+]	67.37	7.370	6.59	60.79

contract, (5) delivery-equivalent price, (6) basis, and (7) repo rate, (8) carrying cost, and (9) net basis from August 9, 1988, to the September T-bond contract's last delivery date (September 30, 1988). The bond prices are given in thirty-seconds, in brackets, with [98.02+] representing a price of $98^{2.5}/_{32}$, as this is how they are normally quoted in the marketplace. Basis, carrying cost, and net basis are all given in 32nds as well—a basis of 26.88 represents $^{26.88}/_{32}$.

With a net basis of $^{2.97}/_{32}$, the most deliverable (buy-and-carry) issue on this date was the UST 7.25 of 5/15/2016. A short-seller of the September T-bond contract who wants to buy-and-carry a cash bond to deliver on the contract's last delivery day (September 30, 1988) should select the 7.25 percent bond because the worst-case loss would be only $^{2.97}/_{32}$ (assuming that the repo rate stays the same). He or she will make a profit if this 7.25 percent bond becomes rich relative to the other deliverable issues.

■

The Effect of Carry.   Because of the forward nature of futures contracts, their prices depend heavily on the cost of carry for the deliverable issues. For example, on 4/21/80 and 4/4/83, long-term rates were comparable—10.9 percent and 10.68 percent, respectively. However, in 1980 the Federal Reserve was tightening credit in its effort to control inflation, and the short term rate was 15 percent (a negatively sloping yield curve), while in April 1983, the short term rate was 9 percent (a positively sloping yield curve). With negative carry, the September 1980 bond contract was trading at $77^{15}/_{32}$, while the September 1983 bond futures contract traded at $75^{23}/_{32}$ in a regime of positive carry. With negative carry, the market makes investors pay more for bonds in the future, because they can earn a higher rate on short term investments; with positive carry, investors would rather own the bonds, and the futures price will be adjusted downward accordingly.

Option-Adjusted Basis.   As noted above, the bond futures contract seller enjoys a number of advantages implicit in the options on delivery against the futures contract. In fact, these advantages can be treated explicitly as *embedded options*. Such embedded options can be valued using option valuation techniques (see Chapter 3), and an *option-adjusted basis* can thereby be calculated. Such an adjusted basis can give the trader or investor valuable additional insight into the fair value of a futures position. There are circumstances when a straight examination of the unadjusted basis between the bond future contract and the cheapest-to-deliver issue may suggest that the future contract is cheap (or rich) relative to the cash market, while a closer examination of the option-adjusted basis may show that it is in fact fairly priced (or vice-versa). Tang (1988) observes that "on March 6, 1987 the June 87 Treasury bond contract was seemingly cheap relative to the cash market using the conventional models in evaluating futures contracts. After adjusting for the effect of the options, however, the bond contract was actually fairly priced."

Each of the delivery-related embedded options has its own terms and value; these particulars must be taken into account when choosing which option pricing techniques to bring to bear. The most important of these embedded options are the following:

- The *quality option:* This is the contract seller's option as to which qualified Treasury bond issue to deliver during the period that the bond contract is still trading. The contract seller will always seek to deliver the issue that is cheapest to deliver (has the smallest basis) at the time of delivery. In an environment of volatile interest rates, however, the cheapest-to-deliver issue may well change during the period that the future contract is trading. This will affect the invoice price to be paid by the long party. The value of this option is actually the maximum of a bundle of option values, one for each potentially deliverable issue.
- The *end-of-month option:* This is the contract seller's option as to which issue to deliver *after trading in the bond contract has ceased.* At this point, the settlement price for the future contract will already have been set; small changes in interest rates can thus affect the choice of cheapest-to-deliver issue. This is a short-term but potentially very volatile American option.
- The *wildcard* or *afternoon option:* This is the seller's option to declare intent to deliver at any time prior to 8:00 P.M. EST during the first 15 days of the delivery month. Since the futures market closes by 2:00 P.M., while the cash market trades actively into the afternoon, there is a window of opportunity for the seller to take advantage of favorable interest rate movements. This is an interesting option, as its strike gets reset each day with the repricing of the futures contract.
- The *timing option:* This is the seller's option to deliver on any chosen day of the delivery month. The emphasis here is not on *which issue* is delivered, but rather on considerations of *carry.* In an environment of positive carry (upward-sloping yield curve), ignoring the possible effects of any of the other delivery-related options, delivery would normally be deferred to the last day. In an inverted yield curve environment, early delivery would be advantageous. The value of this option is contingent on the likelihood of a yield curve inversion.
- The *new issue option:* This is the value associated with the possibility that a new Treasury issue may turn out to be the cheapest-to-deliver against the future contract. While rarely of much value, this option can play a role in environments of high but falling yields, where new issues are likely to have both the lowest coupon and the longest maturity among deliverable issues, factors that combine to give them the longest duration,

making them good candidates for the cheapest-to-deliver issue. It is of more significance for note futures than for bond futures, as Treasury note auctions are more frequent.

While many of these embedded options only rarely take on significant value, the quality and end-of-month options are frequently noteworthy, and the active futures trader ignores any of these factors at his or her own peril. The diversity of characteristics of these options, and the fact, for example, that they must generally be considered as European prior to the delivery period, but American thereafter (but possibly with varying strikes) makes clear the value of some of the more sophisticated option pricing methodologies described in Chapter 4.

Differences Between T-Bond and T-Note Futures Contracts.   Contract terms for the T-bond and 10-year T-note futures contract are identical except for the definitions of deliverable issues. This difference in deliverables has some important consequences, however. Deliverable notes have shorter maturities, and hence lower durations than deliverable bonds. Moreover, because the *range* of deliverable maturities is much narrower for note futures (3 1/2 years as compared with 15 years for bond futures), the range of coupons on deliverable note issues also tends to be narrower, leading to a narrower range of durations. The absence of callable notes among the deliverable issues acts to reduce further the variability in duration. The end result is less sensitivity to market level in T-note futures contracts, and hence a smaller basis.

The lower volatility of note futures prices means that most of the delivery options are worth less than the corresponding options for the T-bond futures contract. The one exception is the *new issue* option, which tends to be potentially more significant for note futures than for bond futures, as note auctions are more frequent and there is a higher probability of a new issue becoming the cheapest-to-deliver. This is especially true of five-year and two-year note futures. In the case of two-year note futures, there is only a four-month range of deliverable maturities, and typically only four or five deliverable issues. These issues usually have very similar coupons and maturities, hence nearly identical durations. There is essentially no quality option for these contracts. On the other hand, there is *always* a new issue that could potentially become the cheapest-to-deliver.

Debt Options Markets

Options on Treasuries and Treasury futures are traded on two different markets. Options on T-bond and T-note futures are traded on the Chicago Board of Trade (CBT). There is also a significant over-the-counter market for cash bond options.

The Role of Debt Options. Interest rate options provide a flexible tool for the investor or speculator in the fixed-income arena. In general terms, they represent a very convenient repackaging and reallocation of interest-rate related risk, and thus lend themselves to both hedging and speculation. As a speculative instrument, interest-rate options are highly leveraged, and thus provide a high potential rate of return for the trader who wishes to gamble on market trends. Options also lend themselves to so-called "volatility plays," combining options at different strikes and/or expirations to take advantage of anticipated changes in the volatilities imputed by the market to the various options. As hedging instruments, puts provide a relatively cheap form of insurance against market-level risk that does not require the liquidation of an underlying position.

The option market on interest-rate *futures* is much larger and more liquid than that on cash bills, notes, and bonds. Although there are certainly situations in which an options positions in the cash instrument is preferred, and profit opportunities exist in this market for market makers, strategic traders, and investors, the futures option market is a much more active arena for the interest-rate options player.

Exchange-Traded Options on T-Bond Futures. The CBT bond futures option market, initiated in 1982, has been very successful. With the volume of trading in one options contract equal to about a third of the volume in the underlying futures contract, these have become the second most active exchange-traded options in the world. Volume on the bond futures option in December, 1988 was 1,193,987 contracts, or over $119 trillion. Open interest for the month was a little less than half of that. Volume in options on the 10-year note future was 67,638 contracts, or $6.76 billion.

CBT bond (note) futures options are traded on the nearest three futures contracts, and are struck at even, round-number prices centered around the current futures price. Expiration is on the third Friday of the month preceding the futures contract delivery month. Option prices are quoted in 64ths.

If an option buyer exercises a call (or put), a long (or short) position in the underlying futures contract is assigned. The option seller is assigned a corresponding short (or long) position. If the strike price equals the futures contract price, the transaction is complete. If the strike price is lower (or higher) than the futures price, the call (or put) seller must pay the buyer the difference.

Over-The-Counter (OTC) Options on Cash Bonds. As we have noted, exchange-traded options on cash Treasury notes and bonds are not very liquid. Institutional investors wishing to trade options on cash bonds often do so on an over-the-counter (OTC) basis. This is a market made by government securities dealers, who will often create options contracts tailored to the needs of the investor. Because the participants are not trading listed contracts, strike prices, expirations, and face value may be freely specified. OTC markets also currently have an advantage over the exchange-traded cash bond options market in that the dealers themselves maintain quotes on a variety of underlying notes and bonds at all times. They are therefore in possession of up-to-the-minute pricing information, and are also usually able to directly hedge their options positions with positions in the underlying bonds. The average daily volume in OTC cash bond options is unofficially estimated to be $750 million to $1 billion.

Differences between Exchange-Traded and OTC Options. The most obvious difference between the exchange-traded and OTC options markets is that in the OTC market, contract terms are set entirely by the two parties, whereas exchange-traded options have pre-determined strikes, expirations, and contract sizes. In the OTC market, options may also be European or American, whereas the exchange-traded options are always American. There are some other important differences, however, that the potential OTC options market participant should keep in mind. An investor who wants to hedge a cash bond position using options on futures is exposed to *basis risk*, as option exercise results in the assignment of a long or short futures contract position. In the OTC market, where all options are on specific securities, there is no such risk. On the other hand, because futures prices represent a cash transaction at a future date, positive or negative carry is already factored into the futures price, whereas in the OTC market, changes in the yield curve or financing costs for a particular security can have a major impact on the option price.

As in the case of exchange-traded options on cash bonds, the OTC market is generally not as liquid as the bond futures option market. Spreads in the OTC market are accordingly wider than those quoted in the exchange-traded futures option market; this difference, however, can vary widely depending on the maturity of the underlying cash issues, the volatility of the market, and how far out of the money the options are struck.

A Note on Agency Issues

In addition to those debt securities directly issued by the U.S. Treasury, there are a number of securities issued by government agencies and sponsored corporations, known collectively as *agency issues*. These issues all enjoy the implicit backing of the U.S. government, although not necessarily the "full faith and credit" of direct UST issues. Like UST issues, they are generally exempt from state and local taxes. Agency issues tend to be smaller than UST issues, so they are somewhat less liquid. For this reason, and because of their slightly higher credit risk, agencies trade at a spread to UST issues of the same maturity.

During the 1980s, this spread ranged from as little as 3 basis points up to almost 90 basis points for shorter maturities and more than 125 basis points for longer maturities. The sometimes extreme behavior of such spreads can offer occasional profit opportunities to patient relative-value traders.

While UST issues are offered at public auction, agency issues are underwritten by investment banking firms, much like corporate debt. A syndicate and selling group are assembled; the coupon is set in consultation with the agency's fiscal agent, and the issue is bought by the syndicate at par less a selling concession for resale in the secondary market. The secondary market in agency securities is very similar in structure and function to that for USTs, and is made up mainly of the same dealers.

ASSET-BACKED SECURITIES AND THEIR DERIVATIVES

Over the past 10 years, a major secondary market has emerged in **asset-backed securities.** Various kinds of **mortgage-backed securities (MBS)** make up the bulk of this market, but other "securitized" receivables, such as car loans and credit card payments, have also grown in recent years. In this selection, we will describe a few of the most common varieties of mortgage-backed securities and some of their derivatives.

The Mortgage-Backed Securities Market

The predominant and most important form of mortgage-backed security is the **pass-through security.** Pass-through securities consist of *pools* of mortgages that are serviced by either the originator or another banking institution that *passes through* both principal and interest payments, less a service fee, to the security holders. Security holders thus receive a share of the actual cash flow for the securitized pools proportional to the share held. Note that constituent mortgages in the pools may be prepaid at any time, with potentially significant impact on the price and yield of the pass-through security.

The best known and most common pass-through securities are those guaranteed by the Government National Mortgage Association. GNMA is a government-owned corporation set up in 1968 to support Federal Housing Administration (FHA) and Veterans' Administration (VA) housing loans. It operates under the auspices of Housing and Urban Development (HUD). GNMA pools thus consist of FHA-insured and VA-guaranteed mortgage loans, backed by the full faith and credit of the U.S. government. The holder of a GNMA certificate is guaranteed full and timely payment of both principal and interest *regardless of whether individual mortgage payments are actually made.*

All mortgages in a GNMA pool must be of a common type, and less than 12 months old. Type I GNMA pools must also consist of mortgages with a common interest rate, issued by a common lender. Type II GNMA pools, introduced in 1983, may include multiple issuers and a range of interest rates (which are leveled to the lowest rate in the pass-through process, with the issuer or servicer claiming excess interest payments as part of servicing fees). Type I GNMA securities are issued for pools with a minimum pool size of $1 million, and have a 15-day delay in pass-through payments; Type II GNMA securities have a minimum pool size of $7 million principal value, and a pass-through delay of 20 days.

The most common GNMA pass-throughs represent 30-year maturity, fixed-rate mortgages on single-family residential homes. Ninety percent of the individual mortgages backing a 30-year GNMA pass-through must have original maturities of 20 years or more. GNMA pass-throughs are also issued based on 15-year single-family mortgages; these are known in the industry as "GNMA Midgets." Markets for other GNMA securitized loans, such as graduated payment mortgages and adjustable rate loans, are much smaller and less liquid, and the special characteristics of such mortgage-backed securities make their analysis different in significant respects from the more common GNMA pass-throughs.

Along with GNMA, two other federal agencies play a major role in the mortgage market. The Federal Home Loan Mortgage Corporation (FHLMC, or "Freddie Mac"), formed in 1970, supports certain mortgages not guaranteed by either the VA or the FHA. Unlike GNMA, FHLMC is not backed by the full faith and credit of the U.S. government, but it does have Federal Reserve borrowing rights and the implied credit of the U.S. government. FHLMC guarantees timely payment of interest and eventual payment of principal to security holders. (In industry parlance, FHLMC securities are said to be "modified" while GNMA securities are "fully modified.")

The Federal National Mortgage Association or FNMA has been in existence since the 1930s, buying and selling FHA mortgages, but only began issuing pass-through securities in 1981. FNMA is a semi-private government-sponsored corporation—its stock is traded on the New York Stock Exchange. FNMA guarantees timely payment of both interest and principal payments on all pass-through securities it issues (they are "fully modified"), but because it has somewhat looser ties to the U.S. government, its securities frequently trade at a slight yield spread to FHLMC's.

The price and yield behavior of pass-through securities can only be understood in relation to the cash-flow properties of the securities and their underlying pools. Traditional mortgages are fixed-rate, level-payment loans, in which equal monthly payments are made; early payments will consist mainly of interest. Over time, the proportion of principal will very gradually rise until it surpasses the interest portion in later years. Assuming homogeneity of individual mortgages in the pool, and ignoring for the moment any prepayment effect, the cash flows from a pool of traditional mortgages will be simply the aggregate of the individual mortgage cash flows, The cash flows from a pass-through certificate backed by such a pool will be very similar, modified only to reflect service charges and pass-through payment delay. However, note that because service fees are a percentage of *outstanding principal,* the total cash flow to pass-through certificate holders gradually increases.

The major complication in the analysis of pass-through certificates, and most mortgage-backed securities, is the possibility of *prepayment.* The possibility of prepayment means that the cash flows of mortgage-backed securities cannot be predicted with certainty; there is an element of *prepayment risk.* Certain assumptions are made about prepayment behavior, but these are only approximations to empirically observed prepayment patterns, and more sophisticated prepayment modeling plays a major part in the analysis and trading of mortgage-backed securities. For details, see Fabozzi (1988) or Bartlett (1989).

The simplest and standard prepayment assumption is that *a constant fraction of remaining principal is prepaid each month.* This fraction is known as the Constant Prepayment Rate (CPR). The Public Securities Association (PSA) has developed a slightly more sophisticated set of prepayment assumptions for use in valuing mortgage-backed securities, especially Collateralized Mortgage Obligations (CMOs). The PSA Standard Prepayment Model consists of a series of monthly CPRs, starting at 0.2 percent per year in the first month and increasing by 0.2 percent per year each month until month 30, thereafter remaining flat at 6 percent per year through maturity. This model is based on detailed "experience tables" compiled by the FHA based on empirical experience, but includes improvements on some aspects of the FHA tables. For more details, see Fabozzi (1988) or Bartlett (1989).

Because of the uncertainty associated with prepayment risk, calculation of yield and other sensitivity measures for mortgage-backed securities is more complex and involved than for simple, fixed-coupon bonds. Some of the techniques required to analyze mortgage-backed securities, such as mortgage duration and weighted average maturity (WAM), are dealt with in Chapter 4.

Adjustable-Rate Mortgage Securities

Over the past decade, there has been a significant shift away from the issuance of traditional, fixed-rate, level-payment mortgages and toward the issuance of more flexible, adjustable-rate mortgages (ARMS). By the late 1980s, high or uncertain interest rates had made such mortgages so attractive that annual originations of ARMs began exceeding those of conventional fixed-rate mortgages. As expected, an active secondary market has grown up around these newer securities, along with market pressures to standardize such contracts for convenient securitization.

The basic difference between an ARM and a conventional fixed-rate mortgage is that an ARM's interest rate is periodically adjusted up or down, whereas that of a fixed-rate mortgage, as the name suggests, is fixed throughout the life of the mortgage. That said, several other contract features are significant, including:

- Frequency of adjustment: how often interest rate is "reset." The most common reset frequency is one year, but periods of one month, six months, three years, or five years occur.
- Index of adjustment: the prevailing rate to which the mortgage rate is "pegged." For one-year reset ARMs, a common index has been the yield on one-year T-bills. Six-month T-bills and three- and five-year T-note rates have also been popular index rates. Other indices, such as the Federal Home Loan Bank Board's national average mortgage contract rate, have also been used.
- Initial rate: The availability of low initial rates is one of the features that has made ARMS increasingly popular, particularly for families with relatively low current income but expectations of higher family income.
- Fees and caps: There are frequently up-front fees of a certain percentage of the principal. There may also be a cap or floor on the mortgage interest rate or on the total interest-rate movement over the life of the mortgage.

As is to be expected, ARMs frequently exhibit more complex behavior than conventional fixed-rate mortgages. The indexing of ARM rates to prevailing interest rates can simplify matters in some respects. ARMs can be thought of as *short-term* loans with a commitment to "roll over" at prevailing interest rates every N years (or months) for the life of the contract. The initial rate offered will therefore tend to depend on the reset period and the shape of the yield curve (reflecting market expectations about term rates, and hence the price of "reinvestment risk"; see Chapter 3). If all other factors are equal (which they rarely are), an ARM with a shorter reset period will tend to have a *lower* initial rate than one with a longer reset period in an environment with a *positively* (upward) sloping yield curve, and vice versa.

Collateralized Mortgage Obligations

Collateralized mortgage obligations (CMOs) represent another major innovation in the mortgage-backed securities market. These securities made their debut in June 1983, when FHMLC issued its first CMO. Since then, over $200 billion in CMOs of all types have been issued. A CMO issuer typically partitions the cash flows from a large (typically several hundred million dollar) mortgage pool (GNMAs, FHLMCs, or FNMAs are the usual "collaterals") into a series of synthetic bonds called *tranches* with different cash flow characteristics. The different tranches appeal to different investors because they have different maturity and coupon characteristics. CMOs are therefore a very efficient way for mortgage originators or holders of very large mortgage portfolios to sell off assets on their balance sheets. Conversely, they offer prospective investors a variety of risk/reward combinations that were not previously available. A large pool backing a CMO helps stabilize cash flows against inevitable statistical variations in prepayment among individual mortgages. Moreover, many CMOs issued and traded by Wall Street firms are based on pools limited to securities of a given type and coupon—for example, GNMA 8 percent coupons. This makes the prepayment risk of such securities easier to predict, and hence such *generic* CMOs are easier for both issuer and purchaser to evaluate and price. CMOs based on pools made up of a combination of types or, especially, a combination of maturities and coupons can be much more difficult to accurately analyze and price.

CMOs have been issued with anywhere from 4 (the most common) to more than a dozen tranches. The number and size of tranches will significantly affect the predictability of expected tranche maturities, or "average life." In general, fewer and larger tranches translate into less certainty and "fuzzier" average lives, while many smaller tranches tend to translate into more narrowly defined, "bullet" maturities for the tranches.

IOs, POs, and Other Derivatives

As the mortgage sector of the debt market grew and matured during the late 1980s, other derivatives of mortgage-backed securities were structured by innovative securities firms, with special characteristics unavailable in simple pass-through securities. **Stripped mortgage-backed securities** are CMOs in which the interest and principal payments from the underlying mortgages are partially or completely separated out. IOs, or Interest-Only securities consist, as the name suggests, of *interest* payments from an underlying pool of mortgages, whereas POs, or Principal-Only securities, consist of the *principal* payments.

FNMA issued the first IO and PO stripped mortgage-backed securities in early 1987. By the end of the 1980s, the market for such securities had grown to many billions of dollars, and included issues backed by FHLMC and GNMA pools as well. (Various stripped MBSs with synthetic combinations of interest and principal payments, known as "synthetic discount" and "synthetic premium" MBSs, were also issued during the 1980s, but they have mostly given way to IOs and POs today.)

Because of their special characteristics, IOs and POs appeal to those eager to hedge prepayment risk and to those with clear expectations about the future direction of interest-rate movements, and hence of prepayment rates. Only a few of their significant applications will be discussed; for more details, see Bartlett (1989) or Fabozzi (1988). Readers unfamiliar with the notions and significance of "duration" and "convexity" should refer to Chapter 3.

POs tend to have long, positive durations, and therefore are desirable investments in "up," bull markets. They behave essentially like deep-discount MBSs; their value is often *enhanced* by rapid prepayments. IOs, however, have *negative* duration, which means that unlike most debt securities, they will perform well in a "down," bear market. IOs and POs can be engineered from pools with specific characteristics to have special convexity characteristics as well: IOs stripped from high-coupon MBSs and POs stripped from discount MBSs both have positive convexity, which means that they will outperform other MBSs in a high volatility environment, no matter which direction interest rates move. Similarly, negatively convex IOs and POs can be crafted that will perform well in low-volatility environments.

Stripped MBSs can also be used to hedge prepayment risk; when an MBS begins to trade at a premium price, it will also experience an increase in prepayment. This leads to negative convexity and a levelling out or even a drop in price. POs, however, perform extremely well in such an environment, and hence can be used as a very effective hedge against prepayment risk.

Other Asset-Backed Securities

In addition to the derivative securities collaterized by FNMA, GNMA, and FHMLC mortgages and adjustable-rate mortgages (ARMs), there has recently been rapid growth in the securitization of other kinds of collateral, especially receivables such as car loans and credit card payments. Marine Midland Bank has issued securities known as CARS, backed by pools of automobile loans; General Motors has issued securities backed by GMAC loans. A number of financial institutions have issued asset-backed securities collaterized by credit-card receivables. By 1988, the total of such asset-backed securities had reached over $29 billion, with over $24 billion backed by car, truck, and credit-card receivables (Bartlett, 1989).

FOREIGN BOND MARKETS

The Japanese Government Bond (JGB) Market

The rapid growth of the Japanese Government Bond (JGB) market has coincided with the Japanese government's need to finance large budget deficits since the mid-1970s. Such government deficits began with the oil crisis of the 1970s and have continued through the 1980s, with the JGB market now representing the second largest government debt market in the world, after the United States. As of December 1990, the total outstanding volume in Japanese government bonds was ¥163 trillion (US$1.25 trillion). Daily turnover in the JGB cash market has averaged ¥2–3 trillion in recent years—as much as ¥ 7–8 trillion in a bull market. Up to 95 percent of this volume is in large OTC trades involving security houses and banks, with only about 5 percent on the public exchanges.

Japanese government bonds are issued in maturities ranging from short-term (less than one year) discount bonds to the so-called "super-long" 20-year bonds, but the vast majority of outstanding JGB securities—over 80 percent of the total—are coupon bonds with a 10-year maturity at issue date. Medium-term coupon bonds with two- to four-year maturities and a small number of five-year discount bonds make up the rest of the JGB market. Issue sizes have ranged from ¥500 million to ¥3 billion, with benchmark issues typically issued in sizes of at least ¥1.5 trillion.

Japanese government bonds are each identified by a unique trading number. All JGB securities have coupon dates on the 20th of the month, and their maturity dates are on the corresponding coupon date (the 20th of the maturity month) or on the next Japanese business day. Normally, JGB bonds are issued in denominations of ¥100,000.

The JGB Primary Market. Until 1989, many Japanese government bonds were issued through a syndicate system in which a syndicate of 788 financial firms (including about 50 foreign firms) negotiated coupon rate, issue size, and price terms with the Japanese Ministry of Finance (MOF). After negotiation, the MOF had the right to impose terms, and syndicate members had to accept these terms or be expelled from the syndicate. Such negotiations were very difficult at times; the October 1987 auction was cancelled because issuing terms could not be agreed upon. The MOF then moved to auction 20 percent of the issue of 10-year bonds, but only at the negotiated price terms, making the auction a means of reserving greater participation in a given issue. This was of particular interest to foreign syndicate participants. In September 1988, the Ministry of Finance announced that it would start using an auction pricing method for government bond issuances starting in April 1989. The auctions cover 60 percent of each issue, with the remaining 40 percent now priced at the auction average price, meaning that, since 1989, market forces effectively set the cost of Japanese government debt.

Medium term (two- to four-year) coupon bonds and "super-long" 20-year bonds are issued through an auction system very similar to that used by the U.S. Treasury. Secret bids are entered through participating securities houses, and are used to set a reserve price; all bids at or above the reserve price are guaranteed to be met in full.

The dominant 10-year JGB issues are coupon bonds with interest paid semi-annually. These bonds are quoted in the market in simple yield terms. Coupon rates are generally low by U.S. standards, rarely rising over 6 percent in recent years. The bonds have payment dates on the 20th of the month, and are listed on the Tokyo Stock Exchange (TSE) 40 days after payment. Bond issues can be reopened for up to three months, as long as the coupon rate remains the same. Issue size can be quite variable; in 1986 and 1987, issues ranged from ¥300–1,400 billion. Old and new 10-year issues make up more than 80 percent of outstanding JGB volume.

The "super-long" 20-year bond is also a coupon bond with semiannual interest payments. Such bonds are issued four or five times a year by auction, with no fixed schedule of issue dates. The first such issue was in 1986, and the total outstanding amount of such bonds is still relatively small.

Five-year discount bonds are issued quarterly through the government bond syndication process, mostly to private investors. The number of these bonds issued is not large, amounting to no more than 2 percent of the total outstanding JGB volume. Shorter-term discount issues (under 1-year maturity) are also underwritten by syndication and sold most to private investors, and constitute another 2 percent of outstanding volume.

Bonds with two-, three- and four-year maturities are also issued irregularly, by auction. They are all coupon bonds, with semiannual interest payments. As of August 1987, such bonds made up about 7 percent of outstanding JGB volume.

Differences between the UST and JGB Markets.   There are several important ways in which the UST and JGB secondary markets differ. The incompleteness of the JGB market, the lack of liquidity of many issues, the premium attached to high-coupon issues, and tax considerations make it difficult to construct a meaningful yield curve for the JGB market. The lack of a true and efficient repo market and the structure of Japanese settlement dates makes it very difficult—or at any rate very expensive—to short JGBs. The emphasis on speculation and trend-following often leads to excessively high volatilities and to sustained apparent price distortions among related instruments, which initially can be quite misleading to the UST-oriented trader. There are also some technical differences in the way in which JGB and UST market calculations are performed, most notably in the fact that Japanese government bonds are quoted in *simple yield* terms.

Shorting and the Gensaki.   One important difference between the UST and JGB markets is in the difficulty of shorting JGBs. Until June 1989, there was no organized system for borrowing bonds to cover short sales, and failure to deliver brings drastic sanctions. Whereas it is possible to short for a few days, because of the JGB market's delayed settlement system, it is very difficult to borrow bonds for longer periods. The highly liquid benchmark issue commands a hefty premium, whereas side issues are often unavailable. This situation entails significant inventory costs for market makers, making them even more reluctant to trade in side-issues, particularly those with low coupons. This is one of the sources of illiquidity in such issues.

Until June 1989, the only way to borrow securities (to go short) was through a *gensaki* (bond repurchase) agreement, in which bonds are borrowed from an investor in exchange for the loan of cash. Most *gensaki* agreements, however, are used by securities houses to borrow *cash*, using their surplus inventory bonds as collateral. Moreover, there is essentially no *gensaki* secondary market, unlike the well-established repo market in the United States.

Gensaki yield is calculated on a 365-day basis:

$$Gensaki \text{ yield} = \tag{2.15}$$

$$\frac{\text{Repurchase price} - \text{Current price}}{\text{Current price}} \times \frac{365}{\text{Holding period in days}}$$

In late 1988, the MOF announced its intention to introduce a true repo market in 1989, to facilitate short sales for more than a few days at a time. Dealers had been pressing for such flexible bond-borrowing arrangements to rationalize the cash-futures relationship and hedging. This market was opened in June 1989, but its performance proved disappointing. A gap between the rates proposed by investors and those offered by bond dealers, and a lack of clear accounting standards for marking to the market, initially depressed the market, leading to a fall in trading volume from an opening daily level of around ¥10 billion to only ¥500 million within a few days.

Settlement. Japanese government bonds settle every five trading days—on the fifth, tenth, fifteenth, twentieth, twenty-fifth, and the last day of the month. Before August 1987, there were only three settlement days per month. Relatively infrequent settlement encourages speculation and contributes to the domination of the market by the largest trading houses and banks. Combined with the lack of an efficient, liquid repo market, which discourages rolling over short positions, this situation creates the conditions for "bear squeezes" and other market maneuvers at settlement, when short positions generally must be covered.

Coupon Effects. Market makers have been very reluctant to trade bonds with low coupons because of the difficulty of selling short in the JGB market. Moreover, JGBs with high coupons are preferred by certain institutional investors, such as insurance companies, which by law are allowed to distribute coupon income to their policy holders only. Historical prices were therefore systematically distorted, with a premium associated with higher-coupon issues. This situation changed somewhat in early 1989, when bond holdings began to be marked to the market for accounting purposes, but the high-coupon issues have not fallen completely out of favor. Along with other factors, such considerations have made it difficult to construct a meaningful yield curve for JGBs.

The Benchmark Issue. Perhaps the most important characteristic of the JGB market is the overwhelming concentration of trading in what is known as the 10-year *benchmark* issue. Up to 90 percent of cash market trading can take place in this issue, and the benchmark issue has been known to turn over up to four times its total volume in a single day. As a result of this enormous liquidity, the benchmark issue will trade at a very significant premium to the other, or side, issues—sometimes as much as 70 to 80 basis points premium. Trading spreads for the benchmark issue can be as narrow as 1 to 2 basis points, while recent side issues and old benchmark issues tend to trade with a spread of 2 to 5 basis points, and side issues at an even wider spread.

The benchmark issue at any given time is determined through a complex process of market interaction by the largest trading firms. To qualify, an issue must be large, with a remaining maturity of at least nine years, and with a relatively high coupon. Benchmark issues thus are not necessarily the most recent issue, and may persist for up to a year or more. In the absence of good new candidate benchmark issues, an older issue may even persist when its remaining maturity is less than nine years.

Since the benchmark issue trades at such a premium, it is frequently held more for speculative reasons, for short-term gains, than as a long-term investment. Long-term investors are still driven by the benchmark issue, however, as it provides the leading indicator for the direction of the entire JGB market, as its name suggests. Moreover, the transition from one benchmark issue to another can be a painful source of market uncertainty and risk; when confidence in an old benchmark issue erodes, it can suffer a sudden market collapse, as occurred in 1986 when JGB 78 (6.2 percent of July 1995) suffered a rise of 60 basis points relative to the rest of the market within seven trading days. As of September 1989, the benchmark issue was JGB 111 (4.6 percent of June 1998), which became the benchmark in November 1988.

Tax Effects. JGBs are subject to a *withholding tax* of 20 percent. For foreign investors, the amount of the tax depends on nationality and their country's tax agreements with Japan. For U.S. investors, the rate is 10 percent. A 16 percent one-time tax on the difference between face and purchase price is also levied on discount bonds at issue. These taxes directly affect the prices of bonds in the secondary market. There is also a *transfer tax* on all domestic sales of

JGB securities; this tax is one of the factors making the maintenance of a short position so expensive, as it has to be paid each time the short position is rolled over (every five days, as settlement dates are currently structured).

JGB Yield Calculations.   JGB yields quoted as a *simple yield* which is different from the yield-to-maturity used with UST securities. The formula is

$$\text{Simple yield} = \frac{(\text{Par} - \text{Price})/(\text{Remaining term}) + \text{Coupon}}{\text{Price}} \quad (2.16)$$

This is just coupon over price, with any capital gain or loss amortized over the life of the security according to a straight-line amortization. (For comparison with UST securities, calculate the yield-to-maturity of the JGB security starting from its coupon and maturity; there is no simple conversion from simple yield to yield-to-maturity.)

JGB Futures Market.   As part of the rapid development of a more complete financial market, the Japanese government in October 1985 introduced trading in futures on the 10-year "long bond." Trading on the same contract opened on the London International Financial Futures Exchange (LIFFE) in July 1987. Contracts are based on a notional 6 percent 10-year government bond, with a standard contract size of ¥100 million, and contract expiration dates in March, June, September, and December, with the next two contracts trading at any time. Delivery is restricted to listed Japanese government bonds with a remaining maturity of at least seven years on delivery date, which is generally the 20th of the month. Delivery price is determined by multiplying the delivery settle price of the futures contract by a conversion factor determined by the coupon and maturity characteristics of the bond being delivered, in a manner similar to that for UST futures. (Contracts traded on LIFFE are for cash settlement, at the delivery settlement price of the corresponding TSE contract.) Last contract trading day is nine Tokyo business days before the last delivery date. JGB futures contracts are marked to market daily and make use of a margin system similar to that used in the UST futures market.

The JGB futures market has been so successful that within its first year, trading volume surpassed that of the extraordinarily liquid UST bond futures market. In mid-1987, open interest on the TSE in the JGB future contract was $85.9 billion. In part this can be attributed to speculation in a new, highly-leveraged instrument, but it also reflects the fact that with JGB futures contracts, investors could for the first time hedge an open position or effectively sell short (because transfer taxes make shorting cash JGBs prohibitively expensive). By mid-1989, daily turnover in the JGB future contract was running at around ¥10 trillion, and at the end of August 1989 there were over ¥20 trillion in outstanding contracts for the benchmark December JGB future contract. Nevertheless, investors in the JGB futures market should exercise caution, as the lack of liquidity in most issues (except the benchmark issue) can create difficulties for the delivering party. Moreover, it is impossible to adequately track the basis of non-benchmark issues on a day-to-day basis because of their illiquidity; most JGB futures traders use the benchmark issue to track basis although, because of its liquidity premium, it will never itself be the cheapest-to-deliver issue. Most frequently, futures positions are closed out prior to the last trading date, to avoid having to deliver (or take delivery of) highly illiquid non-benchmark issues.

JGB Options Market.   The opening of a JGB options market in June 1989 represented another significant step by the Japanese government and financial institutions toward a more complete financial market. Like the JGB futures market when it was introduced in the mid-1980s, JGB options are rapidly becoming a major market, representing a new, highly leveraged set of instruments for both speculation and hedging. Total OTC JGB option trading turnover exceeded ¥11 trillion in July 1989. Traders and investors in yen-denominated bonds should be prepared for the impact of this new market, and they should recognize and understand some of its special characteristics.

The introduction of a JGB options market adds further pressure on the Japanese government and financial industry to move toward continuous settlement and a more liquid repo market. The lack of these features has made the application of classic option pricing models to the JGB market less certain, as the cost of carry, forward prices, and discounting rates are harder to specify accurately. Since it is difficult for dealers to delta hedge some of their options positions using the underlying bonds, they have tended to use the benchmark issue or the future contract to cross-hedge. In the early stages of the JGB options market, trading was largely concentrated on the benchmark and a few side issues. As one would expect, there have been certain discontinuities in option pricing, including some inconsistencies in implied volatilities for options with different strikes and/or expiration dates, that should not necessarily be taken to indicate the existence of profit opportunities.

Because of the affinity of Japanese financial institutions for current high yields, early trading in JGB options was dominated by selling, and especially by call-writing against cash JGB positions. The net effect was to push implied volatility in the JGB options market during its first few months to unrealistically low levels, around 2 percent. This created a real investment opportunity, since historical JGB volatilities have been around 5 percent. As the market absorbed this fact, implied volatility levels began to correct to more realistic average levels. Bid-ask spreads were also wide at first, but as the JGB market has developed they have settled down to competitive market levels.

Other Foreign Government Bond Markets

Belgium. The Belgian government and the Belgian Road Fund issue Belgian Government Bonds (BGBs) backed by the full faith and credit of the government. Since May 1989, a new security called *Obligation Linéaire–Linéaire Obligatie* (OLO) has been issued, and has become the principal form of state issue. Issues range in size from about BFr80–170 million. Maturities range from 5 to 10 years. There were about BFr3.7 trillion (US$116 billion) outstanding as of December 1990. Most are standard bullet-maturity, annual coupon bonds; there have been a few issues with special features, such as a "stepped" coupon, redemption above par, or put and call features. All OLOs are straight, non-callable issues, however.

Canada. The Canadian government bond market resembles the U.S. Treasury market in many ways. Issue size ranges from C$250 million to C$3.5 billion, with a total of about C$140 billion (US$103 billion) outstanding as of December 1990. Maturities range from 2 to 25 years, with two-year issues auctioned quarterly and other issues as required by the government's debt financing needs. Almost all Canadian bonds have bullet maturities with semiannual coupon payments. The 3.75 percent of 1998 is the only callable issue.

France. The French government has issued several kinds of bonds and notes. Until 1985, *Emprunts d'État* (EEs) were issued, with variable structures and features including bullets, zeros, sinking funds, convertability to variable-rate bonds, and indexing. Subsequently, the French Treasury has issued *Obligations Assimilables du Trésor* (OATs), which are mostly bullet-maturity, fixed-coupon issues, but also include some convertible to fixed or variable-rate bonds and some with warrants and indexing features. OATs are issued in maturities ranging from 5 to 30 years. Issue size for EEs was from FFr1–20 billion; for OATs it can be as large as FFr50 billion or more, because new tranches of existing bonds may be reopened.

The Treasury also issues *Bons du Trésor à Taux Fixe et Intérêt Annuel* (BTANs), bullet-maturity notes with fixed annual coupon payments, in maturities from 1 to 7 years, and discount short-term T-bills. Since September 1989, only 2- and 5-year BTANs have been issued. About FFr398 billion (US$79 billion) in BTANs are currently outstanding.

Germany. The German Federal Government (pre-unification West Germany) and its agencies issue a number of different bonds, known as *Bund, Bahn, Post,* and *Unities*. All recent issues have been fixed annual coupon, bullet-maturity bonds. Maturities range from 8 to 12 years, with 10 years the most common. Issue sizes tend to be in the range of DM2–8 billion. The total outstanding as of December 1990 was about DM281 billion (US$185 billion).

The German government also issues medium-term notes (*Kassenobligatio-nen*, or *"Kassen"*) with maturities from 2 to 6 years. Issue sizes are around DM1–2 billion, and there were about DM43 billion (US$29 billion) outstanding as of December 1990. Since 1979, the German government has also issued certain special 5-year federal notes known as *Bundesobligationen* or *Bobls*. Issue sizes range from DM500 million to DM5 billion, and the total outstanding as of December 1990 was about DM123 billion (US$81 billion).

Italy. The Italian government issues a number of forms of debt instruments, including floating rate notes known as *Certificati di Credito del Tesoro* (CCTs), fixed-rate bonds known as *Buoni del Tesoro Poliennali* (BTPs), fixed-rate ECU-denominated issues known as CTEs, and most recently puttable fixed-rate *Certificati del Tesoro con Opzione* (CTOs). BTPs come in maturities of 2 to 7 years; CCTs mostly in 5-year issues (there was a 10-year issue in 1987); CTEs mostly in 5-year maturities; and CTOs in 6-year maturities, puttable at par after 3 years. Issue sizes range from Lit4–6 trillion for CTOs to Lit8–15 trillion for CCTs. The total outstanding as of December 1990 was Lit644 trillion (US$549 billion) with Lit411 trillion, or almost $2/3$, made up of CCT floating notes and another $1/4$, Lit163 trillion, in BTPs. CTEs and CCTs with maturities over 5 years have annual coupon payments, while issues of shorter maturities pay semiannually.

Mexico. Mexican treasury bills, CETES, are the best known fixed-income instruments for foreign investors. CETES account for more than 50 percent of Mexico's outstanding internal debt. The one-year CETE was yielding approximately 17 percent in December 1991, equivalent to nearly 15 percent in U.S. dollars, assuming a 2.4 percent annual devaluation rate of the Mexican peso against the U.S. dollar. Investing in CETES, however, carries the risk of unexpectedly high inflation in Mexico, which also induces a corresponding devaluation of the peso. Historically, there have been periods where the inflation rate was greater than the CETES' interest rate, resulting in *negative real returns* for CETES investors in those periods. *Ajustabonos* are medium-term (3-year or 5-year) local currency bonds issued by the Mexican federal government. The principal amount of the bonds is *adjusted* upwards quarterly by the previous quarter's inflation rate (Mexico's Consumer Price Index—CPI) until its maturity date; hence the name *Ajustabonos*. In addition, *Ajustabonos* pay a quarterly interest that is the multiplicative product of the fixed interest (coupon) rate and the inflation-adjusted principal at the beginning of the quarter. Since the principal is adjusted by the CPI, the *Ajustabono's* fixed interest (coupon) rate represents its yield over inflation, or a *real interest rate*. (This real interest rate is fixed at the date of issuance; for example, the 3-year *Ajustabono* issued on November 19, 1991, has a 4.35 percent coupon rate.)

The *Ajustabono* was introduced in July 1989. It is auctioned every two weeks under the single-price mode at a nominal value of 100,000 Mexican pesos. The *Ajustabono* has become an important and popular instrument in the Mexican fixed-income market. As of November 1991, there were US$10.35 billion of *Ajustabonos* outstanding, and they accounted for 18 percent of the outstanding debt of the Mexican government at that time.

The Netherlands.   The Dutch government issues bonds in maturities ranging from 6 to 15 years. Most recent issues have been fixed, annual coupon, 10-year bullet-maturity bonds, but earlier issues exhibit a variety of structures, including sinking funds and call features. Issue sizes have ranged from Dfl1.25–1.6 billion, with about Dfl181 billion (US$107 billion) outstanding as of December 1990.

Spain.   The Spanish government issues two forms of debt: *Bonos*, in maturities of 3 to 5 years, and *Obligaciones*, in maturities of up to 10 years. All recent issues have been fixed, annual coupon, bullet-maturity bonds, but many older issues were semiannual and some had put and call features. Issue sizes have ranged up to Pta50 billion, with a total of about Pta4.7 trillion (US$47 billion) outstanding as of December 1990.

Switzerland.   The Swiss government issues bonds (SGBs) and notes (SGNs) with maturities from 7 to 25 years. Issue sizes have ranged from SFr200–700 million, and all issues are fixed-coupon, bullet-maturity; many are callable. As of December 1990, there was a total of about SFr12.4 billion (US$9.8 billion) outstanding.

United Kingdom.   The UK issues debt in the form of "gilt-edged stocks," or "gilts." These come in maturities ranging up to 30 years, but perpetuals ("irredeemables") also exist. UK debt exhibits a lively variety of structure, including convertibles, index-linked issues, and "double-dated" issues in addition to perpetuals. Issue sizes range from £400 million to £1.5 billion, with about £114 billion (US$220 billion) total outstanding as of December 1990.

A Note on Interest Rate Swaps

Most corporate and bank debt issues, especially in the huge Euromarket, are floating-rate notes (floaters or FRNs). Floaters are debt issues with interest payments that float, or are revised, every three or six months. The basis for the rate revision is usually some well-established rate such as the London Interbank Offered Rate (LIBOR), Treasury bill or coupon rate, commercial paper rate, or some other money market index. Each FRN, therefore, has a maturity, a spread to the specified index, and a revision (reset) frequency. For the investor, FRNs are appealing because of their stable principal value and built-in protection against interest-rate hikes. Compared with fixed-coupon debt instruments like Treasury bonds and notes, however, the future cash flow stream of an FRN is much more uncertain. The swapping of a fixed-coupon income stream for a floating interest cost of the same duration is an example of a simple **interest-rate swap.**

The interest-rate swap market emerged in 1981 and has been growing rapidly ever since. Markets in swap options ("swaptions") have also developed rapidly. An interest-rate swap may be defined as an exchange of an income stream of one configuration (either fixed or variable rate) for a differently structured income stream on essentially the same notional principal amount. For corporate debt issuers, swap transactions are often useful as a tool to lower borrowing costs; a highly developed swap market provides easy access for investors in fixed- and floating-rate instruments to alter the shape of future income streams from their investments. (See Walmsley, 1988.)

Interest rate, currency, equity, and asset-backed swaps have become standard financial techniques. These are important off-balance-sheet tools for hedging against adverse interest rates and currency and equity price movements. Fixed-income securities traders must, therefore, be familiar with at least the simpler interest-rate swap transactions. For example, profit opportunities can be found by monitoring the term structure of yield spreads between Treasury coupons and similar-duration LIBOR instruments, and their relationship with the term structure of interest-rate swap spreads.

MARKET PARTICIPANTS

The Leveraged Traders

Dealership and proprietary traders of the fixed-income markets are all leveraged players who depend on the highly liquid repo market. Market makers play the major role in bond trading because they provide liquidity by continually quoting bids and offers for all bonds. They are supposed to make their money by selling at offer what was bought at bid, and not by speculating on market direction. Their profit opportunities are not risk-free, however, because as market prices change continuously, dealers are often caught long (or short) in the market after a bid has just been hit (or an offer has been lifted). This market risk is significant when the price gaps up or down and the order flows are one-sided. Dealers therefore have more profit opportunities when the market prices fluctuate as a large volume of both buy and sell orders come in. Successful market makers are good at distinguishing order flows that will quickly reverse from more permanent market trends. Many of them base their judgments on price movements in related instruments; for example, "off-the-run quotes" are spread off the price of the nearest current issue; cash bond prices are based on bond future prices; and so forth. Many such market makers are therefore well-trained in relative-value analysis. Good market makers are also very quick in adjusting their quotes as market conditions change. Experience does count in market making, and it is certainly more art than science.

Proprietary traders, working for either a dealer or an investment partnership, normally base their trading decisions on one of three types of analysis: *technical, fundamental,* or *relative-value.* Technical analysis is based on the premise that a historical study of the markets will provide a means for anticipating the external factors that affect the supply and demand, and in turn the future price behavior, of a particular financial instrument. Fundamental analysis relies on a direct study of those external factors (such as directly observable econometric variables and "leading indicators"). In contrast, relative-value analysis does not attempt to predict the future prices of financial instruments; instead, it is a mathematical approach that quantifies the *relative* richness or cheapness of, for example, a futures contract with respect to its underlying instrument, or an option on a futures contract with respect to other options on the same or similar instruments. While traders may use drastically different evaluation techniques, most would agree that it is helpful to know what other traders are thinking. All would concur that discipline, patience, and consistency are critical success factors in proprietary trading.

The Buy-and-Hold Investors

Pension funds, insurance companies, and mutual funds are key players in the fixed-income markets. The objective of a fixed-income portfolio manager is to generate superior returns through yield enhancement under a set of investment constraints including, but not limited to, duration and credit risk limitations. To achieve this goal, the manager may actively trade or passively manage his or her portfolio to match a selected bond index. Similar to proprietary traders, most active managers rely on either fundamental, technical, or relative-value analysis for their trading decisions. Relative-value analysis, for example, is often used by portfolio managers as a tool to enhance the return of index funds. The manager's portfolio is often made up of many different bonds. Some of the bonds in the portfolio may be rich compared with other bonds in the same sector. The portfolio's return can therefore be enhanced if the manager sells *relatively rich* bonds and replaces them with *relatively cheap* ones.

REFERENCES

Bartlett, William W. (1989). *Mortgage-Backed Securities: Products, Analysis, Trading*, New York: New York Institute of Finance.

Fabozzi, Frank J., ed. (1987). *The Handbook of Treasury Securities: Trading and Portfolio Strategies*, Chicago: Probus Publishing Company.

Fabozzi, Frank J., ed. (1988). *The Handbook of Mortgage-Backed Securities*, (Revised Edition), Chicago: Probus Publishing Company.

Mayer, M. (1991). "Mystery Market: A Look at Trading in Treasuries," *Barron's*, (September).

Schwarz, E. W., J. M. Hill, and T. Schneeweis (1986). *Financial Futures: Fundamentals, Strategies and Applications*, Homewood, IL: Dow Jones-Irwin.

Tang, E. M. (1988). *The Effects of Delivery Options on Interest Rate Futures and Options Contracts*, San Francisco: Portfolio Management Technology.

Trachtenberg, Andrea J. (1987). "Repurchase Agreement," in *The Handbook of Treasury Securities*, (F.J. Fabozzi, ed.), Chicago: Probus Publishing Company.

Walmsley, J. (1988). *The New Financial Instruments*, New York: John Wiley & Sons.

3
Analytical Tools
for Fixed-Income Securities

This chapter presents the basic analytical tools used in evaluating fixed-income securities. The important "time value of money" concept is introduced first, followed by present value and cash flow analysis. It then covers the fundamentals of price and yield calculations, including the notions of duration, convexity, and other measures of sensitivity. The Treasury yield curve in its various guises is also presented and the relevant analytics explored, including a discussion of arbitrage-free pricing of bonds for forward settlement.

INTEREST RATES

Fundamental to all financial calculations is an understanding of *the time value of money*. This involves understanding the relationship between *interest* and *discounting* rates, the terms in which they are quoted, and the various *compounding* and *day-count* conventions used in the financial industry. These concepts are explained in this section.

Basic Definitions

Perhaps the simplest question about financial calculations one can ask is, *"If I invest a dollar (or a million dollars) today, how much will it be worth tomorrow (or in a year)?"* To answer this question, we must of course know the *amount invested,* which is known as the **principal** (or, in the case of a security, the **face amount**). A round-number nominal sum, for example $100, will be used as the principal for illustrations, but it can equally well be any odd amount.

We must also know the **investment rate.** This is the amount by which the principal will increase, or *appreciate,* over a given span of time. The investment rate is almost always quoted as a *percent* of the principal, and the span of time over which that percent appreciation occurs is the **term** of the rate. Thus, if we are guaranteed that $100 deposited in a savings account at a bank will appreciate at an *annual rate* of 8 percent, this means that in one year that $100 will become $108. The $8.00 by which this investment has increased is known as the **interest** on the principal over the investment period—in this case, one year. The investment rate (8 percent in this example) is also known as the **rate of interest,** or simply **interest rate** of the investment.

(Most of the discussion in this section is phrased in terms of *investment.* All the concepts apply equally well to *borrowing,* however. Investment examples can equally well apply to the interest to be *paid out* on a loan or mortgage.)

Interest rates are often quoted in terms other than the simple, annual rate of this illustration. The most important additional feature of an interest rate is its **compounding period.** An investor rarely knows in advance the exact period for which his or her money is to be invested. In fact, investments that have a fixed investment period, like CDs, typically command a premium (a higher interest rate) because the investor is giving up his or her *liquidity* (the freedom to shift the money to some other use) for the duration. It is therefore essential to be able to calculate the value of an investment after a period different from the term for which the interest rate is quoted. One might want to know the value of the above $100 investment after three months, for example, or after 10 1/2 years. To calculate such a value, one must know *how interest is compounded.*

Simple and Compound Interest

Interest is said to be *compounded* because the simplest way to think about the value of an investment over a period *longer* than the term for which the interest rate is quoted is to suppose that at the end of that term, the money is *withdrawn and reinvested* at the same rate. In the above example, the $108 we receive at the end of one year would be reinvested on the same terms. This means that after *another* year, the entire $108 would increase by 8 percent, to a total value of

$$\$116.64 = \$108 \times 1.08 = \$100 \times 1.08^2$$

Note that this is *not* the same as simply receiving $8 interest each year. The difference is the effect of *reinvesting the interest;* this is called **compound interest,** and it is fundamental to many financial calculations.

Interest that is *not* compounded is known as **simple interest.** With simple interest, the interest on principal is never reinvested. The value of an initial principal investment P after N years at r percent simple interest is given by the formula

$$V = P \times \left(1 + \left(N \times \frac{r}{100}\right)\right) \tag{3.1}$$

The value of an initial principal investment P after N years at r percent interest *compounded annually* is given by the formula

$$V = P \times \left(1 + \frac{r}{100}\right)^N \tag{3.2}$$

The difference between simple and compound interest is crucial, and over long periods it can be quite dramatic. Table 3.1 shows the value of a $100 investment over varying periods under simple and compound interest-rate assumptions.

To make matters more complex, the *compounding period* is not always the same as the term for which a rate is quoted. Because U.S. Treasury notes and bonds pay coupons (which are a form of simple interest) on a semiannual basis, rates associated with bonds are frequently quoted in *annual* terms, but compounded *semiannually*. A one-year investment or $100 at an 8 percent annual rate, compounded semiannually, would return

$$\$100 \times 1.04^2 = \$108.16$$

Table 3.1 Total Return on $100
for 8 Percent Simple and Compound Interest

Investment Period (yr)	Simple Interest	Compound Interest
1	108.00	108.00
2	116.00	116.64
5	140.00	146.93
10	180.00	215.89
20	260.00	466.10
50	500.00	4,690.22

After six months, we receive 4 percent, or half the annual rate, of our initial principal. This is then *reinvested* along with the original principal, and after the second six months, we receive an additional 4 percent of the $104 invested for that period. This amounts to multiplying the original principal twice by 1.04, instead of once by 1.08, as we would in the annually compounding case.

After two years, still compounding semiannually, the $100 would become

$$\$100 \times 1.04^4 = \$116.98$$

Note that this is slightly more than we receive when the interest is compounded annually.

For an annual interest rate of r percent, compounded M times a year, the value of an initial principal investment P after N years is given by the formula

$$V = P \times \left(1 + \frac{r/M}{100}\right)^{N \times M} \tag{3.3}$$

As Equation (3.3) illustrates, more frequent compounding (a shorter compounding period) leads to more rapid growth in an investment. Over a long enough span, a shorter compounding period can make a big difference. Table 3.2 shows the result of investing $100 for varying periods with annual, semiannual, and quarterly compounding.

In order to compare the results of investing a sum at different rates with different compounding periods, it is convenient to convert to a common form. One such comparison yardstick is the **total return** over a given period. This is the total percentage increase in an investment over the given period, taking into account any compounding. For a one-year period, this is also known as the **annualized return**. The annualized return on an investment at 8 percent simple interest is 8 percent. It is still 8 percent with annual compounding. It is

Table 3.2 Total Return on $100 Compounded Variously at 10 Percent

Investment Period (yr)	Annual Compounding	Semiannual Compounding	Quarterly Compounding
1	110.00	110.25	110.38
2	121.00	121.55	121.84
5	161.05	162.89	163.86
10	259.37	265.30	268.50
20	672.73	703.83	720.91
50	11,738.35	13,142.53	13,954.09

8.16 percent with semiannual compounding, and 8.24 percent with quarterly compounding. Because "total return" makes no reference to a compounding period, it is understood to refer to the specified investment period. It is also common to convert rates quoted in different terms to a standard form quoted in annual terms with a specified compounding period, typically annual or semiannual (which is also known as "bond equivalent," since most bonds pay their coupons semiannually).

When one first studies compound interest, it is common to suspect that if only the compounding period were made short enough (weekly, daily, or hourly, for example), the annualized return on an investment could be made arbitrarily high. But this is not true. The annualized return on an investment compounded at shorter and shorter intervals approaches a limit. The effect of compounding more and more frequently is offset by the fact that interest accumulates over each interval at a smaller and smaller fraction of the annual rate. In the limit, interest is said to be **continuously compounded.** The formula for the value of an initial investment of principal P with *continuous compounding* at rate r for one year is

$$V = P \times e^{r/100} \tag{3.4}$$

where e is a mathematical constant that equals approximately 2.718. (This is demonstrated mathematically in Appendix A.)

The annualized return on an investment compounded continuously at 8 percent is 8.329 percent. The continuously compounded rate is another standard form commonly used in more theoretical treatments, as it is mathematically very convenient, but it is not commonly used in practical financial applications.

Interest for Arbitrary Periods

So far, we have been comparing investments over periods that are even multiples of the terms in which the interest rates are quoted. But how do we calculate the result of investing a sum for, say, a year and three months?

For simple interest, the calculation is straightforward. The total return on an investment with original principal P over an investment period T at rate r is given by

$$V = P \times (1 + (T \times r/100)) \tag{3.5}$$

where T is measured in years when r is given as an annual rate (or, in general, T is given in multiples of the term for which r is quoted). Note that T may have a fractional part; $100 invested at 8 percent simple annual interest for 1 $\frac{1}{4}$ years would have a total return for the investment period of

$$\$100 \times (1 + (1.25 \times 0.08)) = \$100 \times 1.10 = \$110$$

The most natural way to handle *compounding* for fractional periods is the **exponential** or **geometric** compounding convention. Using this convention, the result of investing a principal amount P for T years at an annual rate of r would be given by

$$V = P \times (1 + r/100)^T \tag{3.6}$$

If the interest rate r is given in other than annual terms, the investment period T must be expressed as a multiple of the term.

The result of investing $100 for 1$\frac{1}{4}$ years at 8 percent compounded annually would thus be

$$\$100 \times 1.08^{1.25} = \$110.0981$$

For continuous compounding, the corresponding formula is

$$V = P \times e^{T \times r/100} \tag{3.7}$$

where, again, the investment period T must be expressed as a multiple of the term for which the rate r is quoted if this is other than annual.

In some financial applications, other conventions are used to calculate compound interest. These conventions were introduced to simplify calculations in the days before computers and programmable hand calculators, but have now been enshrined in tradition and law. One important type of calculation in which different conventions exist is the calculation of fractions of a year, or **day counts.**

Day Counts

In the preceding examples, we assumed that an investment period of "a year and a quarter" could be expressed as exactly 1.25 years. Unfortunately, the financial world is not always so simple. There are several established conventions for converting a given span of time into multiples and fractions of years. The most straightforward simply divides the actual number of days in the period by 365. This is known as the **actual-actual** day count convention. In some circumstances, it is also known as the **exact** day count method. (365 is usually used as the denominator even if the period in question falls in, or overlaps with, a leap year, although for some long-term investments where rates are calculated based on actual elapsed years, a value of 365.25 is used.)

A second convention, common in calculations related to securities with maturities less than a year, computes the number of days in a given investment period based on 30 days for each month entirely contained in the period, plus any additional days. The total number of days is then divided by 360 (not 365) to get the appropriate fraction or multiple of a year. This is known as the **30-360** day count convention, sometimes called the **ordinary** day count method.

Finally, in some applications a hybrid of the two is used, in which the exact number of days in the period is divided by 360; this is often referred to as the **actual-360** or **Banker's Rule** day count method. In any financial application, it is very important to know the relevant day count conventions and apply them consistently.

Example 3.1

An investment is to be held from July 4, 1991 through April 1, 1992. At a 10 percent annual interest rate, what would be the total return on $100 under each of the three day count conventions? (Assume that the starting and ending dates are both included in the period.)

Using the actual-actual convention, the actual number of days in the investment period is

$$28 + 31 + 30 + 31 + 30 + 31 + 31 + 29 + 31 + 1 = 273$$

Note that we include leap year day in our count. This is divided by 365 to get the investment period T in terms of years

$$T = 273/365 = 0.7479$$

The total return for the period, assuming simple interest, is calculated by using Equation (3.5)

$$V = \$100 \times (1 + (0.08 \times 0.7479)) = \$100 \times 1.059832 = \$105.9832$$

The total return for this period assuming annual compounding is calculated by using Equation (3.6)

$$V = \$100 \times (1 + 0.08)^{0.7479} = \$100 \times 1.059248 = \$105.9248$$

If we use the 30-360 day count convention, the number of days in the period becomes

$$28 + 30 + 30 + 30 + 30 + 30 + 30 + 30 + 30 + 1 = 269$$

and the period T expressed in years is then

$$T = 269/360 = 0.7472$$

The total return, assuming simple interest, would then be

$$V = \$100 \times (1 + (0.08 \times 0.7472)) = \$100 \times 1.059776 = \$105.9776$$

Assuming annual compounding, it would be

$$V = \$100 \times (1 + 0.08)^{0.7472} = \$100 \times 1.059191 = \$105.9191$$

Finally, if we use the actual-360 convention, the period T becomes

$$T = 273/360 = 0.7583$$

The total return assuming simple interest is

$$V = \$100 \times (1 + (0.08 \times 0.7583)) = \$100 \times 1.060664 = \$106.0664$$

And assuming annual compounding

$$V = \$100 \times (1 + 0.08)^{0.7583} = \$100 \times 1.060096 = \$106.0096$$

These results are summarized in Table 3.3. A few pennies' or fractions of pennies' difference may not seem like much, but if the principal involved is $100 million instead of $100, the difference is substantial.

■

Table 3.3 Total Return on $100 at 8 Percent for Different Day Count Conventions for Period from July 4, 1991, to April 1, 1992

Convention	Simple Interest	Annual Compounding
Actual-Actual	105.9832	105.9248
30-360	105.9776	105.9191
Actual-360	106.0664	106.0096

Conversion Between Different Interest Rate Conventions

Where there is no fixed investment period, total return cannot be used as a common basis for comparison. It is therefore important to be able to convert between different conventions for expressing interest rates. There are many formulas for converting back and forth between various formats. The basic method used to derive all these formulas is to equate the corresponding total returns for a common period (usually a year). This method can be used to derive any desired conversion formula.

Simple Interest. For simple interest, conversion is easy. If r_m is a simple interest rate quoted for a term that is $1/m$ of a year, and we want to convert to an annual rate r, we equate the annual returns

$$1 + r/100 = 1 + r_m/100 \times m$$

so

$$r = r_m \times m \qquad (3.8)$$

Thus, a 2 percent quarterly simple interest rate is equivalent to an 8 percent annual simple interest rate.

Compound Interest. A compound interest rate $r_{m,m}$ quoted for a term that is $1/m$ of a year, *and with a compounding period equal to that same term*, can be converted to a rate $r_{1,m}$ quoted in annual terms *but still compounded every* $1/m$ of a year by a similar formula. Equating total returns for one year

$$\left(1 + \frac{r_{1,m}/100}{m}\right)^m = (1 + r_{m,m}/100)^m$$

so

$$r_{1,m} = r_{m,m} \times m \qquad (3.9)$$

That is, the conversion to annual terms is the *same* for simple and compound interest *as long as the compounding period remains the same.*

Some Conventional Assumptions. Since it is so straightforward to convert to annual terms, **we will assume that all interest rates are given in annual terms** whatever their compounding period, unless otherwise stated. It is also convenient to quote interest rates in *decimal* rather than percent form, to avoid cluttering equations with factors of 100. For all equations, **we will henceforth express interest rates in decimal form,** unless explicitly stated otherwise.

Changing the Compounding Period. To convert a rate r_m with compounding period equal to $1/m$ of a year to an annually compounding rate r, we equate the corresponding annual total returns, as usual

$$1 + r = (1 + r_m)^m$$

so

$$r = (1 + r_m)^m - 1 \qquad (3.10)$$

The inverse of this equation gives us a rate compounded m times annually in terms of an annually compounded rate

$$r_m = m \times \left[(1 + r)^{1/m} - 1\right] \qquad (3.11)$$

So, for example, to convert a 10 percent annually compounded interest rate into semiannually-compounded ("bond equivalent") terms, we calculate

$$2 \times (1.1^{1/2} - 1) = 2 \times (1.04881 - 1) = 2 \times 0.04881 = 0.09762$$

(Remember that $x^{1/2} = \sqrt{x}$.) This says that a 9.762 percent semiannually compounded rate will bring the same return as a 10 percent annually compounded rate.

Combining Equations (3.10) and (3.11), we can convert rates from any arbitrary compounding period to any other. Annual, semiannual, quarterly, and monthly rates are all fairly common in practice, so it is useful to be comfortable switching back and forth between rates quoted in these terms.

Variable or Uncertain Interest Rates

The techniques discussed so far can be used to analyze the behavior of investments over periods during which interest rates *change.* For example, suppose we invest \$100 at 8 percent for one year, at the end of which time rates have risen, and we reinvest for a second year at 10 percent interest. What will our total return for the two year investment period amount to? At what annually compounded rate would we have to have invested initially to match this return?

The total return for the two year period is given by

$$\$100 \times 1.08 \times 1.10 = \$118.80$$

We want to know what rate r would produce this return when compounded annually. That is, we seek r such that

$$\$100 \times (1 + r)^2 = \$118.80$$

This is just

$$r = \sqrt{1.188} - 1 = 0.08995$$

Our *effective annually compounded interest rate* for the period is 8.995 percent. If we were able to borrow money at 8.5 percent, or even 8.75 percent for the duration to finance our investment, we would make a profit. A rate of 8.995 percent is the **breakeven financing rate** for this investment. This is a very simple example of **total return analysis,** which is a fundamental financial technique used in many contexts.

In our discussion so far, we have implicitly assumed that all investments have a *known* interest rate. When you deposit money in a savings account or CD, or buy a U.S. Treasury bond as a long-term investment, you usually know what interest rate you will receive. But when you buy stock or real estate, or take out an adjustable-rate mortgage, the relevant interest rate is far from certain. Even an asset with a known coupon rate, such as a Treasury bond, has an uncertain rate of return if it is bought *speculatively*, that is, with the expectation of price appreciation and profitable resale after a relatively short holding period. The tools developed in this section are still useful, however. We can analyze the *functional relationship* between any appreciation in the value of an investment and the corresponding rate of return over the investment period. This is the essence of *bond price-yield analysis*. Where future uncertainty can be quantified, we can analyze the *expected* rate of return on such investments. This is an important aspect of the valuation of *options* and other contingent claims.

DISCOUNTING, PRESENT VALUE, AND CASH FLOW ANALYSIS

Most investments will not just sit like a pumpkin, quietly growing until they are "plucked" and converted to some other use. (Some do—CDs, zero-coupon bonds, and non-rental real estate are examples.) More commonly, an investment will produce periodic **cash flows** in the form of dividends or coupon payments, rent, or some other form. An enormous part of financial theory and practice is concerned with the planning and analysis of such cash flows. Fundamental to all cash flow analysis is the notion of the *present value* of a future cash flow.

Present Value of a Future Cash Flow

In this section, we consider the question:

What is the value of a dollar to be received tomorrow, or in one or ten years, today?

As in the previous section, we will for the time being assume that there is a known, fixed interest rate for the period in question. One approach to valuing future cash flows is to ask:

What sum today would result in the projected cash flow if invested at available rates?

That is, how much money would we have to invest today to *finance* that future cash flow—to be sure of having the exact sum required on the specified date? For example, suppose we want to find the current value of $100 to be received one year from today, under the assumption of 6 percent annually compounded interest rates. We want to find sum X such that

$$X \times 1.06 = \$100$$

Clearly,

$$X = \$100 \times \frac{1}{1.06} = \$100 \times 0.9434 = \$94.34$$

The factor $1/1.06 = 0.9434$ here is known as the **discounting factor** for the period in question. We are *discounting the future cash flow back* at a 6 percent rate to get its **present value.** Naturally, the discounting factor is less than 1; this corresponds to the fact that a dollar deferred is worth less than a dollar today. In general, we can use Equation (3.6) to calculate the appropriate discounting factor for an arbitrary period T

$$\mathrm{DF}(T) = \frac{1}{(1 + r)^T} \qquad (3.12)$$

where T = period measured in years
   r = annually compounded interest rate

Note that using this discounting factor, the present value of the future cash flow resulting from investing $100 at the "going rate" of r for any given period T is exactly $100, as we would expect

$$\$100 \times (1 + r)^T \times \mathrm{DF}(T) = \$100 \times (1 + r)^T / (1 + r)^T = \$100$$

Table 3.4   Present Value of $100 in N Years at 8 Percent Compound Interest Rate

N (years)	Present Value
1	92.59
2	85.73
5	68.06
10	46.32
20	21.45
50	2.13

The value of a dollar dwindles rapidly as it recedes into the future, exactly as the value of a dollar invested today at compound interest balloons with the years. Table 3.4 illustrates this fact.

Valuation Principle

It is indeed common sense to say that a dollar next year is only worth what it would cost today to finance the receipt of that future dollar. Now comes the payoff: *any* investment with known future cash flows can be valued by taking the *sum* of *all* its future cash flows. Think of the investment as being "unbundled" into its component cash flows. The value of the investment is just the sum of the values of its components, each of which can be valued using the above techniques. *It does not matter that the various cash flows may occur on different dates.* This is one of the fundamental principles of financial analysis:

> **VALUATION PRINCIPLE: The value of an investment with known future cash flows is just the aggregate present value of all those future cash flows.**

Annuities

An **annuity** in its most general form is a contract to pay out agreed-upon payments at equal intervals over some fixed period. Rental agreements, mortgage payments, interest on loans, and coupon payments on bonds can all be viewed as annuities. (Originally, the term referred only to *annual* payments, but with time it has come to include other regular payments as well.) For simplicity, we will first consider annuities with *fixed annual* payments.

What is the value of an annuity A paying $100 each year for five years? Once again, the present value depends on our assumptions about interest rates.

Let us assume an 8 percent annually compounded interest rate. Then the present value of our annuity will be the sum of the present (discounted) values of its component cash flows

$$A = \$100 \times \frac{1}{1.08} + \$100 \times \frac{1}{(1.08)^2} + \$100 \times \frac{1}{(1.08)^3}$$

$$+ \$100 \times \frac{1}{(1.08)^4} + \$100 \times \frac{1}{(1.08)^5}$$

$$= \$92.59 + \$85.73 + \$79.38 + \$73.50 + \$68.06$$

$$= \$399.26$$

Notice that in this formula, the fixed payment \$100 occurs in each term; it will be a lot easier if we *factor out* the constant annuity payment, treating the general annuity with constant payments as if each payment were just \$1. In general, the value of an annuity A paying \$1 each year for N years will be given by the formula

$$A = \frac{1}{1 + r} + \frac{1}{(1 + r)^2} + \cdots + \frac{1}{(1 + r)^N}$$

which we can also write as

$$A = \sum_{i=1}^{N} \frac{1}{(1 + r)^i}$$

(The $\sum$ symbol is used to abbreviate such summations, thus making the use of "$\cdots$" unnecessary.)

This expression can be simplified. First, we will simplify the discounting factor for one year

$$x = \frac{1}{1 + r}$$

Our expression for the present value of the annuity then becomes

$$A = \sum_{i=1}^{N} x^i \tag{3.13}$$

It turns out that we can get rid of the "summation" in this formula and write it in a simple closed form

$$A = \sum_{i=1}^{N} x^i = x \times \frac{1 - x^N}{1 - x} \qquad (3.14)$$

This is because

$$\sum_{i=1}^{N} x^i = x + x^2 + \cdots + x^N = x \times \left(1 + x + x^2 + \cdots + x^{N-1}\right)$$

and

$$\left(1 + x + x^2 + \cdots + x^{N-1}\right) \times (1 - x) = 1 - x^N$$

because all the terms except the first and last in the product cancel out.

We can even simplify Equation (3.14) a little more, using the fact that from Equation (3.13),

$$\frac{x}{1 - x} = \frac{1/(1 + r)}{1 - [1/(1 + r)]}$$

$$= \frac{1/(1 + r)}{r/(1 + r)} = \frac{1}{r}$$

so

$$A = \frac{1 - x^N}{r} \qquad (3.15)$$

Equations (3.14) and (3.15) are very useful simplifications, since annuities with fixed payments are very common in one form or another. (For example, the coupon payments on a U.S. Treasury note or bond can be viewed as such an annuity.)

Lottery Payments. When a state lottery or a sweepstakes offers a "$10 million" prize, they do not usually have the state treasurer (or Ed McMahon) hand the lucky winner a certified check for $10,000,000. They usually pay out the prize money in stages, typically over 20–40 years. We now have the tools to determine **how much the lottery sponsors must set aside to fund a given**

prize (or, equivalently, **how much winning the lottery is really worth in today's dollars**).

For simplicity, let us assume a $10 million prize, to be paid out in equal annual payments over a period of 40 years. If we assume a fixed interest rate of 8 percent for the entire period, we are asking for the value of

$$\$250,000 \times \sum_{i=1}^{40} = \$250,000 \times \frac{1 - x^{40}}{r}$$

Since $r = 0.08$ and $x = 1/(1+r) = 0.9259$, this works out to be $2,981,314.36, or just under $3 million. So it is entirely possible for a lottery to sell *far fewer* than 10 million $1 tickets and still make a profit.

Of course, the lottery sponsors must be able to **lock in** the rate r to guarantee this result. This is typically accomplished by buying *zero-coupon bonds,* one maturing on each payment date. Zero-coupon bonds, as described in Chapter 2, are bonds with no coupon payments—just a lump sum at maturity. A $100 zero-coupon bond of maturity n years is worth just $100 \times x_n^n$, where $x_n = 1/(1 + r_n)$ is the discounting factor corresponding to the annualized investment rate r_n currently available on an n-year basis. Because the r_n may vary with n, lottery sponsors may actually be able to *improve* on the value calculated, which is based on a single, fixed rate r for all payment dates.

Perpetual Annuities.   A **perpetual annuity** is an annuity that continues paying a regular amount forever (or possibly until redeemed by the recipient of the payments under some previously agreed-upon terms). A life annuity, which pays a regular dividend to the bearer until death, can best be analyzed as a perpetual annuity, since it is uncertain what its true term will be.

What is the present value of a perpetual annuity paying one dollar a year forever? One might be tempted to say that the value is infinite, because in principle the amount actually paid out grows without bound, but when discounting is taken into account, even a perpetual annuity has a definite present value. To see why this is so, consider a sum of $100 invested at a fixed rate of 8 percent. Every year, this investment will pay $8.00. The principal will remain untouched, so in effect we have *created* a perpetual annuity with a current value of $100. Of course, this result depends on the assumption that the rate of return on the investment will remain the same forever. In practice, almost all investments have some fixed or limiting *term*—even if it is rather long, such as 30 years in the case of a long-term U.S. Treasury bond. At the end of the investment term, the investor faces *reinvestment risk*—the risk that the interest rate at that juncture will be unfavorably low. But for the purposes of this example we ignore reinvestment risk.

The algebra for valuing a perpetual annuity is similar to that for an annuity with a fixed, finite term. The resulting formula is even simpler. We have

$$A = \sum_{i=1}^{\infty} x^i = x + x^2 + \cdots$$

$$= x \times (1 + x + x^2 + \cdots)$$

$$= x \times (1 + A)$$

so

$$A = \frac{x}{1-x} = \frac{1/(1+r)}{1-[1/(1+r)]} = 1/r \qquad (3.16)$$

where, as before, x is the discounting factor $1/(1+r)$. In our example above, the investment rate r is 8 percent, $x = 1/1.08 = .9259$, and $A = \$12.50$. That is, $\$12.50$ invested at 8 percent will fund a $1 annual payment in perpetuity, and $100 will fund an $8 perpetual annuity.

An Application: Valuing a Life Memebership.   Once the algebra required to value perpetual annuities is understood, one can analyze a surprising variety of investment scenarios. To take one simple example, consider a membership organization that wants to offer *life memberships*. If the annual membership fee is currently $25, what would be a reasonable price for a life membership? To answer this question, some additional information about the expected levels of interest rates is required. We need to know the *investment rate, r*, at which the sum received for a life membership will be invested. We also need to know the *inflation rate, i*, at which the cost of an annual membership will grow. Finally, we need to make an actuarial assumption about the average life span of a member. What we would like to be able to do is to fund a perpetual annuity in which the annual payments would be constantly adjusted up to take inflation into account. Under certain circumstances—if the investment rate r is greater than the inflation rate i—this may be possible. If the investment rate is less than or equal to the inflation rate, however, it will not be possible, no matter how much is initially charged. To see this, we calculate the amount remaining after n years on the assumption that the initial sum to be invested (the value of the life membership) is M, and that each year the organization takes out the amount of an annual membership, m, adjusted up to take inflation into account. The amount left after the first year would be

$$A_1 = M \times (1+r) - m \times (1+i)$$

After two years, the amount left would then be

$$A_2 = [M \times (1 + r) - m \times (1 + i)] \times (1 + r) - m \times (1 + i)^2$$

And after n years, the amount left would be:

$$
\begin{aligned}
A_n &= M \times (1 + r)^n - m \times (1 + i) \times (1 + r)^{n-1} \\
&\quad - m \times (1 + i)^2 \times (1 + r)^{n-2} - \cdots - m \times (1 + i)^n \\
&= (1 + r)^n \times \left[M - m \times \sum_{k=1}^{n} \left(\frac{1 + i}{1 + r} \right)^k \right]
\end{aligned}
$$
(3.17a)

$$
= (1 + r)^n \times \left[M - m \times \frac{1 + i}{1 + r} \times \frac{\left(\dfrac{1 + i}{1 + r} \right)^n - 1}{\dfrac{1 + i}{1 + r} - 1} \right]
$$
(3.17b)

It is convenient for some purposes to rewrite this expression in terms of the *spread* $s = r - i$ between the investment and inflation rates. We have

$$\frac{1 + i}{1 + r} = 1 - \frac{r - i}{1 + r} = 1 - \frac{s}{1 + r}$$

Letting $s' = s/(1 + r)$ be the *adjusted spread* (which, unless rates become hyperinflationary, will be very close to s) we have

$$A_n = \left[M + m \times (1 - s') \times \frac{(1 - s')^n - 1}{s'} \right] \times (1 + r)^n$$
(3.18)

In order for the life membership to finance the necessary payments over a long enough span, it is necessary and sufficient that A_n be positive for all n up to the critical term; if A_n is positive for *all* n, we have a perpetual membership (a perpetual annuity with the annual payments adjusted for inflation).

Clearly, if $s' < 0$, that is, if the inflation rate is greater than the rate at which the funds can be invested, then the term $(1 - s')^n$ will grow without bound, so $[(1 - s')^n - 1]/s'$ will get increasingly negative, and A_n will eventually turn negative too; that is, it will be impossible to fund a perpetual membership no matter how large M is made relative to m. On the other hand, if $s' > 0$, that is, if we are able to beat inflation by a spread of s' in investing the life membership funds, then the term $(1 - s')^n$ will tend to zero as n grows, and A_n will tend to $[M - m/s' \times (1 - s)] \times (1 + r)^n$ as n grows.

What this says is that if we can guarantee a spread of s' between the investment rate and inflation, then we should charge $1/s' \times m$ in order to fund a *perpetual membership*. If we expect to beat inflation by 2 percent, for example, and if the current investment rate is 8 percent, so $s' = 0.02/1.08 = 0.0185$, we should charge 54 times the cost of an annual membership, or \$1,350, for a life membership. (Note that this analysis holds even if investment and inflation rates *change* over the course of time, as they certainly will. What matters is the *spread s* between the two rates.)

What will happen if we are wrong in our projections, and fail to maintain this favorable spread between r and i? This could happen, for example, if we were to lock the investment into a long-term CD or some other fixed-income security, and inflation were to skyrocket. If the inflation rate i is *equal* to the investment rate r, then $s' = 0$, and Equation (3.18) tells us nothing, because we cannot divide by zero. Going back to Equation (3.17a), we see directly that

$$A_n = (1 + r)^n \times [M - (m \times n)]$$

This means that after M/m years, the initial funds will be exhausted, and the organization will have to begin to pay the costs of membership out of other funds for the balance of the life of the member. If we continue to assume $M = 54 \times m$, as suggested by an expected investment-inflation spread of 2 percent, this would mean that the "life membership" would be fully funded for 54 years—still a reasonably conservative assumption.

Another, more intuitive way to see this result when $r = i$ is to think of the original sum to be invested, M, as divided into M/m little pieces, each of size m; each of these pieces will obviously exactly fund a payment of $(1 + i)^k \times m$ after k years. One piece is paid out each year. After M/m years, all the pieces are gone.

What if inflation increases, and the spread s of investment to inflation turns negative? How long would we have before going into debt? From Equation (3.18), we must have

$$0 = \left[M + m \times (1 - s') \times \frac{(1 - s')^n - 1}{s'} \right]$$

or

$$\frac{M}{m} = -(1 - s') \times \frac{(1 - s')^n - 1}{s'}$$

If we assume an unfavorable spread of $s' = -2$ percent, then, still taking $M = 54 \times m$, we have

$$54 = 1.02 \times \frac{1.02^n - 1}{.02}$$

so

$$2.06 = 1.02^n$$

and

$$n = 36.5$$

That is, after about 36.5 years, the fund would be exhausted and the organization would have to start paying the annual cost of the life membership out of other funds.

The actual behavior of such a fund under three scenarios: $i = 8$ percent, $r = 6$ percent; $i = 8$ percent, $r = 8$ percent; and $i = 8$ percent, $r = 10$ percent, is shown in Table 3.5.

Table 3.5 Funding a Life Membership
under Different Interest Rate Scenarios*

	$r = 6\%$	$r = 8\%$	$r = 10\%$
1	1,324.53	1,325.00	1,325.45
2	1,298.58	1,300.00	1,301.36
3	1,272.13	1,275.00	1,277.69
4	1,245.19	1,250.00	1,254.46
5	1,217.74	1,225.00	1,231.66
10	1,072.53	1,100.00	1,123.68
15	913.09	975.00	1,025.18
20	738.03	850.00	935.31
25	545.82	725.00	853.32
30	334.79	600.00	778.51
35	103.07	475.00	710.27
40	−151.34	350.00	648.00
45	−430.68	225.00	591.20
50	−737.39	100.00	539.37
51	−802.24	75.00	529.56
52	−868.32	50.00	519.94
53	−935.65	25.00	510.48
54	−1004.25	0.00	501.20
55	−1074.14	−25.00	492.09
60	−1443.88	−50.00	448.95

* Columns show amount remaining/owed in today's dollars discounted back at the rate r with $i = 8\%$.

THE PRICE-YIELD RELATIONSHIP FOR BONDS

Because the present value, or fair price, of a bond is sensitive to interest rates, and because bonds with the same price can have very different coupon characteristics, players in the fixed-income market often look at a different measure of value, the **bond yield.** There are several different kinds of yields, but by far the most commonly used is the **yield-to-maturity.**

The yield-to-maturity of a bond or note is often quoted along with the market price; this yield is defined as the semiannually-compounded discounting interest rate that makes the net present value of an issue's future income stream equal to its current market price. The formula connecting price and yield is

$$IP = \frac{100}{[1 + (y/2)]^{N-1+(d/D)}} + \sum_{k=1}^{N} \frac{C/2}{[1 + (y/2)]^{k-1+(d/D)}} \qquad (3.19)$$

where   IP = invoice price (including accrued interest)
N = number of remaining coupon payments
C = annual coupon in percent terms
d = actual number of days to the next coupon payment
D = number of days in the current coupon period
y = annual yield in decimal terms

If this calculation is performed on a coupon date, it simplifies to

$$IP = \frac{100}{[1 + (y/2)]^{N}} + \sum_{k=1}^{N} \frac{C/2}{[1 + (y/2)]^{k}} \qquad (3.20)$$

In the terminology of financial theory, this yield is the bond's "internal rate of return."

(Actually, Equation (3.20) gives what is known in the industry as the "true" yield-to-maturity. There is another, slightly different formula used by the U.S. Treasury to calculate the "treasury" yield-to-maturity, and both formulas must be complicated slightly to take into account the possibility of an *odd first coupon period.* The details of these two approaches, including the handling of an odd first coupon period, are explained in Appendix B.)

Qualitative Behavior of Bond Prices and Yields

The relationship between the bond's price and its yield is determined by three factors: the bond's face value, its coupon rate, and the remaining time to maturity. Given these three factors, Equation (3.19) (or (3.20) on a coupon date) allows us to determine the bond's theoretical invoice price given the yield, or to solve for the bond's yield, given the invoice price. These formulas also give us important information about the *qualitative behavior of bond prices and yields*.

A bond trading at 100.00 has a price equal to its face value, and is said to be trading at **par.** One of the fundamental facts about bond price-yield relationships is that:

[BPY1]: The price of a bond will be equal to 100.00 (par) exactly when the yield is equal to the coupon rate.

One way to see this is to rewrite Equation (3.20) in terms of a *unit* face value, dividing through by 100 and letting c equal the coupon rate in *decimal:*

$$IP = \frac{1}{[1 + (y/2)]^N} + \sum_{k=1}^{N} \frac{c/2}{[1 + (y/2)]^k} \qquad (3.21)$$

Now, if we set $y = c$ in this equation, we have

$$IP = \frac{1}{[1 + (c/2)]^N} + \sum_{k=1}^{N} \frac{c/2}{[1 + (c/2)]^k} \qquad (3.22)$$

But the summation term can be simplified

$$\sum_{k=1}^{N} \frac{c/2}{[1 + (c/2)]^k} = \sum_{k=1}^{N} \frac{1 + (c/2) - 1}{[1 + (c/2)]^k} = \sum_{k=1}^{N} \frac{1 + (c/2)}{[1 + (c/2)]^k} - \sum_{k=1}^{N} \frac{1}{[1 + (c/2)]^k}$$

$$= \sum_{k=0}^{N-1} \frac{1}{[1 + (c/2)]^k} - \sum_{k=1}^{N} \frac{1}{[1 + (c/2)]^k}$$

$$= 1 - \frac{1}{[1 + (c/2)]^N}$$

So after combining with the first term in Equation (3.22), $1/[1 + (c/2)]^N$, we see that $IP = 1$, and the bond is indeed trading at par.

A more intuitive, if less rigorous, way to see this is to recall that the *yield-to-maturity* y of a bond is defined to be the rate at which the sum of all future cash flows properly discounted at the semiannually compounding rate y gives the current invoice price. But this is *equivalent* to asserting that the yield is the rate y at which *the current invoice price would be adequate to finance all future cash flows, if invested at y percent paid semiannually.* And it is obvious that 100 (or the face value of the bond) invested *at the coupon rate C* will be exactly adequate to finance all the coupon cash flows, leaving 100 (or the face value) to be paid out at maturity. Paying semiannual interest at the rate *C* is *by definition* the same as paying half the coupon amount, *C*/2, twice annually. Viewing the yield alternatively as a *discounting* rate and as an *investment* or *financing* rate can be very helpful in understanding the qualitative behavior of bond prices and yields.

Another fundamental fact about bond price and yield is that they move *inversely* to each other; that is:

[BPY2]: A bond's price rises when the bond's yield falls, and vice versa.

This should be evident from Equations (3.19) and (3.20); the yield appears only in the denominators, in the discounting terms. If the yield *y* is increased, the discounting term $1/(1 + y/2)$ will become smaller, so the price, which is the sum of the discounted cash flows, will shrink. (Since prices *fall* when yields *rise,* a **bear market** in bonds is one in which yields are *rising.* You have to be careful when you ask a bond trader whether the market is "up"!)

As an extension of principles [BPY1] and [BPY2], we have:

[BPY3]: A bond will trade at a *discount* (less than par) precisely when its yield is *above* the bond's coupon. It will trade at a *premium* (above par) precisely when its yield is *below* the bond's coupon.

DURATION, CONVEXITY, AND OTHER SENSITIVITY MEASURES

Duration and the Value of a Basis Point

In examining the price sensitivity of an individual bond or note to interest-rate movements, traders often refer to its **duration,** a cash flow–weighted average maturity measure. For historical and technical reasons, the measure most frequently used is known as the **modified duration.** On a coupon date, modified duration is given by the formula

$$D_{\mathrm{mod}} = \left(\frac{1}{1 + y/2}\right)\frac{\text{Sum of time weighted cash flows}}{\text{Invoice price}} \qquad (3.23)$$

$$= \left(\frac{1}{1 + y/2}\right)\frac{\displaystyle\sum_{t=1}^{M} \frac{tC/2}{(1 + y/2)^t} + \frac{100M}{(1 + y/2)^M}}{\displaystyle\sum_{t=1}^{M} \frac{C/2}{(1 + y/2)^t} + \frac{100}{(1 + y/2)^M}}$$

where D_{mod} = modified duration
M = number of coupon periods to maturity
C = annual coupon in percent terms
y = annual yield in decimal terms

(D_{mod} is called the *modified duration* to distinguish it from the original definition of this measure by Macaulay (1938), which differed from modified duration by the factor $1/(1 + y/2)$.)

The above formula may look formidable, but the concept is rather straight-forward. A bond's modified duration is, in fact, its **percent change in dollar price per basis-point change in yield**

$$\frac{100}{P} \frac{\Delta P}{\Delta y} = -D_{mod}$$

(Because price *decreases* as yield *increases*, the negative sign is required.)

Thus, a bond's duration is a measure of its *sensitivity to changes in interest rates*. A related sensitivity measure is a bond's **value-of-a-basis-point (VBP)**, which is the *actual* price change per basis point change in yield. It is this aspect of duration and VBP that makes them most significant to traders in general, and to arbitrage traders in particular: where all other values are equal, *a bond with a higher duration (VBP) will respond more rapidly to changes in interest rates*, and hence will generally be more risky. Conversely, instruments with similar durations or VBPs (even if they have different coupon and/or maturity characteristics) are often used to hedge one another, as they show similar price response to shifts in interest rates.

This is conventional wisdom and part of the day-to-day practice of most bond traders. Nevertheless, it must be taken with a grain of salt; as we noted above in our example comparing the value of two instruments with different coupon and maturity characteristics, when valuing a set of cash flows spread over a considerable time span, one must make an implicit or explicit assumption about the behavior of term reinvestment/discounting rates. The usual, and simplest, assumption is that term rates, and short-term rates in particular, remain the same for equal intervals throughout the life of the security in question. As we will see in slightly more detail, this is equivalent to assuming a *flat yield curve,* and when examining sensitivity to changes in interest rates, it amounts to restricting attention to **parallel shifts** in the yield curve. In practice, the yield curve is rarely flat and its movements are rarely parallel. Some more sophisticated techniques for compensating for these oversimplifications in the definition of duration will be discussed. Duration as defined here is so widely used, however, that the savvy trader should be fully comfortable with its uses and meaning while still keeping an eagle eye on its potential abuses in those special circumstances (such as a rapidly steepening yield curve) where conventional assumptions about the term structure of interest rates may be violated. For more on the possible abuses of duration, see Winkelmann (1989).

Convexity

One corrective to the limitations of duration is a second measure of sensitivity known as *convexity*. The convexity of an instrument is sometimes described as a *time-squared weighted average maturity measure,* and, analogously to duration, is defined as

$$\text{Convexity} = \left(\frac{1}{1+y/2}\right)^2 \frac{\text{Sum of time squared weighted cash flows}}{\text{Invoice price}}$$

$$= \left(\frac{1}{1+y/2}\right)^2 \frac{\displaystyle\sum_{t=1}^{M} \frac{t^2 C/2}{(1+y/2)^t} + \frac{100M}{(1+y/2)^M}}{\displaystyle\sum_{t=1}^{M} \frac{C/2}{(1+y/2)^t} + \frac{100}{(1+y/2)^M}} \tag{3.24}$$

(Actually, this definition should be modified slightly, but the changes are unimportant for a qualitative understanding of the concept of convexity.)

At first glance, this may seem even more counter-intuitive than the definition of duration, but convexity is nothing more than a measure of *how duration changes with yield*. (In mathematical terms, duration is the *first derivative* of price with respect to yield, and convexity is the *second derivative* of price with respect to yield.)

Since duration tells us how price changes with yield, we can use the duration of a security to project a *correction* for a given change in yield; if the yield changes by a quantity Δy, then the price P will change by the quantity $-D\Delta y(100/P)$. But this is a *linear* correction—for every basis point y moves away from current yield, we correct P by the *same* amount. We know this can't be quite right; as the yield changes, the price doesn't change *linearly*. Convexity helps us make a more reasonable approximation of the price behavior of a security for small changes in yield, as it estimates the *curvature* of the price/yield function near the given yield value y. This is why it is called *convexity*.

As with duration, however, convexity as defined here depends on the customary assumptions of a flat yield curve and parallel yield-curve shifts. It is only with the introduction of more sophisticated analytic concepts that we will be able to determine the sensitivity of prices under more general assumptions about the term structure of interest rates (the shape of the yield curve) or in response to arbitrary changes in the *shape* of the yield curve.

Other Sensitivity Measures

While duration and convexity are by far the most frequently used measures of sensitivity of bonds and notes, there are other, more important sensitivity measures for derivative securities such as options. As discussed in Chapter 4, option values depend critically on the *volatility* of the underlying security's price or yield; they also depend on short-term interest rates or, in the case of long-term options, on the term structure of interest rates over the life of the option. Futures and mortgage-backed securities possess option-like characteristics that make them sensitive to changes in these parameters as well. A variety of models have been developed for valuation and sensitivity analysis of such derivatives, and along with such models comes a range of sensitivity measures. Some of these, such as *stochastic duration,* can be applied to simple bonds and notes in a way that compensates for some of the shortcomings of the traditional notions described in this section. Before we can adequately discuss such techniques, however, we need more background on the yield curve and the term structure of interest rates.

THE TREASURY YIELD CURVE

The Empirical Yield Curve

In many ways, the state of the U.S. Treasury market at a given time can best be captured by plotting the **empirical Treasury yield curve.** This is the graph of **yield-to-maturity** against **term-to-maturity** (or sometimes duration) for all current Treasury issues. (In the case of Treasury bills, the discount yield must be converted to a bond-equivalent yield for consistency.)

Treasury issues with longer maturities generally have higher yields. Because the prices of longer maturity bonds fluctuate more than the prices of shorter ones for the same change in interest rates, longer bonds have a greater price risk, and investors accordingly demand a higher yield from these bonds. The empirical yield curve will thus normally be upward sloping; see Figure 3.1 for an example of a normal treasury yield curve, based on actual yields on June 12, 1992. Yields on short-term issues do, however, rise above long-term bond yields at times, creating what is known as an **inverted yield curve.** This usually happens when most market participants anticipate that interest rates are going to *fall* in the future. Figure 3.2 shows an example of an inverted yield curve, based on actual yields on April 3, 1989.

The **current issue** Treasury securities—the most recent issues at each maturity—are the determinants of the empirical yield curve most frequently referenced by traders. The yields of older issues (known as **off-the-run** issues)

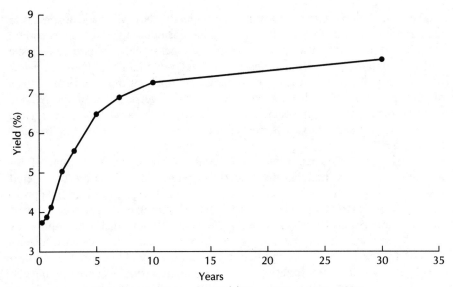

Figure 3.1 Treasury Yield Curve, June 12, 1992

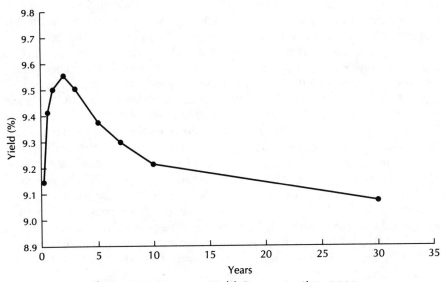

Figure 3.2 Treasury Yield Curve, April 3, 1989

can be plotted along with the current ones; typically, they will trade at spreads to the current issues, as they are less liquid and hence command a yield premium (which is equivalent to a price concession). Occasionally, a particular issue will face extraordinary demand and go "special"; its yield may then fall *below* the current yield curve, at least temporarily. By tracking the historical spreads of off-the-run issues to the current issues, traders get a sense of the relative richness or cheapness of specific issues in the various sectors of the yield curve. Such spread analysis is one of the fundamental tools of the Treasury bond trader.

The empirical Treasury yield curve contains an immense amount of information about the market. Because U.S. Treasury securities are considered essentially immune to default, the empirical yield curve gives us a good approximation of the market's perception of the **term structure of risk-free interest rates.** Comparison of current Treasury yields at different maturities allows us to derive implied forward rates for given intervals; thus, the market's "expectations" for forward rates are implicit in the empirical yield curve. We can also derive a **term discount function** from the empirical yield curve, giving the implied discounting factors for valuing future cash flows of any given maturity. This function is also known as the **zero-coupon bond (ZCB) price curve**; the present value of a zero-coupon bond, a bond with a single cash flow at maturity, is the product of the bond's face value with the term discounting factor for that maturity. We will see more detail on how some of these curves are related.

To a very crude approximation, a fitted yield curve given by a particular functional form can be specified by its short rate value (the 3-month yield), its slope (the spread of the long rate—30-year yield—to the short rate) and a curvature parameter. When traders and investors consider the sensitivity of their holdings to interest-rate movements, they most often think in terms of *parallel shifts* in the yield curve—movements up or down by the entire yield curve that keep the spread between the long and short rates constant. When dealing with some of the more complex and long-term interest rate–sensitive instruments, such as interest rate caps, floors, and options on swaps, however, the *slope* of the yield curve, and even its shape (curvature), become very important considerations. Such shifts in shape are probably more common than truly parallel yield-curve shifts in the long run; for example, between December 31, 1990, and December 31, 1991, the Treasury yield curve steepened significantly, with the 2-year to 30-year spread-widening from 110 basis points to 265 basis points.

It is sometimes useful to refer to a duration-based yield curve, plotting yield-to-maturity against the *duration* of each Treasury security rather than against the maturity itself. Since securities of similar duration tend to have similar price sensitivities, and hence similar price-risk premiums, such a curve can help clarify the true relationship between current and off-the-run securities.

The Zero Curve

One of the most useful transformations of the yield curve is the so-called **zero-coupon bond (ZCB) price curve** or "zero curve" for short. Since zero-coupon bonds have only a single "bullet" cash flow at maturity, their analytics are particularly simple: their duration is always equal to their maturity, and their price is the product of their face (redemption) value with the *term discounting factor* for that maturity. Each such discounting factor implies a *term discounting rate* for that maturity, and it is the curve of these rates that is referred to as the zero curve.

To the extent that there is an active, liquid market for ZCBs of a given maturity, the zero curve can be constructed directly. But such markets do not necessarily exist for all maturities, so it is often necessary to *derive* the zero curve from information on rates *implicit* in other markets. This is possible through a kind of "bootstrapping" process that calculates the shortest discounting rates first, then uses the knowledge of those rates to find the rates for successively longer terms. For example, if we know that the price of a six-month zero-coupon bond is 97.00, the implied discounting rate for that period (ignoring details of day-counts) will be given by

$$1 + r_{1/2} = \frac{100}{97.0} = 1.030928$$

so 3.09 percent would be the six-month discounting rate expressed in semiannually compounded terms.

Suppose there were no market for 1-year zero-coupon bonds, but that we knew that the price of a bond with exactly one year to run and coupon 8 percent was, say, $101\,{}^{21}/_{32}+$ (or 101.672 in decimal). We have

$$\text{IP} = 101.672 = 4.0 \times 0.97 + 104.0 \times \left(\frac{1}{1 + r_1}\right)^2$$

and we can solve for r_1, giving $r_1 = 0.03125$ or 3.125 percent for the one-year discounting rate. We can continue in this fashion calculating discounting rates for ever longer terms.

Of course, nothing is ever as simple as we would like it to be; in reality, there are *many* coupon bonds with about one year to run (and perhaps none with *exactly* one), and the values of r_T will vary depending on which set of bonds we use. The solution usually taken is to use *all available bonds* (or some representative basket, perhaps excluding those one suspects are "special" due to a liquidity crunch or some other factor) and *simultaneously* estimate all the r_T using techniques from statistics and linear algebra to achieve a "best fit" for the available data. The fit is usually rather good—if it weren't, there would be obvious arbitrage opportunities to be exploited by stripping certain bonds. And the result is a zero curve or discount curve that gives us a very good picture of the term discount rates implied by the market.

The technique used here, which implicitly depends on the assumption that the markets under consideration are theoretically *arbitrage-free*, is fundamental to fixed-income trading. Of course, we know that few markets are *truly* arbitrage-free, but any market that offers significant arbitrage opportunities quickly attracts market players whose profit-generating activities are focused on the elimination of those opportunities. Stated in other terms, the *theoretical* (or "fair") basis for pricing should assume a market that is *theoretically* free of arbitrage (or price discrepancies). This kind of technical assumption often looks like a trick, but it is used again and again—particularly in option pricing—and has been shown to give results corresponding very well with empirical data.

The Par Curve

Another approach to understanding the yield curve is to consider the so-called *par* curve, the curve of yields-to-maturity associated with bonds currently selling at par. As noted earlier, a bond selling at par will generally have a yield equal to its coupon. (Odd coupon periods and day-count conventions may lead to slight variations.) Bonds selling at a high premium or deep discount are often assumed to be subject to special forces that can distort their price/yield; high-coupon bonds may be considered especially desirable investments in an environment in which the interest rate may have bottomed out, for example. It is often considered more accurate to construct a zero curve from the par curve, rather than trying to fit all issues, because bonds selling at or near par are likely to be more representative of the underlying term discounting rates implicit in the market. The derivation is essentially the same as that described above, with the added advantage that if prices are truly par, there will be no need to worry about "fitting"; the "bootstrap" process will give *exact,* unambiguous values for each maturity. Of course, just as there is no liquid market in ZCBs across all maturities, there may well be gaps in the range of maturities for which true par bonds are available. Techniques exist for interpolating values for such gaps if they are neither too wide nor too frequent.

The Implied Forward Curve

Another very important concept related to the yield curve is that of *implied forward rates* and the *implied forward curve*. The zero curve can be thought of as representing *term discounting rates* for all terms across the span of maturities in the market, but these are all terms starting *from the present*; in other words, they are useful in telling us the *present value* of a quantity to be received at some future date, but they do not necessarily tell us the "one-year-from-today" value of a million dollars to be received 10 years from today. Or do they?

In fact, complete knowledge of the zero curve (or any equivalent) allows us to compute *forward rates* $r_{t,t'}$ for discounting between any two given times t and t' within the span of maturites for which we have term rates. The key here is in the principle of **multiplicativity of rates**: if r_1 is the discounting rate for 1 period, and r_2 that for 2 periods, each expressed in terms of periods and compounded in terms of the same periods, then we must have

$$(1 + r_1) \times (1 + r_{1,2}) = (1 + r_2)^2 \tag{3.25}$$

(If not, there would be an *arbitrage opportunity*.) Equation (3.25) allows us to solve for $r_{1,2}$, the 1-period *forward rate* one period in the future. Similar equations allow us to solve for *any* forward rate in the range of maturities covered by r_t. Moreover, if we solve two different such equations for the same forward rate, we should get the *same* value. In other words, the zero curve is itself arbitrage-free.

ARBITRAGE-FREE PRICING OF BONDS FOR FORWARD SETTLEMENT

In the fixed-income securities markets, traders are often required to quickly evaluate the *forward price* of a security, based on the security's *spot price* and its financing costs. Spot price is used for **regular settlement**, which means that the price is good for settlement in the following trading day. A security's forward price is the price of that security if the trade is to be settled on a future date, possibly three months or more from the actual trading day. In options trading, for example, the accurate determination of a bond's forward price at the option's expiration date is essential; in evaluating a futures contract, the trader must know how to calculate the deliverable issue's forward price during the delivery month. Although the implied forward curve analysis discussed in the last section is useful in providing estimates of the forward rates, and therefore forward prices, implied by the empirical yield curve, it is **not** appropriate for calculating arbitrage-free pricing of bonds for forward settlement, because it does not explicitly take into account the **carrying costs** of a specified security.

Suppose that a Treasury security with a coupon rate of 6 percent is trading at a spot price of $99\,16/32$. With an accrued interest of $2,500 per million, the security's invoice price is $997,500. Assuming that the current overnight repo rate for this security is 4 percent, the one-day financing cost of a $1 million long position in this bond would be $110.83. (Repo interest = 0.04 × $997,500 × ($1/360$).) With a coupon of 6 percent, the bond holder would receive a daily coupon income of $167.75. (Coupon income = 0.03 × $1,000,000 × ($1/181$), where 181 is the number of days in the current coupon period.) The daily *carrying cost* of this bond is therefore $54.92, which is equal to $165.75 − $110.83. Following this analysis, if a trader is willing to buy this bond at the spot price of $995,000 for *regular settlement* (on the following trading day), then he or she would be willing to pay only $995,000 − $52.92, or $994,947.08, for this bond if the trade settled one day after regular settlement, because the later settlement would cause him or her a carrying cost "loss" of $54.92. In other words, the *arbitrage-free forward price* of this security is computed from the formula

Forward price = Spot price − Carrying cost to forward date

Remarks

1. Carrying cost is usually defined as the difference between coupon income and repo-based financing costs. This definition works fine for notes and bonds with long maturities. For securities with maturities less than two years, however, the price convergence to par at maturity would be ignored by this definition, and a security's carrying cost so defined can therefore be very misleading.
2. As noted in Chapter 2, the term repo market is not always liquid, especially beyond three months; forward pricing beyond three months may, therefore, involve an educated guess at the forthcoming effective term repo rate.
3. For more detailed treatment of forward pricing, see Hull (1989) and Ritchken (1987).

APPENDIX 3A: CONTINUOUS COMPOUNDING AND LOGARITHMIC RATES

Earlier in Chapter 3, we stated that the total return on an investment approaches a limit if compounding is performed at shorter and shorter intervals, and that this limit is known as the *continuously compounded* rate of interest. In this appendix we will prove this, and establish that the result of investing a sum P at the continuous compounding rate r for one year is

$$V = P \times e^r \tag{A.1}$$

where e is a mathematical constant (named after the mathematician Leonhard Euler) having value approximately 2.718.

The total return over one year at a rate r compounded n times a year is

$$\left(1 + \frac{r}{n}\right)^n$$

We want to show that this quantity approaches some limit as n grows very large. Expanding, we have

$$1 + n \times \frac{r}{n} + n\frac{n-1}{2} \times \frac{r^2}{n^2} + \cdots \qquad (A.2)$$

The general term in this expansion will be

$$\frac{n(n-1)(n-2)\cdots(n-k+1)}{k!} \times \frac{r^k}{n^k}$$

Where $k! = k \times (k-1) \times \cdots \times 1$ is the product of all the integers from k down to 1 (called k *factorial*). For n large, the term $n(n-1)(n-2)\cdots(n-k+1)$ will be approximately equal to n^k, so we can cancel it with the n^k in the denominator, leaving

$$1 + r + \frac{r^2}{2} + \cdots + \frac{r^k}{k!} + \cdots \qquad (A.3)$$

Those with some exposure to calculus may recognize this as the *Taylor series expansion* of the function e^r. We basically have an expression that gives a value—the limit of our compounding process—for every value of r we plug in. That is, Equation (A.3) defines a *function* of r, which for conciseness we will temporarily call $f(r)$. We want to show that this function is really the exponential function e^r, for a special constant e. We have that $f(1) = 1 + 1 + \frac{1}{2} + \frac{1}{6} + \cdots$, which must turn out to be equal to our special constant e. (In fact, just these first four terms sum to $2.\overline{6666}$, which is already getting very close to $e = 2.718$.)

The first step is to convince ourselves that the infinite series in Equation (A.3) *converges*—that is, that it defines a definite number. But the factorials $k!$ in the denominators of the terms of Equation (A.3) eventually grow much faster than the powers of r in the numerators, since the powers of r grow by adding the (constant) factor r, while the factorial grows by adding bigger and bigger factors. So eventually the terms in Equation (A.3) become so tiny as to be insignificant—in short, Equation (A.3) converges for all values of r. We now *define* e to be the value $f(1)$.

Next, we look at the behavior of $f(r)$. We claim that $f(r+s) = f(r) \times f(s)$. Expanding the product, we have

$$1 + r + \frac{r^2}{2} + \cdots \times 1 + s + \frac{s^2}{2} + \cdots = 1 + (r + s) + \left(rs + \frac{r^2}{2} + \frac{s^2}{2}\right)$$

$$+ \cdots 1 + (r + s) + \frac{(r + s)^2}{2} + \cdots = f(r + s)$$

as claimed. This is really the key to proving our result, because now we can see that $f(2r) = f(r + r) = f(r) \times f(r) = f(r)^2$, and in general that $f(nr) = f(r)^n$, for n any integer. But we also have $f(r) = f(r/2 + r/2) = f(r/2) \times f(r/2) = f(r/2)^2$, so $f(r/2) = f(r)^{1/2}$, and in general $f(r/n) = f(r)^{1/n}$, and $f[r \times (m/n)] = f(r)^{m/n}$. But we can get as close as we like to an arbitrary s with a rational approximation m/n, so we must have $f(r \times s) = f(r)^s$ for all s. Using the fact that $f(1) = e$, we therefore have

$$f(r) = f(1 \times r) = f(1)^r = e^r \qquad (A.4)$$

We have proved that the expression in Equation (A.3) is really e^r, and established the relationship of Equation (A.3).

Note that if the total return over a period is given by $1 + r'$, then the continuously compounding rate r for that period must be such that

$$1 + r' = e^r$$

The inverse of the exponential function e^r is called the *natural logarithm*, or *natural log* (to distinguish it from other logarithms, such as to the base 10 or 2). It is sometimes written **ln(x)**. Thus, we have that **the continuously compounding rate for a period is the natural log of the total return** for that period

$$r = \ln(1 + r')$$

This is why the continuously compounding rate is sometimes referred to as the *logarithmic rate*. (The period used in determining this rate is most frequently a year, of course, and is understood to be such if not stated otherwise.)

APPENDIX 3B: TRUE VS. TREASURY BOND PRICE-TO-YIELD CALCULATIONS

This section shows how the two principal conventions for bond price-to-yield calculations are derived, and how they differ. It also describes the different motivations behind the two approaches.

Price-to-Yield Calculations

The principle underlying all price-to yield calculations is the rule that **the value of a security is the net present value of all its future cash flows.** For a bond, this is the sum of all the coupon cash flows and its face value, appropriately discounted. If we know the price of a bond, we can solve for its yield as the rate that, when used to discount the cash flows, would produce the given price. *On a coupon date,* the formula for price in terms of yield is thus given by

$$\text{IP} = \sum_{i=1}^{N} \frac{1}{[1 + (y/2)]^i} \times \frac{c}{2} + \frac{1}{[1 + (y/2)]^N} \times 100 \tag{B.1}$$

where   IP $=$ invoice price of the bond,
   c $=$ annual coupon,
   y $=$ bond yield (in annual decimal terms),
   N $=$ number of remaining coupon payments (or coupon periods).

This is just Equation (3.20) rewritten a little. (Note that the present value of all future cash flows gives the *invoice price,* which in this case, on a coupon date, is equal to the market price.)

Handling of Fractional Coupon Periods

Equation (B.1) includes both the true and the treasury calculations; that is, the two coincide in this best-behaved of all cases. The complications arise when we move away from a coupon date, and especially if we find ourselves performing this calculation in an odd first coupon period.

   Let us first consider the case where we are in a normal coupon period, but between two coupon payments. One of the ways the true and treasury algorithms differ is in their conventions for handling day-count calculations. We are going to use d to denote the number of days from settle to next coupon payment, and B to denote the total number of days in the current coupon period.

- In the true yield calculations, d will be the *actual* number of days to the next coupon payment, and B the *actual* number of days in the current coupon period, even when it's an *odd* coupon period.
- In the treasury calculations, d will be the number of days to the *theoretical* next coupon payment date; this only makes a difference if we are in an odd first coupon period, as we'll see below. Similarly, in the treasury calculations, B is the number of days in the current *standard* semiannual coupon period. In either case, the fraction of a coupon period remaining is given by

$$\theta = \frac{d}{B}$$

In the true yield calculations, θ can sometimes be greater than 1; in the treasury calculations, it will always be between 0 and 1. To avoid confusion, we will use θ only in the true yield calculations; in the treasury calculations, we'll use d/B.

Last Coupon Period

Note that if a bond is in its *last* coupon period, the treasury convention is to use a *simple yield* calculation

$$IP = \frac{1}{1 + (d/B)(y/2)} \times \left(\frac{c}{2} + 100\right) \tag{B.2}$$

(The true yield in this case will be given by the same formula, Equation (B.5), as is used for any fractional normal coupon period.)

Normal Coupon Period

Assume our settle date falls between two normal coupon payment dates, with more than a single coupon payment to go. To avoid having to write the term $1/(1 + y/2)$ too many times, let

$$x = \frac{1}{1 + y/2} \tag{B.3}$$

Then the value of the bond on the *next* coupon date ("ex-coupon," that is, after that coupon payment) can be calculated using Equation (B.1)

$$IP_{next} = \frac{c}{2} \times \sum_{i=1}^{N-1} x^i + 100 \times x^{N-1} \tag{B.4}$$

To get the value of the bond *today*, we must discount this value back over the fractional period θ, also taking into account the first coupon payment. There are two conventions for performing this discounting over a fractional coupon period. The true yield calculation uses *exponential* discounting; the treasury calculation uses *linear* discounting. The true yield formula for this case is thus

$$IP = x^\theta \times \left[\frac{c}{2} \times \sum_{i=0}^{N-1} x^i + 100 \times x^{N-1} \right] \tag{B.5}$$

where we are now summing from $i = 0$ to incorporate the first coupon payment. The treasury formula is

$$IP = \frac{1}{1 + (d/B)(y/2)} \times \left[\frac{c}{2} + \frac{c}{2} \times \sum_{i=1}^{N-1} x^i + 100 \times x^{N-1} \right] \tag{B.6}$$

where we have kept the term $c/2$ from the first coupon payment separate from the sum for reasons soon to be evident.

If we write Equation (B.6) in terms of the *market* price P, we have

$$P = \frac{1}{1 + (d/B)(y/2)} \times \left[\frac{c}{2} \times \frac{d}{B} + \frac{c}{2} \times \sum_{i=1}^{N-1} x^i + 100 \times x^{N-1} \right] \tag{B.7}$$

where the term $c/2$ representing the next coupon payment has now been replaced by the fractional coupon payment $(c/2) \times (d/B)$ one receives after subtracting off the accrued to date.

This formula can be further simplified if we note that

$$1 - x = 1 - \frac{1}{1 + y/2} = \frac{y/2}{1 + y/2} = x \times y/2$$

so

$$\frac{x}{1 - x} = \frac{1}{y/2}$$

now,

$$\sum_{i=1}^{N-1} x^i = x \times \sum_{i=0}^{N-2} x^i = x \times \frac{\left(1 - x^{N-1}\right)}{(1 - x)} = \frac{\left(1 - x^{N-1}\right)}{y/2}$$

so we can write Equation (B.7) as

$$P = \frac{1}{1 + (d/B) \times (y/2)} \times \left[\frac{c}{2} \times \frac{d}{B} + \frac{c}{2} \times \frac{\left(1 - x^{N-1}\right)}{(y/2)} + 100 \times x^{N-1} \right] \quad (B.8)$$

We have captured the key difference between the true and treasury yield calculations—all we have to do is look at what happens in an odd first coupon period.

In an odd first coupon period, one will receive a first coupon payment that is either larger than normal (long first coupon period) or smaller than normal (short first coupon period). (See Figure 3B.1) The true yield calculation takes this into account by adjusting Equation (B.5) by a factor δ, which is just the difference between a normal coupon payment and the actual first coupon payment

$$\delta = \text{Odd coupon payment} - \frac{c}{2}$$

This over- or underpayment is then discounted back to the settle date using the same exponential discounting convention used throughout the true calculations, for a final formula given by

$$IP = x^\theta \times \left[\delta + \frac{c}{2} \times \sum_{i=0}^{N-1} x^i + 100 \times x^{N-1} \right] \quad (B.9)$$

(a)   ^---^-----^------^--...--^-----^coupon periods
        ----^-----^------^--...--^-----^coupon payments
        --^-----------------------------settle date

(b)   ^---^-----^------^------^--...--^-----^coupon periods
        -----------^------^------^--...--^-----^coupon payments
        --^-----------------------------settle date

Figure 3B.1   Odd First Coupon Period:
(a) Odd Short First Coupon Period;
(b) Odd Long First Coupon Period

In the case of the treasury calculations, the odd coupon payment is handled a little differently. For a short first coupon period, so distinction is made; since Equation (B.7) is based on the *market* price P, the missing portion of the first coupon payment is hidden in the accrued, which is ignored. For a long first coupon period, if the settle date falls after the initial "stub" period (if the time remaining to the next (first) coupon payment is actually less than or equal to a normal semiannual coupon period), the same formula still applies, for the same reasons. It is only when the settle date falls within the extra stub portion of the odd, long first coupon period that a different formula must be used. The correct treasury formula is

$$P = \frac{1}{1 + (d/B) \times (y/2)} \times \left[\frac{c}{2} \times \frac{d}{B} \times x + \frac{c}{2} \times \frac{\left(1 - x^N\right)}{(y/2)} + 100 \times x^N \right] \quad (B.10)$$

In keeping with the full-coupon-period bookkeeping conventions of the treasury calculations, the index N, which counts the number of full coupon payments to maturity, is increased by one, since there is now actually an *extra* full coupon period to count (even though there's no extra *coupon*).

With just this adjustment (N for $N - 1$), the summation term in Equation (B.10) would now count *all* the coupon payments, including the first, but it would not take into account the excess amount included in that first coupon payment. The first term of Equation (B.7), $(c/2) \times (d/B)$, is now modified slightly to correctly account for this excess; it is multiplied by x to discount it back once over the standard semiannual coupon period contained within the long odd first coupon period; the factor in the denominator discounts it back the rest of the way, according to correct treasury linear discounting conventions. (Note that d is now the number of days from settle to the *theoretical* first coupon payment date—just to the end of the first, stub portion of the long, odd first coupon period, and *not* to the actual first coupon payment date.)

Conclusions

To summarize, the main differences between the two calculations are:

1. Discounting: True yield uses exponential discounting for the stub term; treasury yield uses linear discounting.
2. Day count conventions: True yield uses "actual" coupon periods; treasury yield always uses "theoretical" or "normal" coupon periods.
3. Handling of accrued: The true yield calculation always solves an equation involving the *invoice price*; the treasury calculation solves an equation involving the *market price*.

True yield appeals to the mathematician, because it is based on a continuous view of calendar time, and uses exponential discounting, which is always more convenient mathematically. Treasury yield appeals to the accountant, because it is based on a coupon-period view of calendar time, and uses linear discounting, which is more convenient for manual calculation.

REFERENCES

Hull, John (1989). *Options, Futures and Other Derivative Securities*, Englewood Cliffs, NJ: Prentice Hall, Inc.

Macaulay, F. (1938). *Some Theoretical Problems Suggested by the Movements of Interest Rates, Bond Yields and Stock Prices in the United States Since 1856*, Cambridge, MA: National Bureau of Economic Research.

Ritchken, Peter (1987). *Options: Theory, Strategy and Applications*, Glenview, IL: Scott, Foresman and Company.

Winkelmann, Kurt (1989). "Uses and Abuses of Duration and Convexity," *Financial Analysts Journal*, (September–October).

4
Advanced Models and Algorithms

Fixed-income financial analysis is a rather sophisticated affair, and entire books have been devoted to the valuation techniques for bond options and mortgage-backed securities alone. It is important for relative-value traders to familiarize themselves with some of the essential techniques. This chapter covers analysis of the term structure of interest rates, option pricing methodologies, and some evaluation techniques for mortgage-backed securities.

ANALYSIS OF THE TERM STRUCTURE OF INTEREST RATES

Definitions

The **term structure of interest rates** refers to the fact that discounting rates for different maturities, or terms, are not usually equal, as many simple formulas and models implicitly assume. The interest-rate markets incorporate expectations about the probable directions of interest rates, and each *term* has an associated discounting rate. The **spot interest rate** for a given maturity is the discounting rate appropriate for valuing future cash flows of that maturity; the **term structure of interest rates** is the aggregate of spot rates considered as a function of maturity.

As noted in Chapter 3, if a zero-coupon bond of a given maturity exists its price should reflect the term discounting rate for that maturity. If there were a consistent, liquid market for zero-coupon bonds of all maturities, it would be possible to read off the term structure of interest rates from their prices. Unfortunately, such a market does not exist, so various techniques have been developed to extract the *implied term structure of interest rates* from data on a variety of instruments readily available in the markets. The discussion of the yield curve in the previous chapter indicates some of the more straightforward techniques for extracting a zero curve, or term structure, from data on coupon Treasury bond prices. For some purposes, however, the **functional form** of the term structure is as important as the closeness of fit at a given maturity.

For technical reasons, it may be easier to model the **forward curve** or **discounting function** than it is to model the term structure of interest rates (zero curve) directly. Recall from Chapter 3 that just as spot rates give the appropriate interest rates for a range of maturities, **forward rates** give the one-period, or more generally n-period rate expected or implied at a given future date. The two are related by the formula

$$(1 + r_t)^t = (1 + f_1)(1 + f_2) \cdots (1 + f_t)$$

(4.1)

where r_t is the spot rate for a term of t periods, and f_k is the one-period rate k periods in the future.

Rates are conventionally quoted in terms of a convenient compounding period, which may vary with the market and instruments under consideration. Note that r_t and f_k are quoted *in terms of the conventional period* and *not* necessarily in annualized terms. If, for example, we are concerned with the Treasury market and choose a conventional period of six months, we might have forward rates of 3.95 percent and 4.15 percent, giving rise to a two-period term spot rate of 4.05 percent quoted in terms of a six-month period; in simple annualized terms this would be 8.264 percent, and in bond-equivalent (semiannually compounded) annualized terms, it would be 8.10 percent.

The **discounting function** is a given by the formula

$$D_t = \frac{1}{(1 + r_t)^t}$$

(4.2)

or

$$D_t = \frac{1}{(1 + f_1)(1 + f_2) \cdots (1 + f_t)}$$

(4.3)

Mathematical Model

The valuation principle emphasized in Chapter 3 (value = present value of future cash flows) suggests the importance of the discount function in modelling the term structure of interest rates. Moreover, the discount function has a convenient functional form; since the one-period forward rates f_k can usually be expected to change relatively slowly from period to period, Equation (4.3) suggests that the discount function should follow an *exponentially declining curve*. A curve of such a simple functional form lends itself particularly well to fitting.

Fong and Fabozzi (1985) give a nice exposition of a fairly general model of the term structure of interest rates developed originally in Vasicek and Fong (1982), which involves just such fitting of the discount function. Their mathematical model is given by

$$P_k + A_k = D(T_k) + \sum_{j=1}^{L_k} C_k D(T_k - j + 1) - Q_k - W_k + \epsilon_k, \quad k = 1, \ldots, n \quad (4.4)$$

where n = number of bonds used in the estimation
T_k = term of the kth bond, in semiannual periods
$D(t)$ = discounting function; $D(t) = e^{-tR(t)}$, where t = time in semiannual periods, and R(t) = spot rate in continuously compounded terms
C_k = semiannual coupon of the kth bond
P_k = price of the kth bond
A_k = accrued interest of the kth bond
L_k = number of coupon payments to be received
Q_k = a measure of tax-related price discount
W_k = a measure of call-related price discount
ϵ_k = a measure of residual error

The model assumes that the *variance* of the residual error ϵ_k on *yields* is the same for all bonds. The residuals for different bonds are assumed to be uncorrelated, and various other simplifying assumptions are made about the terms Q_k and W_k. Finally, the discounting function itself, $D(t)$, is *fitted* to a convenient functional form.

Curve-Fitting Methodology

Vasicek and Fong point out that while so-called *polynomial splines* (piece-wise polynomial functions with smooth "joints") have traditionally been used to fit the discount function, they are not really the most appropriate family of curves for a variety of reasons, including the basically exponential nature of the discount function itself. Instead, Vasicek and Fong transform the discounting function into a function of a new variable x: $D(t) = G(x)$, where

$$t = \frac{1}{\alpha} \log(1 - x), \qquad 0 \le x < 1 \qquad (4.5)$$

with the result that where $D(t) \approx e^{-\gamma t}$, $G(x) \approx (1 - x)^{\gamma/\alpha}$; $G(x)$ is approximately a *power* function where $D(t)$ is approximately exponential.

$G(x)$ can then be fitted by polynomial splines (Vasicek and Fong use cubics) according to well-established techniques. We substitute the functional form

$$G(x) = \sum_{i=1}^{m} \beta_i g_i(x) \qquad (4.6)$$

into Equation (4.4), where the $g_i(x)$ form a basis for the space of fitting polynomials, and, taking into account the various simplifying assumptions on the components of Equation (4.4), we find the set of values for the regression coefficients β_i giving the best least-squares fit for the empirical data (bond prices) driving the whole parameter estimation process.

When transformed back into terms of t and $D(t)$, we have

$$D(t) = a_0 + a_1 e^{-\alpha t} + a_2 e^{-2\alpha t} + a_3 e^{-3\alpha t} \qquad (4.7)$$

That is, $D(t)$ has been fitted by a *cubic exponential spline*. (It turns out that α represents the *limiting value of forward rates* for the term structure in question.) For more details, see the original paper by Vasicek and Fong (1982) or the exposition in Fong and Fabozzi (1985).

PRICING MODELS FOR DEBT OPTIONS

As noted in Chapter 2, options on bonds and bond futures are fundamental tools for both hedging and speculation in the fixed-income markets; they are also key components of many arbitrage strategies. However, as options represent *contingent claims,* they introduce a new element of uncertainty and associated risk into the valuation process, and their associated analytics are correspondingly more complex. The good news is that theoretically sound analytical models for both valuation and sensitivity analysis have been developed and tested over the past 20 years, particularly for relatively short-dated (six months or less) options. The bad news is that more and more complex options and option-like features of fixed-income securities and their derivatives, including American options, long-dated options, and such "exotic" features as "look-back," "average-strike," "down-and-out," and "up-and-in" options are increasingly common, and provide a rich source of arbitrage opportunities and techniques.

This section describes the basic option-pricing models applicable in the fixed-income markets, their most important applications, and some of the pitfalls and abuses to watch for in option pricing. A brief survey of some of the more advanced techniques used to evaluate long-dated and "exotic" options is included, with signposts to the literature for those requiring more detail.

Option-Pricing Models: An Overview

An option-pricing model provides a formula for valuing an option contract, given the terms of the contract and other relevant market data (including, for example, the price of the underlying security and its anticipated price volatility). In general, the terms of the contract will be known, while other inputs, such as the current price of the underlying security and its volatility, must be specified and/or estimated by the user.

The known factors in most option-pricing formulas include the following:

- The contract settlement date
- The expiration date
- The strike price
- Whether the option is a put or a call
- Whether the option is American or European
- The current price of the underlying security
- Current risk-free and term repo rates

The unknown factors may include:

- The price of the underlying security at expiration (for American options, the entire behavior of underlying prices between contract date and expiration date).
- The yield of the underlying bond at expiration and/or at all intervening dates (Note that this yield will correspond to a different point on the yield curve for each date, as the underlying bond matures).
- Short-term interest rates at expiration and/or on intervening dates.
- Projected price or yield volatilities.

What distinguishes one option pricing model from another is the way it captures (or models) the uncertainty in the values of its parameters. There are three classes of option-pricing models:

1. The well-known Black-Scholes model and its variants, which provide closed analytic formulas for option prices and sensitivities.
2. Lattice-based models, sometimes known as "binomial" models, which do not generally lead to closed analytic formulas, but rather to numerical computational algorithms.
3. Term structure–based option-pricing models, which may involve more than one fundamental parameter and do not generally lead to closed analytic formulas.

These option-pricing models assume that one or more of their parameters, such as underlying price, evolve through time according to some statistical rule, which is usually specified by giving the assumed probability distribution for that variable at expiration. Such a parameter is known as a stochastic variable, and the associated models are known as stochastic models. Different assumptions about the ways in which variable values are distributed give rise to different pricing models. There are also differences in the mathematical techniques used to derive the option-pricing formulas or algorithms based on these statistical assumptions.

A simple stochastic option-pricing model assumes that there is a single driving variable, such as the price of the underlying security, or frequently in the case of cash bond options, the yield of the underlying bond. The analytic pricing model provides a closed formula based on the values of known variables (such as strike price and time-to-expiration) and of parameters specifying the particular statistical distribution assumed for the driving variable (such as price volatility). This closed pricing formula will be an exact or approximate solution to the stochastic differential equations specifying the driving process. Such models are highly accurate when applied to short-term (less than six months) European options. For options with features such as early exercise (American options) and intervening cash flows, lattice-based models are more accurate. Both classes of models are generally inadequate for longer-dated options (more than six months), where variations in interest rates over the life of the option become significant.

Option Sensitivities: Delta, Gamma, Vega, Theta

Option-pricing models also provide additional analytics, such as the hedge ratio, or delta, of the option and other such measures of sensitivity in the option price to changes in one of the parameters to the pricing formula. Such sensitivity measures are frequently at least as important as the option-pricing formula itself, as they allow the holder of an option to quantify the risk exposure to changes in the value of the holdings due to shifts in market variables and time decay, and to determine how such risk can be hedged away. In particular, if the price of the underlying security changes by a unit, the price of a call option will change by delta, the hedge ratio. Thus, a holding consisting of long one call and short delta of the underlying security will be **delta neutral**—for small changes in the price of the underlying security, the value of the holding will not change.

Other important option sensitivities include gamma, the change in delta per small change in underlying price; vega, the change in option value per small change in volatility; and theta (also known as time decay), the change in option value per small change in time. (Because an option with longer to run is naturally worth more, theta is always negative, hence the name time decay.) Another sensitivity, kappa, measures the effect on option value of changes in the short-term discounting rate.

Where an option-pricing model has an explicit, closed analytic expression for option value, delta, gamma, and other sensitivity measures may be computed directly from the option-pricing formula; if this is too cumbersome, or if there is no closed expression, they may be calculated by varying the parameter in question by a small quantity and computing the resulting variation in the option price.

The Role of Volatility

The key parameter in most option-pricing models not directly determinable from the option contract or the market is the **volatility** of the underlying security. Options are *contingent* claims; they are a bet against the future behavior of the underlying security. The valuation of an option therefore involves estimating the *expected* value; this means that we must somehow associate a *probability distribution* with all the possible outcomes and their values (some of which will be zero, of course). This is typically done by assuming that the price (or yield) of the underlying will be distributed according to some well-known (and well-behaved) probability function on the expiration date (for American options, on all intervening dates as well). Most commonly this is a *normal* or *lognormal* distribution; in either case, it is specified essentially by a single parameter: the standard deviation of the distribution. This is what traders call the *volatility* of the underlying security. Intuitively, it is a measure of how much the price or yield of the security moves around over time—how "jumpy" or volatile the security is. Even without delving into the math, we can understand that an estimate of the volatility of the underlying security is important in trying to determine how likely it is that one will end up in the money, and by how much.

Unfortunately, as noted, volatilities are not given *explicitly* in the markets; there is nothing that can help us determine with certainty just how volatile a given security will be in the future. There are two techniques for estimating volatilities: **historical volatility analysis,** which assumes that the recent volatility level of a security is likely to continue for the relevant future; and **implied volatility analysis,** which derives an implied volatility from the market prices for options and other related derivative products. The assumption here is that volatilities for similar securities are similar, which is usually, but not universally, true.

Volatility estimation is both an art and a science, and many research articles have been written about the subject. The fixed-income arbitrageur for whom options play a major role, either directly or in hedging, should be conversant with the major volatility estimation techniques and their possible pitfalls, as this is generally the key parameter in any option-pricing model. For more details, see Wong (1991) or Natenberg (1988).

Put-Call Parity

Many option-pricing models satisfy a very general relationship known as "put-call parity," which allows us to derive the price of a European put option from that of a European call with the same strike price and expiration (or vice versa). For options on equities, zero-coupon bonds, or other instruments with no intervening cash flows (dividends or coupon payments), this relationship is stated as follows

$$P = C - S + DF(K) \qquad (4.8)$$

where
P = price of the put option
C = price of the call option
S = current price of the underlying security
DF = the discounting function that calculates the net present value of the variable in parentheses at expiration
K = strike price

This relationship is traditionally established by considering a simultaneous position in European puts and calls on the same underlying security consisting of writing one call, buying one put, buying one unit of the underlying bond, and borrowing DF(K) in cash. At expiration, what is the value of this position? If we assume that the value of the underlying bond at expiration is S', there are two outcomes: either the call finishes in the money ($S' > K$), and the put out of the money, or the call finishes out of the money ($S' < K$), and the put in the money. Where coupon accrual is not an issue, the values of the various components of the holding in each case are

Now	$S' > K$	$S' < K$
C	$S' - K$	0
P	0	$K - S'$
S	S'	S'
DF(K)	K	K

where S' = value of the underlying instrument at expiration.

Because the total value at expiration is zero in every case, the initial investment required to create this position must also have a value of zero; otherwise, it would be possible to arrange a perfect arbitrage (something for nothing). Thus the put-call parity relationship is established.

When put-call parity holds, it is unnecessary to have separate pricing formulas for European puts and calls. This relationship does *not* hold in general, however, for *American* options, where the possibility of early exercise introduces an asymmetry in the relationship of puts and calls. For options on coupon-bearing bonds, where coupon accrual must be taken into account, a reformulation is necessary. In general, the price of the option will depend on the *forward* price of the underlying at the expiration date (spot price minus carrying cost), which takes into account financing costs and coupon accrual. For European options on coupon-bearing bonds, it can be shown that put and call values obey the following modified form of put-call parity

$$P = C - \text{DF}(\text{Fwd} - K) \tag{4.9}$$

where Fwd is the forward price of the underlying on the expiration date and the other variables are as above. (Note that $P = C$ when the strike is equal to the forward price.)

For a general exposition of put-call parity and many other aspects of option pricing theory in an equities setting, see Cox and Rubinstein (1985); for an exposition including discussion of options on debt instruments, see Ritchken (1987).

Black-Scholes and Related Models

By far the most popular pricing model for short-term options is the *Black-Scholes* model, in which the *log* of the underlying price is assumed to be normally distributed. Such a model arises naturally if one assumes that the price of the underlying security is equally likely to move up or down by the same *proportion* in a given time interval; that is, up from 100.00 to 110.00, or from 110.00 to 121.00; or down from 100.00 to 90.90, or from 90.90 to 82.64. Many traders feel that this is a natural assumption for many markets—that the expected size of changes should be proportional to market level—and this assumption gives rise to the classic Black-Scholes option-pricing model, the earliest and best known of all the closed-form option-pricing models.

Undoubtedly, the Black-Scholes model is a milestone in options-pricing theory. In theoretical terms, this model first established that the expected cash flows of any continuously traded asset obeying a reasonable stochastic process can be replicated for a risk-neutral cost, and laid the groundwork for a consistent theory of the pricing of contingent claims. Practically, Black-Scholes introduced the first closed analytic options-pricing formula to gain wide currency in the financial industry. Introduced in the mid-1970s as an equity option-pricing model (Black and Scholes, 1973), and subsequently extended and modified to handle a variety of other instruments (see Cox and Rubinstein, 1985), the Black-Scholes model has proven extraordinarily accurate and consistent in those markets where its basic assumptions are met, and has become a standard tool for all options traders. The classic Black-Scholes option-pricing model is a "lognormal price" model. It assumes that the underlying price at expiration obeys a lognormal probability distribution—that the natural log of the price is normally distributed. This distribution is specified by a *price-relative* volatility, which might typically be quoted in average percent annual price change terms.

The assumptions of this model are:

- That the underlying price follows a lognormal process—that is, that the log of the price obeys a normal distribution at expiration.
- That volatility remains constant over the life of the option.
- That the risk-free discounting rate is constant over the life of the option.
- That the market is continuous (liquid), and that transaction costs can be ignored.

The resulting option-pricing formula for a European call option with strike price K and time to expiration t in years is

$$C = SN(z) - Ke^{-rt}N(z - \sigma\sqrt{t}) \qquad (4.10)$$

where $z = (\log(S/K) + rt + \sigma^2 t/2)/(\sigma \sqrt{t})$

C = value of a European call option with strike K and t years to expiration

S = current price of the security

K = strike price

σ = annualized relative price volatility

$r = \log(1 + r_{rf})$ = logarithmic risk-free (r_{rf}) rate

The option's hedge ratio is given, simply, by

$$\delta C = N(z) \qquad (4.11)$$

Despite the great success and familiarity of the Black-Scholes model in pricing equity options, and the convenience of its closed analytic form, there are some important qualifying assumptions in applying this model to bond options. Coupon accrual complicates matters, but can be accounted for (as can the payment of dividends in the equity option pricing case) by replacing the underlying price S by the present value of the forward price $e^{-rt}F$. F incorporates the coupon effect; note that r is the *continuously compounded* discounting rate.

Adjustments must also be made to compensate for the undervaluation of American call options due to the failure of Black-Scholes to take into account the possibility of early exercise. However, the Black-Scholes model depends fundamentally on the assumption of a constant risk-free rate, and on the assumption that price volatility is not time dependent; neither of these assumptions can consistently be sustained in the world of cash bond options. It is certainly unreasonable to assume that T-bill yields, for example, follow a lognormal process while the short-term risk-free rate remains constant. Perhaps less obvious is the fact that bond volatilities, whether price- or yield-based, *must* be time dependent, since the price of the bond must ultimately converge to par. Nevertheless, for short-term options on bond futures and on longer maturity bonds, where one can assume a low correlation between the bond's yield (or price) levels and the short rate, suitable versions of the Black-Scholes model are applicable.

Example 4.1: Pricing a Call on a Cash Bond

Assume that we are given a three-month (90-day) call option on an 8 percent cash bond maturing in 20 years, which is currently priced at 98.00. Let the option be struck at the money—98.00—and assume an annual volatility of 12 percent. Finally, assume a risk-free discounting rate of 6 percent, and a term (three-month) repo rate of 5 percent for the bond. What should be the price of the option, according to Black-Scholes?

The time interval, t, is 0.246 years, and $K = 98.00$. We have

$$\sigma = 0.12; \quad r = \log(1 + 0.06) = 0.058269; \quad e^{-rt} = 0.985745$$

The forward price of the bond, assuming the bond currently has no accrued interest, is given by

$$F = \text{Price} - \text{Carry} = 98.00 - \left[\left(\frac{0.08}{365} - \frac{0.05}{360}\right) \times 90 \times 98.00\right] = 97.28$$

The replacement for S is

$$e^{-rt}F = 0.9857 \times 97.28 = 95.888$$

and we have

$$\sigma = 0.12; \quad r = \log(1 + 0.06) = 0.0583$$

Therefore,

$$z = \frac{\log(95.88/98.00) + 0.0583 \times 0.246 + 0.12^2 \times 0.246/2}{(0.12 \times \sqrt{0.246})}$$

$$= \frac{-0.0229 + 0.0144 + 0.0018}{0.0596} = -0.1136$$

so

$$N(z) = N(-0.1136) = 0.4612;$$
$$N(z - \sigma\sqrt{t}) = N(-0.1136 - 0.12 \times \sqrt{0.246}) = 0.4376$$

and we have

$$C = e^{-rt}F \times N(z) - K \times e^{-rt} \times N(z - \sigma\sqrt{t})$$
$$= 95.899 \times 0.46119 - 98.00 \times 0.9857 \times 0.4376 = 1.9405$$

or $1\,{}^{30}\!/_{32}$, and

$$\delta C = N(z) = N(0.46119) = 0.461$$

Note that if the option is struck at the forward price, 97.28, one has

$$C = 2.875 \ or \ 2\,{}^{28}\!/_{32}; \qquad \delta C = 0.512$$

which gives a hedge ratio closer to 0.500. From put-call parity, one would expect the hedge ratio of an option to be about 0.500 when struck at the money; but to be at the money, an option on a cash bond must be struck at the *forward price*. (Put-call parity also implies that at this strike level, the call and put options will have the same price.)

■

A slight but important modification of the Black-Scholes option-pricing model was made by Merton (1973); it takes into account explicitly the holding cost or cost of carry b; the resulting pricing formula is

$$C = S e^{(b-r)t} N(z) - K e^{-rt} N(z - \sigma\sqrt{t}) \qquad (4.12)$$

where

$$z = \log(S/K) + bt + \sigma^2 t/2/\sigma\sqrt{t}$$

The option's hedge ratio is now given by

$$\delta C = e^{(b-r)t} N(z) \qquad (4.13)$$

Although Black-Scholes is by far the most popular, there do exist other closed-form option-pricing models. One worth mentioning is the *normal price* model, which assumes that the prices of the underlying security are equally likely to move up or down by the same *absolute* amount. This has the disadvantage of theoretically allowing *negative* prices, but for most securities at empirically observed volatility levels, this is not really a problem. The normal price model has a simple analytic solution, simpler even than Black-Scholes.

The pricing formula using this model for a European call option with strike price K and time to expiration in years t is

$$C = \mathrm{DF}(\sigma[zN(z) + n(z)]) \qquad (4.14)$$

where

C = value of a European call option with strike K and t years to expiration

DF = discounting function over the interval t

$z = (F - K)/\sigma$ = normalized difference between strike K and forward (or future) price F. (For cash bonds, the arbitrage-free forward price can be found by taking F = spot price − carry.)

$n(z)$ and $N(z)$ = the standard normal density function and the cumulative normal distribution function at z, respectively

σ = absolute price standard deviation for the interval t. (This can be derived from the annualized percent price volatility, v, by setting $\sigma = v \sqrt{t} \times F$.)

The option's delta or hedge ratio, which is the derivative of the call price with respect to the underlying bond price, is

$$\delta C = \text{DF}(N(z)) \tag{4.15}$$

Another model uses *yield* as the driving variable. As has been pointed out, one major difficulty with any price-based model is in the "amortization toward par," and the concomitant reduction in variance over time. Normal and lognormal price dynamics fail to deal with this time-dependence of variance, but yield dynamics reflect it automatically. One justification for using yield as the driving variable is the empirical observation that yield volatilities are fairly uniform within a given region of the yield curve. A five-year bond will in time become a 4¾-year bond, and will be subject to changing price dynamics, but its yield dynamics will not change significantly. Yield-based dynamics are also of interest because they provide a more natural basis than do price dynamics for the analysis of long-dated options, although a simple one-parameter stochastic model, whether yield- or price-driven, is no longer appropriate for such options.

Of course, price and yield are linked by a deterministic relationship (given one, and the standard bond characteristics—coupon and maturity—the other can be determined), but what is significant for the option-pricing model is the *process* postulated for the evolution of bond price/yield through time. If bond *yields* are presumed normally or lognormally distributed, bond *prices* *cannot* obey any such simple distribution. In particular, the mean of the implied price distribution will not, in general, correspond to the mean of the yield distribution. One must therefore be careful, for example, in converting price volatility figures to yield volatility figures too freely. Traders should be aware of the modelling assumptions underlying their own and others' figures, or they may find themselves comparing apples and oranges!

If one assumes a yield-based process, it is most realistic to assume that rates move up or down in proportion to the current yield, rather than by absolute steps—that is, according to a lognormal rather than a normal process. This obviates the possibility of negative rates, and gives rise to a rather interesting yield-based model. In general, yield-based models are somewhat more analytically involved than are the price-based models.

It is important to note that for the arbitrage trader, *relative-value analysis is essential for spotting profit opportunities,* and that for this purpose, *the consistent use of a single appropriate model* is more important than squeezing the last decimal of accuracy out of the model. In particular, traders in an environment where multiple models are in use (or where values and comparisons are frequently compared with those produced by other firms) should avoid comparing prices, sensitivities, **and particularly volatilities** from different models.

Lattice-Based Models

While the closed-form option-pricing models have the advantage of simplicity and are generally analytically tractable, they cannot handle certain features of many bond options contracts, such as the early exercise feature of American options. This is because the decision to exercise before expiration depends on the behavior of the price of the underlying security *throughout* the life of the option, and cannot be reduced to a single parameter. While adjustments can be made to take into account the premium associated with early exercise, as discussed above, these adjustments are only approximations. These models are also increasingly inaccurate as the term of the option lengthens because of their inability to take into account variations in short-term interest rates, and/or the time-dependence of volatilities. To deal with such features, more discriminating pricing models have been developed, which are generally known as binomial or (more accurately) lattice-based models.

The key to a lattice-based model is the division of the span from settle to expiration into discrete intervals or steps; for example, for a one-month option the step size might be a single day. The model then assumes that the key parameter, typically the price or yield of the underlying security, evolves through time on a step-by-step basis, moving up or down by a fixed amount or proportion in each interval. If we allow only two possible movements (up and down) at each step, the result is a double-branched, or binomial, lattice; however, we can equally well allow three or more possible movements (up, flat, and down) at each step, giving rise to more complex lattices. (It is important to note that the price or yield movements must be such that successive up and down steps cancel, so that the result of up followed by down will be the same state as down followed by up. This allows the model to incorporate a true lattice, and not a rapidly branching tree, which would be computationally much more demanding.)

The lattice-based model derives an option value by working backward through the lattice from the final step, the expiration date, at which the option value is known, to the initial step, the contract settle date. It is assumed that the states achieved in the lattice are all arbitrage-free, and on this assumption it is possible to solve backward for the implied value of the option contract at each previous step. Thus, a lattice-based model gives rise to an algorithm, rather than a closed formula, for determining the option value.

Assume that at any node in the lattice the price S of the underlying security may go up by a factor u with probability q, or down by a factor d with probability $(1 - q)$

$$
S
\begin{array}{l}
\nearrow \; uS \text{ with probability } q \\[2ex]
\searrow \; dS \text{ with probability } (1 - q)
\end{array}
$$

We also assume a constant short-term interest rate r_0, set $r = 1 + r_0$, with $u > r > d$, and assume a coupon accruing at c per period. Finally, we assume that we can value the option at the up and down nodes, which will be true at the terminal nodes, as the option will be expiring, and will be either worthless or *intrinsic* (worth the difference between the price of the underlying and the strike price)

$$
C
\begin{array}{l}
\nearrow \; C_u \text{ with probability } q \\[2ex]
\searrow \; C_d \text{ with probability } (1 - q)
\end{array}
$$

where C_u and C_d are the option values at the up and down nodes, respectively.

Suppose we create a position consisting of some proportion of the underlying security and cash (or a riskless bond): $S\Delta + H$. (Note that H may be negative— that is, it may represent *borrowing*.) We will choose Δ and H in such a way as to *replicate* the price behavior of the option in both up and down scenarios. At the end of one step, this position will have the value

$$
S\Delta + H
\begin{array}{l}
\nearrow \; uS\Delta + rH + \Delta c \text{ with probability } q \\[2ex]
\searrow \; dS\Delta + rH + \Delta c \text{ with probability } (1 - q)
\end{array}
$$

where c is the one-period accrued interest.

We will choose Δ and H in such a way as to ensure that

$$uS\Delta + rH + \Delta c = C_u$$

$$dS\Delta + rH + \Delta c = C_d$$

Solving for Δ and H, we have

$$\Delta = \frac{C_u - C_d}{(u - d)S}$$

$$H = \frac{uC_d - dC_u}{(u - d)r} - \frac{\Delta c}{r}$$

If there is to be no perfect arbitrage available during the step in question, the value C of the option must be equal to $S\Delta + H$; otherwise we could make a riskless return by buying the option and selling the combination of underlying and riskless bond (or vice versa). We have *replicated* the option contract by a properly leveraged position in the underlying security and cash. Our portfolio $S\Delta + H$ goes up (or down) precisely as much as the value of the option contract in the up and down scenarios. (Δ is thus the *price sensitivity* or *hedge ratio* of the option.)

The value of the option can thus be determined at a given node from the values at the up and down nodes by the formula

$$C = S\Delta + H = \frac{C_u - C_d}{(u - d)} + \frac{uC_d - dC_u}{(u - d)r} - \frac{\Delta c}{r} \qquad (4.16)$$

Now, the value of the option is known *completely* at the terminal nodes of the lattice; it is 0 if the option expires worthless (out of the money), and it is the intrinsic value of the option (the amount it ends up in the money) otherwise. We can therefore apply the above argument at each node in the lattice, until we eventually work our way back to the value of the option at the initial node. Note that the values of Δ and H will generally be different at different nodes; this means that we must adjust the proportions of the underlying security and cash in our replicating portfolio as we move through the lattice. This is only to be expected, as the price-sensitivity of the option naturally changes as it moves further in or out of the money. This pricing method is therefore commonly known as *dynamic replication* of the option value. (An application of this methodology is given as follows.)

The key binomial pricing Equation (4.16) can be rewritten as

$$C = \left[\left(\frac{r-d}{u-d} \right) C_u + \left(\frac{u-r}{u-d} \right) C_d - \Delta c \right] / r$$

or

$$C = [pC_u + (1-p)C_d - \Delta c]/r \tag{4.17}$$

where

$$p = (r-d)/(u-d) \tag{4.18}$$

Note that Equations (4.16) and (4.17) *do not involve the transition probability q;* the value of the option is *independent* of investors' expectations about market trends. Nor does the option value depend on investors' attitudes toward risk; the formula gives the same option value whether the investor is bull or bear, risk-averse or risk-seeking.

In fact, it is easy to see that for p in Equation (4.18), $0 \le p \le 1$, so p can be treated as a kind of *probability.* Equation (4.17) then expresses the option value at a given node as the *expected present value* of the option one lattice step into the future (adjusted for coupon accrual). The probability p is in fact the value of the transition probability q that would lead to the one-period riskless rate of return r as a return on S; that is, it is the solution of the equation

$$q(uS) + (1-q)(dS) = rS$$

Thus, p is the *risk-neutral probability* and Equation (4.17) can be interpreted as asserting that *the value of an option is its risk-neutral expected present value.*

By iterating Equation (4.17), we can work out algebraically what the option value must be in terms of its values two lattice steps into the future, three steps into the future, or N steps into the future. We can thus write an explicit formula for the value of the option at the initial lattice node in terms of its values at the terminal nodes. The algebra is cumbersome, but the final formula sheds some light on the relationship between the price-driven binomial lattice pricing model and the Black-Scholes closed-form analytic model. Ignoring coupon accrual, the full binomial formula is

$$C = S\Phi(a, n, p') - Kr^{-n}\Phi(a, n, p) \tag{4.19}$$

where

$$\Phi(a, n, q) = \sum_{i=a}^{n} \left(\frac{n!}{i!(n-i)!} \right) q^i (1-q)^{n-i}$$

and K = option strike price
       $p = (r-d)/(u-d)$, as above
       $p' = (u/r)p$
       a = the smallest nonnegative integer greater than
       $\log(K/Sd^n)/\log(u/d)$.

For a derivation of this formula, originally from Sharpe (1979), see Cox and Rubinstein (1985), which contains a detailed and lucid exploration of the relationship between the binomial and Black-Scholes pricing models. This presentation of the price-driven lattice-based pricing model is based on theirs.

Relationship Between Lattice-Based and Analytic Models.   The simplest binomial lattice models assume the same driving parameters and statistical rules for their distributions as do the closed-form models: either the price or the yield moves up or down by a fixed absolute or relative step. It can be shown, and should be expected, that such models in fact converge to the closed-form models for European options "in the limit," as the lattice step is made smaller and smaller. (This is natural, because the lattice-based approach is a discrete approximation of the underlying stochastic differential equation solved or analytically approximated in the closed-form models.) In particular, for suitable specification of the limiting behavior of the parameters q, u, and d as n approaches infinity, the binomial pricing Equation given by Equation (4.19) converges to the Black-Scholes pricing Equation (4.10). Recalling that the option delta, or hedge ratio, is given by $N(z)$ in Equation (4.11), we see that the first term on the right hand side of Equation (4.10) (or (4.19)) represents *the amount invested in the underlying security* in creating a position dynamically replicating, or hedging, the option payoffs; the second term represents *the amount borrowed* to finance the replicating, or hedging, position.

Since the closed-form models seem to give the same result, one may question why lattice-based models are even necessary. For *American* options, lattice-based models allow for an accurate valuation of the early exercise option, something the simpler closed-form models cannot achieve. This is accomplished by checking the desirability of early exercise at each node, setting the American option value $C'_{s,t}$ at each node (s, t) to Max $(C_{s,t}, S_{s,t} - K)$ for a call, Min $(C_{s,t}, K - S_{s,t})$ for a put, where $S_{s,t}$ is the value of the underlying at node (s, t) and

$$C_{s,t} = [pC'_u + (1-p)C'_d - \Delta c]/r$$

as in Equation (4.17), with C'_u and C'_d the *American* call values at the up and down nodes. The lattice-based models are also capable of incorporating irregular and path-dependent intermediate cash flows during the life of the option into their calculations. Of course, when such additional features are taken into account, there is usually no closed algebraic expression such as Equation (4.19) associated with the model. In fact, Equation (4.19) is generally of greater theoretical than practical interest, as implementations of lattice-based models generally calculate the prices of options and other contingent claims by explicitly working backwards through the lattice from the terminal nodes to the initial node.

Example 4.2: Pricing a 6-Month Call on a Cash Bond

Consider a bond with initial price par (100.00) and 12 percent coupon, and a six-month call option on it struck at par. Assume that the price of the bond will move up by a factor of 1.1, or down by a factor of $1/1.1 = 0.9091$ over the life of the option. (The fact that the up and down steps are inverse means that we assume there is no "drift" in the median bond price over the life of the option.) We will price the option using a three-step lattice, so that at each step the price goes up by a factor of $u = (1.1)^{1/3} = 1.0323$, or down by a corresponding (inverse) factor of $d = 0.9687$ with equal probability $p = 0.5$. We also assume a six-month risk-free rate r_0 of 5 percent, giving a discounting factor for a single step of $r = (1.05)^{1/3} = 1.0164$. (In practice, many more steps would be used for greater accuracy.)

Bond prices follow the lattice in Figure 4.1. Using the above equations, call prices follow the corresponding lattice, shown in Figure 4.2. and hedge ratios follow the lattice in Figure 4.3.

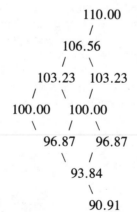

Figure 4.1   Bond Price Lattice

```
                    1.000
                      /
                   6.2057
                    /    \
              3.4729      3.2280
               /    \     /
          1.8089    1.3827
               \     /    \
              0.5784      0.0000
                    \     /
                   0.0000
                         \
                        0.0000
```
Figure 4.2 Call Option Price Lattice

For example, the call value of 1.3827 and its corresponding hedge ratio 0.5079 are obtained as follows:

$$\Delta = \frac{C_u - C_d}{(u - d)S}$$

$$= \frac{3.228 - 0.00}{(1.0323 - 0.9687) \times 100.00} = \frac{3.228}{6.360} = 0.5079$$

$$H = \frac{uC_d - dC_u}{(u - d)r} - \frac{\Delta c}{r}$$

$$= \frac{(1.0323 \times 0.00) - (0.9689 \times 3.228)}{0.0636 \times 1.0164} - \frac{0.5079 \times 2.00}{1.0164} = -49.412$$

```
                    1.000
                      /
                   1.0000
                    /    \
              0.7352      1.0000
               /    \     /
          0.4555    0.5079
               \     /    \
              0.2246      0.0000
                    \     /
                   0.0000
                         \
                        0.0000
```
Figure 4.3 Hedge Ratio Lattice

and

$$C = \Delta \times S + H = (0.5079 \times 100.00) + -49.412 = 1.3827$$

where $c = 2.0$ is the coupon accrual over a single step (two months).

■

Yield-Driven Lattice-Based Models. To handle variations in short-term interest rates over the life of the option, we can let interest rates themselves drive the model; instead of moving the bond price or yield up and down through the lattice, we move the interest rate r through the lattice

$$
\begin{array}{l}
\quad\quad r_u \text{ with probability } p \\
\quad / \\
r \\
\quad \backslash \\
\quad\quad r_d \text{ with probability } (1 - p)
\end{array}
$$

The bond price at each node can then be determined from the assumed bond values at the succeeding nodes, but some additional assumptions are necessary. If we assume that the bond price should always be such that expected return over the next period will be that of a riskless bond (the so-called expectations hypothesis), we have

$$B = \frac{pB_u + (1 - p)B_d + c}{(1 + r)}$$

where B = bond price, and B_u, B_d its up and down values
  p = probability of an upward movement in the interest rate r
  c = coupon accrual for the period

On the other hand, one can price the bonds so that they provide a common risk-adjusted return for the period in question; all bonds will then be priced so that

$$\frac{E(r_B) - r}{\sigma(r_B)} = \rho$$

where $E(r_B)$ = expected return of the bond for the period in question
  $\sigma(r_B)$ = volatility of the return
  ρ = a constant, the market price of risk

We have

$$E(r_B) = \frac{pB_u + (1 - p)B_d + c - B}{B}$$

and

$$\sigma(r_B) = \frac{\sqrt{p(1 - p)}(B_u - B_d)}{B}$$

so

$$\rho = \frac{pB_u + (1 - p)B_d + c - B - rB}{\sqrt{p(1 - p)}(B_u - B_d)}$$

and

$$B = \frac{B_u\left(p - \rho\sqrt{p(1 - p)}\right) + B_d\left((1 - p) - \rho\sqrt{p(1 - p)}\right) + c}{(1 + r)}$$

If $\rho = 0$, this reduces to the previous case (the bond pricing scheme derived from the expectations hypothesis). In any case, derivation of the lattice of bond prices from a given lattice of short-term interest rates requires some assumptions about investor attitudes toward risk. Finally, note that since we know the current price of the underlying bond, the up and down parameters u and d, together with the probability p and the assumed market price of risk ρ must be constrained such that the bond price at the initial node coincides with the known price.

Example 4.3: Evolution of Interest Rates and Bond Prices

Consider a bond maturing in five years, with a coupon of 10.00, and assume a current risk-free rate of 10 percent, and up and down parameters of 1.05 and 0.95. Using a probability $p = 0.5$, under the expectations hypothesis, we have the lattice of rates and corresponding bond prices shown in Figures 4.4 and 4.5. (Note that the price B of a bond goes *up* when the interest rate at the corresponding node goes *down;* that is, B_d is *greater* than B_u.)

For example, $7.738 = 8.145 \times 0.95$ and $8.552 = 8.145 \times 1.05$ in the interest-rate lattice, and the bond price 100.917 is determined by

$$B = \frac{(0.5 \times 100.915) + (0.5 \times 100.045) + 10.00}{(1 + 0.09476)} = 100.917$$

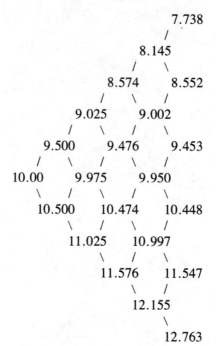

```
                        7.738
                         /
                       8.145
                       /   \
                   8.574     8.552
                   /   \     /
                9.025     9.002
                /   \     /   \
             9.500     9.476     9.453
             /   \     /   \     /
         10.00     9.975     9.950
             \   /     \   /     \
          10.500    10.474    10.448
              \   /     \   /
             11.025    10.997
                 \   /     \
                11.576    11.547
                    \   /
                  12.155
                      \
                    12.763
```

Figure 4.4 Interest Rate Lattice

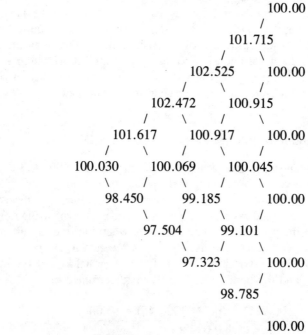

```
                              100.00
                                /
                            101.715
                             /    \
                       102.525     100.00
                        /    \      /
                   102.472     100.915
                    /    \     /    \
               101.617     100.917     100.00
               /    \     /    \      /
         100.030     100.069     100.045
              \     /     \     /     \
           98.450     99.185      100.00
              \     /     \     /
            97.504     99.101
                 \     /     \
               97.323      100.00
                   \      /
                 98.785
                     \
                   100.00
```

Figure 4.5 Bond Price Lattice

Note that the price of the bond at the initial node is 100.030, or $100\,\frac{1}{32}$; if we were constrained to an initial bond price of par, for example, we could determine that a probability $p = 0.504$ would give a tree of bond prices with an initial node bond price of almost exactly par.

We can now derive the price of a call at any point in the lattice similarly to the case of a bond price-driven lattice. Consider a holding consisting of a long position in the bond, and a short position of Δ calls. This position will have a current value of

$$V = B - \Delta C$$

and a value in the up and down nodes of

$$V_u = B_u - \Delta C_u + cV_d = B_d - \Delta C_d + c$$

In order for this holding to be riskless—independent of interest rate movements—these two values must be equal; we can then solve for Δ

$$\Delta = \frac{B_u - B_d}{C_u - C_d}$$

(Note that here Δ is the *reciprocal* of the hedge ratio.)

Since we are assuming that this holding is riskless, it must have a rate of return over the next period equal to the riskless rate r for that period

$$(1 + r)V = V_u = V_d$$

or

$$(1 + r)(B - \Delta C) = B_u - \Delta C_u + c$$

Solving for C, we have

$$C = \frac{\theta C_u + (1 - \theta)C_d}{(1 + r)} - \frac{c}{\Delta(1 + r)}$$

where

$$\theta = \frac{B_d - B(1 + r)}{(B_d - B_u)}$$

As in the price-driven case, we work backward from the nodes at expiration, at which time the call prices are all known (they are either 0 or intrinsic; that is, equal to $B - K$), to the initial node. Note that we derive the hedge ratio at the same time we derive the call price.

■

Example 4.4: Lattice-Based Pricing of a Call Option on a Cash Bond

We can now illustrate the pricing of an at-the-money call option on the above bond, which for simplicity we will assume to expire after four lattice steps. The lattice of call prices generated according to the above algorithm is shown in Figure 4.6.

For example, the call price of 0.24526 at the initial node can be derived as follows:

Because $B = 100.03$, $r = 10$ percent or 0.10, $c = 10.0$, $B_u = 98.45$, $B_d = 101.617$, $C_u = 0.09867$, and $C_d = 0.44089$, we have

$$\theta = \frac{B_d - B(1 + r)}{(B_d - B_u)}$$

$$= \frac{101.617 - (100.030 \times (1 + .10))}{(101.617 - 98.45)} = -2.657$$

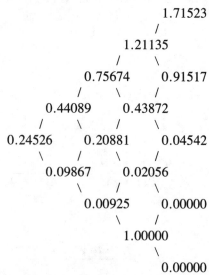

Figure 4.6 Lattice of Call Option Prices

and

$$\Delta = \frac{B_u - B_d}{C_u - C_d}$$

$$= \frac{98.45 - 101.617}{0.09867 - 0.44089} = 9.2543$$

Therefore

$$C = \frac{\theta C_u + (1 - \theta)C_d}{(1 + r)} - \frac{c}{\Delta(1 + r)}$$

$$= \frac{-2.657 \times 0.09867 + ((1 + 2.657) \times 0.44089)}{(1 + 0.10)} - \frac{10.00}{(1 + 0.10) \times 9.2543}$$

$$= 0.24508$$

■

Conclusions.   Lattice-based models can provide greater accuracy than the simpler closed-form models where intermediate cash flows and/or early exercise are an issue. Such an approach is required because there are no known simple closed-form analytic formulas for option prices in such contexts. Another approach, mentioned below, uses *analytic approximations* to option prices and sensitivities. Lattice-based models have the advantage that they can be made arbitrarily precise by increasing the number of lattice steps, whereas analytic approximations generally have some irreducible margin of error. Other numerical methods, such as finite-difference techniques for approximating solutions to the underlying stochastic differential equations governing the evolution of the key parameters over time, are sometimes also feasible, and like the lattice-based models can be made arbitrarily precise, but at a cost.

Although lattice-based models are essential for some applications, their accuracy is dependent on the number of lattice steps employed, and the computational demands of such models increase roughly as the square of the number of steps. There is thus an unavoidable tradeoff between increased accuracy and computational expense. Moreover, although some lattice-based models automatically generate the option delta, or hedge ratio, along with the option price, other sensitivities, such as the rate of time decay or the sensitivity to change in volatility, must be computed numerically by recomputing the option price for slightly different values of the parameter in question. Sensitivity analysis may thus further increase the computational demands of such models.

As we have noted, (and as is proven in references such as Cox and Rubinstein, 1985) the option values calculated by lattice-based and closed-form models such as Black-Scholes will be *exactly the same* in the limit for European options. Under some circumstances, the difference between the values calculated by lattice-based and closed-form models will be small enough to be ignored for most practical applications. (It may be less than a pricing tick—the smallest pricing increment—or at least within the market bid-asked spread.) The simpler, closed-form models should therefore not be discarded. For short-dated European options they are extremely accurate, and there are many other contexts, such as short-dated American options, where they may be perfectly adequate, and their cost and speed far superior to lattice-based models.

The original exposition of the binomial lattice approach to option pricing, building on the ideas of Professor William Sharpe of Stanford University, can be found in Cox, Ross, and Rubinstein (1979) or Cox and Rubinstein (1985). Certain modifications of the original models and arguments are necessary in dealing with bond options. Our exposition is based on that of Ritchken (1987), which includes a presentation of such models in a bond options context.

In any case, both the closed-form and lattice-based models discussed so far share some common limitations. These limitations have generally to do with the implicit assumptions about the behavior of interest rates and volatilities over the life of the option, and become particularly critical in pricing *long-dated options* with terms of up to several years. A discussion of some of the models that have been developed in recent years to deal with these considerations is given below. Before going on to such advanced models, however, a simple analytic approximation for the value of American options is presented.

Approximate Valuation of American Options

Barone-Adesi and Whaley (1987) give a simple analytic approximation for the value of American options that is quite accurate in many circumstances and far easier to implement than any lattice-based model. Building on earlier work by MacMillan (1986), they show that by simplifying the differential equation for the early exercise premium on an American option, one can derive a set of equations that can be solved directly (although not explicitly) for a critical value S^* (S^{**}) of the underlying security above which (below which) an American call (put) will always be exercised; an explicit formula for the early exercise premium below (above) that critical value is then derived. (It is this explicit formula that involves solving an auxiliary quadratic equation; hence the name of the model.)

The pricing formula for an American call option using the quadratic American model is

$$C(S, T) = c(S, T) + A_2\left(\frac{S}{S^*}\right)^{q_2}, \qquad S < S^* \qquad (4.20C)$$

$$C(S, T) = S - X, \qquad S \geq S^*$$

where

$$c(S, T) = S e^{(b-r)T} N(d_1(S)) - X e^{-rT} N(d_2(S))$$

is Merton's formula for the value of a European call option (reducing to Black-Scholes when the holding cost b is equal to the risk-free rate r; compare Equation (4.12)),

$$A_2 = \left(\frac{S^*}{q_2}\right)[1 - e^{(b-r)T} N(d_1(S^*))],$$

$$q_2 = \frac{-N - 1 + \sqrt{(N-1)^2 + 4M/K}}{2},$$

$$d_1(S) = \frac{\ln(S/X) + bT + \sigma^2 T/2}{\sigma\sqrt{T}},$$

$$d_2(S) = d_1(S) - \sigma\sqrt{T},$$

and

$$M = \frac{2r}{\sigma^2}, \qquad N = \frac{2b}{\sigma^2}, \qquad K = 1 - e^{-rT}.$$

The American put option value is given similarly by

$$P(S, T) = p(S, T) + A_1\left(\frac{S}{S^{**}}\right)^{q_1}, \qquad S > S^{**}$$

$$P(S, T) = X - S, \qquad S \le S^{**} \qquad \text{(4.20P)}$$

where

$$p(S, T) = X e^{-rT} N(-d_2(S)) - S e^{(b-r)T} N(-d_1(S))$$

is Merton's formula for the value of a European call option (reducing to Black-Scholes when the holding cost b is equal to the risk-free rate r), S^{**} is the critical exercise level of the underlying for an American put,

$$A_1 = -\left(\frac{S^*}{q_2}\right)[1 - e^{(b-r)T} N(-d_1(S^*))],$$

and

$$q_1 = \frac{-N - 1 - \sqrt{(N-1)^2 + 4M/K}}{2}$$

Since the A_i and q_i do not depend on S, the current price of the underlying security, it is easy to calculate delta, the hedge ratio, from Equations (4.20C) and (4.20P). Sensitivities to changes in r, σ, and T are trickier because S^*, and hence the A_i and q_i, *do* depend on these parameters. Such sensitivities can be calculated indirectly by testing the actual change in option price for small shifts up and down in the parameter in question, which is often referred to as the "up-down delta" method.

Readers seeking more details on this useful model should refer directly to Barone-Adesi and Whaley (1987); readers of the exposition in Natenberg (1988) should beware of errors in the transcription of key formulas from the original paper.

Model Limitations. While the option pricing models described above are adequate and appropriate for a wide variety of applications, including most short-dated bond options, they share some important limitations in the context of longer-dated options and option-related contingent claims (embedded options):

Variable interest rates. Long-dated bond option prices will necessarily be highly sensitive to variations in interest rates over the life of the option. Both the closed-form analytic pricing models like Black-Scholes and the simple price-driven binomial pricing models explicitly assume a constant short-term rate over the life of the option. They are therefore inappropriate for pricing long-dated options, whether *European* or *American*. Even yield-driven binomial lattice pricing models of the sort described above are generally inadequate, as they ignore any potential variation in the *relative* interest rates for differing terms during the life of the option—that is, they ignore changes in the *term structure* of interest rates.

Multi-step arbitrage opportunities. It can be shown that while such simple models are arbitrage-free over a single lattice step, they are susceptible to more subtle, multi-step arbitrage relationships among implied forward interest rates for different terms at different nodes of the lattice. Bookstaber, Jacob, and Langsam (1986), for example, take as their point of departure an analysis of some of the often overlooked sources of arbitrage in traditional binomial pricing models. They point out that while most such models are carefully designed to avoid the possibility of arbitrage locally, over a single lattice step, they are all susceptible to arbitrage globally, over multi-step periods. The source of these arbitrage opportunities is the *overdetermination* of such binomial models when they deal with instruments of multiple maturities.

Bookstaber, Jacob, and Langsam initially propose resolving this difficulty by moving to a *multinomial model,* in which there are $N + 1$ possible interest-rate scenarios when there are N remaining periods. However, this leads to a lattice in which, as they note, "the number of paths will grow factorially, and the size of the equation system will be quadratic in the number of periods." Noting that the source of the difficulty is the existence of N *independently-priced* instruments, the discount bonds of term $1, \ldots, N$, the authors observe that by imposing certain restrictions on the yield curve, it is possible to resurrect a binomial lattice framework. While the authors do not completely specify an arbitrage-free model in their paper (they are mainly concerned with illustrating the multiple sources of arbitrage inconsistencies in the simpler binomial option pricing models in common use), the constraints they impose on the yield curve look a lot like those introduced by Ho and Lee (1986) and by Dattatreya and Fabozzi (1989) in the models discussed below.

Variable volatilities.   The price-based models are also inadequate where the term of the option is significant in relation to the maturity of the underlying bond, because the *amortization to par* in the price of the underlying bond implies that *price volatilities cannot be constant over the life of the option.* For example, the range of possible outcomes at expiration (payoff scenarios) for a 3-year option on a bond with 3½ years to maturity is *narrower* than for a 1-year option on the same bond, because the price of the bond must approach par as it nears maturity.

Path dependence.   Another important limitation of these models is their inability to handle *path-dependent* effects. The values of certain kinds of options depend critically on the *path* followed by the price of the underlying security over the life of the option. For example, *down-and-out options,* which have existed since the mid-1960s, behave like ordinary European options except that a call (put) contract is cancelled, possibly with a rebate payment, if the underlying security price ever falls below (rises above) a certain level; see Cox and Rubinstein (1985) for details. More recently, so-called *look-back* and *average-strike* options have been introduced. These option contracts have *uncertain strike prices:* a look-back call (put) option is European, but the strike price is the *minimum (maximum)* daily closing price of the underlying security over the life of the option. The strike price of an average-strike option is the *average* of the daily closing prices over its life. Clearly, evaluating the fair price of such an option requires examination of the path followed by prices over the entire life of the option.

There are a number of possible techniques for overcoming these limitations. Perhaps the most popular approach in recent years has been to adapt the lattice-based approach to take into account variations in the term structure while constraining interest rates at the various lattice nodes in order to avoid any arbitrage relationship. Two such classes of models are outlined and compared below. Of course, such models are more technically involved and computationally intensive than simpler models, but they are also more powerful. Properly applied, they allow the accurate pricing of a very wide range of complex options and other contingent claims.

Simulation techniques have been used where it is necessary to fully capture *path-dependent* effects, although such methods are computationally expensive and are subject to certain theoretical limitations. Finally, a variety of alternative models based on different assumptions about the driving price or yield dynamics have also been proposed to handle these limitations.

Term Structure–Based Models

To adequately handle long-dated options, including interest-rate caps and floors, and other more complex bond and interest-rate options, one must take into account the potential variability among interest rates at different maturities. Instead of tracking the evolution of a single parameter, such as price or short-term interest rates, the *entire term structure of interest rates* is tracked, either continuously or by specifying a term structure at each node of a lattice, with appropriate up and down shifts. This allows the model to take into account the subtler dependencies of option value on variations in short-term interest rates as well as in the actual price or yield of the underlying security, the maturity of which may change significantly during the life of the option.

Lattice-Based Term-Structure Models. In general, these models require as input the current yield curve (term structure). The term structure will be "modelled" by one or more model parameters, such as a short rate and a long rate. The model then specifies a stochastic process for shifting these rates up or down at successive nodes in the lattice and modifying the projected term structure accordingly. The rates themselves, the lattice transition probabilities, and the volatilities (step size) at each level are adjusted to ensure that the lattice is arbitrage-free, and that the relevant underlying instruments are properly priced at the initial node. Option prices are then calculated by working backwards through the lattice very much as in the simpler binomial models.

These models share certain common assumptions, which Ho and Lee (1986) aptly describe as "the standard perfect capital market assumptions in a discrete state-time framework":

1. The market is *continuous and frictionless*, with no transaction costs.
2. The market is *discrete*, clearing at regular intervals or periods $1, \ldots, T$ in time.
3. The market is *complete*, with riskless discount bonds of every maturity T.
4. The market has only a *finite number of states* at a given time period t. The market at state s and time t is completely characterized by a vector of interest rates $r_{s,t}(T)$ (the *yield curve* at node (s, t)), or by the equivalent *discount function* $\mathrm{DF}_{s,t}(T)$ at node (s, t). $\mathrm{DF}_{s,t}(T)$ is the price of a zero-coupon bond of maturity T. It tells us the value today of a dollar T periods in the future. Given a complete yield curve $r_{s,t}(T)$, one can solve for the discount function $\mathrm{DF}_{s,t}(T)$ and vice versa.

The general scheme of such a model is given in Figure 4.7.

Note that $\mathrm{DF}_{i,j}$ stands for the entire discount function $\mathrm{DF}_{i,j}(T)$ at node (i, j), not just a single rate.

Ho and Lee's Arbitrage-Free Rate Movement Model. Since 1986, Thomas Ho and his collaborators have developed a class of what they call AR (arbitrage-free rate movement) models for pricing long-term contingent claims. In these models, an initial term structure is determined from a set of benchmark bonds covering all relevant maturities, and the evolution of the term structure as it moves through the lattice is then constrained in such a way that all the bonds so used are themselves automatically properly priced at the initial node. Such models can simultaneously and consistently price a wide range of bonds and bond options in a *common* arbitrage-free universe.

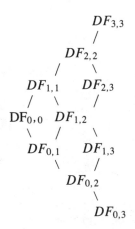

Figure 4.7 Term Stucture–Based Lattice

The Methodology. Ho and Lee (1986) present a simplified version of the general AR model that illustrates the general principles on which these models are based. The central features of the methodology employed are as follows:

1. **Estimation of the initial term structure:** First, a starting specification of the term structure of interest rates, or the corresponding discount function, must be determined. This can be accomplished in a number of ways: see Vasicek and Fong (1982). Typically, what is involved is choosing a basket of bonds covering the relevant range of maturities for which good empirical pricing data are readily available; moreover, a particular *functional form* for the discount function or yield curve must be specified. (Vasicek and Fong use "exponential splines.") Estimates of the unknown parameter values for the specified functional form are obtained from empirical data using standard statistical techniques. The empirically determined discount function is thus one of the important inputs to the model.

2. **Arbitrage constraints on rate movements:** The term structure of interest rates is assumed to evolve in such a way as to satisfy certain natural constraints. Ho and Lee (1986) give the term structure at a node (s, t) of the lattice by specifying the discount function $\mathrm{DF}_{s,t}(T)$ at that node. (In the notation of their paper, this discount function is given by $P_i^{(n)}(T)$, at the ith state of the nth period in the lattice.) They assume that the discount function evolves through time according to the rules

$$\mathrm{DF}_{s+1,t+1}(T) = \frac{\mathrm{DF}_{s,t}(T + 1)}{\mathrm{DF}_{s,t}(1)} h_u(T) \qquad \text{(UP)}$$

and

$$\mathrm{DF}_{s,t+1}(T) = \frac{\mathrm{DF}_{s,t}(T + 1)}{\mathrm{DF}_{s,t}(1)} h_d(T) \qquad \text{(DOWN)}$$

for all nodes (s, t) and all periods $T = 1, \ldots, N$. (See Figure 2.7). The functions $h_u(T)$ and $h_d(T) - h(T)$ and $h^*(T)$ in Ho and Lee's terminology—are called the *perturbation functions*.

Note that $\mathrm{DF}_{s,t}(T + 1)/\mathrm{DF}_{s,t}(1)$ is the t-period *forward rate* that would be implied at the node (s, t) in a *risk-free* (certain) universe. The perturbation functions $h_u(T)$ and $h_d(T)$ respectively measure how the up and down states of the term structure differ from these implied forward rates. The *volatility* of the term structure is therefore embedded in these perturbation functions. (In general, $h_u(T)$ and $h_d(T)$ could depend on the node (s, t), but for simplicity Ho and Lee assume that these functions are independent of s and t.)

In order for a lattice to be arbitrage-free, we must first have

$$\text{DF}_{s,t}(0) = 1 \quad \text{and} \quad \text{DF}_{s,t}(T - 1) > \text{DF}_{s,t}(T) \qquad (4.21\text{a})$$

at all nodes (s, t) and for all periods T. (That is, the value of a dollar today must be a dollar, and a dollar tomorrow must never be worth *more* than its value today.) In addition, any *portfolio* of fairly priced bonds must itself be fairly priced. This implies that there must exist at each node (s, t) a parameter $\pi_{s,t}$ such that the prices $\text{DF}_{s,t}(T)$ of the T-period discount bonds at (s, t) are all equal to π-weighted linear combinations of the bond values one period forward, suitably discounted at the one-period rate for (s, t), *independent of T*. That is

$$\text{DF}_{s,t}(T + 1)/\text{DF}_{s,t}(1) = \pi_{s,t}\text{DF}_{s,t+1}(T) + (1 - \pi_{s,t})\text{DF}_{s+1,t+1}(T)$$

$$(4.21\text{b})$$

for all T. (See Ho and Lee, 1986.)

To ensure the arbitrage-free character of the lattice of term structures, Ho and Lee therefore assume that the perturbation functions obey the relationship

$$\pi h_u(T) + (1 - \pi)h_d(T) = 1 \qquad (4.22)$$

for some constant π independent of time T and the initial discount function $\text{DF}_{0,0}(T)$. From the up and down equations defining $\text{DF}_{s,t}$ in terms of the perturbation functions, Equation (4.22) clearly implies that Equation (4.21b) will be satisfied. (Again, although π could depend on s and t, for simplicity Ho and Lee assume it does not.)

3. **Path-Independence Constraints on Rate Movements:** To ensure *path independence*, a condition in which the term structure resulting from an up step followed by a down step is the same as that resulting from a down step followed by an up step, we must have

$$\text{DF}_{s+1,t+2}(T) = \frac{\text{DF}_{s,t}(T + 2)}{\text{DF}_{s,t}(2)} \frac{h_u(T + 1)h_d(T)}{h_u(1)}$$

$$= \frac{\text{DF}_{s,t}(T + 2)}{\text{DF}_{s,t}(2)} \frac{h_d(T + 1)h_u(T)}{h_d(1)}$$

and hence

$$h_u(T + 1)h_d(T)h_d(1) = h_d(T + 1)h_u(T)h_u(1)$$

Together with Equation (4.22), this constraint implies that there must exist a parameters δ (again assumed for simplicity to be independent of the node (s, t)) such that

$$h_u(T) = \frac{1}{\pi + (1 + \pi)\delta^T} \quad \text{for } T \geq 0 \quad (4.23a)$$

and

$$h_d(T) = \frac{\delta^T}{\pi + (1 + \pi)\delta^T} \quad (4.23b)$$

Together with the initial discount function $DF_{0,0}(t)$, the parameters π and δ completely specify the evolution of the term structure. (More complex AR models may have π and δ dependent on state s and time t as well, as we have noted.) Ho and Lee show that under these assumptions, an interest-rate contingent claim $C_{s,t}$ can then be evaluated by working backward through the lattice using the following equation:

$$C_{s,t} = (\pi C_{s,t+1} + (1 - \pi)C_{s+1,t+1})DF_{s,t}(1) \quad (4.24)$$

Interpretation of Parameters. The parameter π in Ho and Lee's AR model can be interpreted as a kind of "risk-neutral probability"—it is precisely the probability at which the price of a T period bond today is equal to the present value of its expected value in one period. Equation (4.21) can be interpreted as stating that

$$\pi = (r - d)/(u - d)$$

where r is the one-period riskless return and u and d are the one-period returns in the up and down scenarios. This relationship should be familiar from our discussion of the simpler binomial lattice models—see Equation (4.18). Equation (4.24) thus says that, as in those simpler models, the value of the option or contingent claim in state (s, t), $C_{s,t}$, is its *expected present value* in a risk-neutral universe.

The interpretation of the parameter δ is slightly less straightforward. As Ho and Lee note, δ determines the *spread* between the two perturbation functions, $h_u(T)$ and $h_d(T)$. The larger the spread, the greater the variability in the term structures. Thus, δ is connected with the *volatility of the term structure*. Note, however, that this volatility varies *inversely* with δ.

Estimation of Parameters. Ho and Lee note that one must "use a nonlinear estimation procedure to determine π and δ such that the theoretical prices of a sample of contingent claims can best fit their observed prices. The estimated values of π and δ are then used to price other contingent claims." This is not a trivial procedure. A very simplified approach would be to take two securities, such as a 2-year option on a 5-year bond and a 3-year option on a 10-year bond, and calculate their values according to the model using an initial guess at values for π and δ. The resulting theoretical values will generally differ from the observed market values for both securities, so π and δ must then be modified to give new theoretical values better fitting the observed market prices. This process is repeated until the theoretical prices are "close enough" to the market prices, or until further improvement becomes impossible. At least two different securities are required, as there will generally be a range of pairs of values for π and δ giving the *same* price for any single given security. In general, a basket of several securities would be used. As Ho and Lee note, this process is similar to the estimation of implied volatilities for bonds or bond futures from market prices of options on those securities.

Properties of the Model. The Ho and Lee AR model allows us to model the variability in the term structure of interest rates with time in a relatively straightforward fashion, driven by the two parameters π and δ, which can be estimated from market data. It provides consistent, arbitrage-free prices for a specific universe of bonds and options. Because it is driven by an empirically derived initial term structure, it is a *relative* pricing model. The initial term structure is specified *exogenously.* This differs from some other models that generate *endogenous* yield curves driven, for example, by a short-rate stochastic process. This can be a strength where a measure of the relative richness or cheapness of securities within the given universe is required.

Because of the way in which the term structures are constrained, this model automatically accounts for the "amortization to par" experienced by all bonds. A T period bond will initially have a price determined by the initial, empirically determined term structure. As it matures, it will show greater price variability up to a certain point—that is, there will be a considerable range of implied prices for T/2 period bonds at time $t = T/2$, for example. But as the bond approaches maturity, its price variability will decline again; there will be very little price variability among 1-period bonds at time $t = T - 1$. What this means is that the assumed dynamic for term structures (or discount functions) implies a price distribution for bonds that *automatically* converges to par as the bonds approach maturity. Of course, this also implies that implied *price volatilities* for individual bonds are time-dependent in these models.

These AR models have limitations. The term-structure process imposed by the constraints and initial conditions can sometimes lead to implied negative forward rates, at least in the simplified version specified in Ho and Lee (1986). It has also been pointed out that Ho and Lee's model implies a common volatility for all interest rates (see Hull, 1989). In practice, long-term interest rates are normally less volatile than short-term rates.

Estimation of model parameters is not always easy; it is assumed that the parameters π and δ are properties of the term structure of interest rates, rather than of any one bond or class of bonds. It is therefore assumed that one can "back out" appropriate values for these parameters by adjusting their values until some appropriately chosen class of securities for which market prices are readily available is properly priced by the model. It is assumed that this estimation process is stable with respect to changes in the choice of reference securities used in the estimation process, and that the parameter values will not change rapidly with time. All these assumptions require further testing and verification.

Moreover, like all lattice-based models, these AR models are computation-intensive. The production versions of these models, as marketed by Global Advanced Technology Corporation, make use of a customized vector processor board, making them dependent on proprietary hardware and software technology. Nevertheless, their power and theoretical consistency has led to wide use by many financial firms.

Dattatreya and Fabozzi's Rate-Movement Model. Dattatreya and Fabozzi (1989) present a simplified debt options valuation model that is essentially a one-parameter, binomial model driven by an initial yield curve, with the resulting moving term structure adjusted and constrained to avoid arbitrage relationships and properly price a selected universe of bonds at the initial lattice node. Variants of this model are in common use in the securities industry.

The Methodology. Dattatreya and Fabozzi break their approach down into four separate methodological steps:

1. **Determination of the initial yield curve:** As in Ho and Lee's AR model, the initial yield curve is defined as a *discount function*, derived from the prices of current-coupon Treasury securities, statistically fitted and interpolated to give a smooth curve for all intermediate maturities.
2. **Generation of the basic interest-rate process:** Dattatreya and Fabozzi assume that the evolution of the term structure through their lattice is driven *explicitly* by the short rate. They point out that their model framework can accommodate a variety of choices for the stochastic process governing the evolution of the short rate. In their exposition, they choose

a lognormal process, with a fixed volatility (independent of time). A preliminary lattice of short-rate values is then generated according to the specified process.

3. **Assurance of internal consistency in the basic valuation algorithm:** Dattatreya and Fabozzi's basic valuation algorithm defines the value of any security to be the *path average* of its values over all possible paths through the lattice to the terminal level. This is equivalent to the result of *sequential backward averaging:* working backward through the lattice, calculating the *expected present value* of the security at each node. That is, the value $C_{s,t}$ of a security at node (s, t) is given by

$$C_{s,t} = (pC_{s+1,t+1} + (1 - p)C_{s,t+1})/1 + r_{s,t}/100 \qquad (4.25)$$

where p = probability of an up step in the lattice
           $r_{s,t}$ = short rate at node (s, t) in percent terms

(This formula can be adjusted to take into account intermediate cash flows such as coupon payments.)

4. **Calibration for external consistency:** Given the initial lattice of short rates, theoretical prices can be calculated for the zero-coupon bonds of varying maturities using this process of backward averaging through the resulting lattice. The resulting prices will *not* usually correspond to those in the initial discount function fitted to empirical data. To ensure consistency with the empirically given external data, the rates in the lattice are modified to meet the given constraints. The rates at each level t in the lattice are successively adjusted by a level-specific *drift* parameter, chosen to ensure that the $(t + 1)$-period zero-coupon bond is properly priced by the backward averaging process.

Consider the initial lattice of short rates shown in Figure 4.8. Suppose that the one- and two-period zero-coupon bonds are priced respectively at

Figure 4.8 Original Lattice of Short Rates

96.15 and 92.86. The one-period zero-coupon bond is already properly priced because the unique discounting rate for the first period, $r_{0,0}$, is *defined* by the one-period zero-coupon bond. To ensure that the two-period zero-coupon bond is properly priced, the rates at level 1 in the lattice are adjusted. For example, using the initial lattice of rates, we find that the *theoretical* price of the two-period zero-coupon bond is

$$ZCB_2 = \left(\frac{100}{1.044} + \frac{100}{1.03635}\right)/(2 \times 1.04)$$

$$= \frac{95.7854 + 96.4925}{2.08} = 92.4413,$$

which is different from the actual price of 92.86. It is therefore necessary to add a drift constant of -0.938 at level 1, so that the theoretical price is the same as the actual price (see Figure 4.9)

$$ZCB_2 = \left(\frac{100}{1.03931} + \frac{100}{1.03166}\right)/(2 \times 1.04)$$

$$= \frac{96.2177 + 96.9312}{2.08} = 92.8600$$

Next, to ensure that the three-period zero-coupon bond is properly priced, the rates at level 2 are adjusted, and so forth. Note that *we use the one-period rates just calculated to discount over the first period;* only the rates at a single level are adjusted at each step.

Dattatreya and Fabozzi note that one could also calibrate the model by modifying the *transition probabilities,* but that this would also change the volatility and lognormal distribution assumptions. By adjusting the rates by an additive drift constant, the volatility and distribution assumptions are preserved.

```
                  9. 68
                    /
                 7.862
                 /    \
             8.00     8.00
                 \    /
                 6.332
                      \
                      6. 61
```

Figure 4.9 Adjusted Lattice of Short Rates

Once the lattice of rates has been properly adjusted and calibrated, options—or any other security with clearly defined contingent cash flows—may be priced using the backward averaging approach (always discounting at the appropriate local short rate, of course). The essential pricing algorithm is given in Equation (4.25), iterated through the lattice back to the initial node.

Interpretation of Parameters. The Dattatreya and Fabozzi model has the advantage that its parameters are quite intuitive—the short rate is governed by a lognormal process with a specified volatility. The moving term structure generated by this process is, however, initially *endogenous* rather than exogenous—it is entirely determined by the short-rate stochastic process. The empirical yield curve enters only through the somewhat ad-hoc calibration process, so it is somewhat less explicit than in the Ho and Lee model just how the entire term structure of interest rates evolves with time. (What is the implied volatility of *long*-term rates, for example?) In this respect, Dattatreya and Fabozzi's model is closer to the simple rate-driven lattice-based models.

The transition probabilities also play an explicit role in this model, through the backward averaging process, and a different choice of transition probabilities may lead to different prices. Dattatreya and Fabozzi assume transition probabilities of ½ throughout in their exposition, but it is unclear why other probabilities might not be chosen. (A choice of transition probabilities other than ½ would imply a market drift, and hence a bullish or bearish view of the market.) Of course, this would imply a different rate distribution and would lead to different calibrated rates. Calibration guarantees that the universe of zero-coupon bonds is always properly priced, but it is unclear whether the resulting prices of other contingent claims would still be the same.

Properties of the Model. The Dattatreya and Fabozzi model provides a relatively straightforward approach to pricing long-term and path-dependent interest-rate contingent claims. Like the Ho and Lee AR models, this approach guarantees proper pricing of the initial universe of bonds used to specify the empirical yield curve—the calibration process forces such pricing. Parameter estimation is likely to be simpler than in the case of the Ho and Lee models, if only because the short rate is more immediately accessible than supposed structural properties of the term structure as a whole.

As the authors of this model point out, it can also be used to calculate an *option-adjusted spread* (OAS) for non-Treasury securities. Such a spread arises from the fact that higher discount rates must generally be used in discounting cash flows from lower-quality (riskier) non-Treasury securities, or the resulting prices will be too high. By solving iteratively for the appropriate spread to the short rate, to be added uniformly throughout the lattice in order to generate observed market prices for such securities, an implied OAS can be calculated.

(Note that such an OAS is spread to the *short rate,* and may be somewhat different from OAS values as defined by other models. It will have much the same qualitative behavior and significance, however.)

Dattatreya and Fabozzi also note that one of the consequences of the arbitrage-free constraints is that "the average or expected return from all securities for any horizon is the same."

This model is similar in many ways to the simpler lattice-based models, and it shares some of their limitations. Volatilities are assumed to be constant through time. The evolution of the term structure of interest rates is driven directly by the short-rate stochastic process. It is unclear how some traditional measures of sensitivity (to changes in the price or yield of the underlying security, for example, or to changes in the volatility of the underlying) could be evaluated. (The authors address this problem by introducing a new sensitivity measure called the *stochastic duration,* defined as the *price sensitivity to variations in the level of short-term rates.* This is an interesting measure, but lacks the intuitive appeal of traditional duration, and is unlikely to replace the option delta in most traders' minds.)

Simulation Methods

There are times when an option contract (or some other contingent claim) depends on one or more parameters in a way that is intrinsically "path-dependent"; that is, in such a fashion that one *cannot* assume that up and down steps cancel out. This will be true, for example, when we deal with *look-back options,* the strike prices of which are based on the *minimum* or *maximum* daily closing price of the underlying security over the life of the option. In such a case, the lattice opens out into a tree of possibilities, and one must resort to simulation techniques.

Simulation methods, like all pricing models, make certain assumptions about how key parameters evolve through time. Like the lattice-based models, a simulation method will typically break time (the term to option expiration, or to maturity of a mortgage, for example) into some number N of discrete steps. At each step, the key parameter or parameters (such as price, yield, short term rate) are assumed to move as random variables according to certain specified probability distributions. If we were to proceed as in the lattice-based models, the parameters would move up or down (or possibly to one of three or more states) at each step. If we were to attempt to evaluate all possible paths through such a tree, however, we would need to evaluate at least 2^N terminal states, since we cannot assume that any two sequences of up and down steps bring us to a common node. For even relatively small values of N, this is computationally prohibitive; for $N = 20$, there are over a million terminal nodes, and for $N = 30$ there are over a billion.

Simulation models avoid this exponential proliferation of paths by sampling the set of all possible paths—they compute some large but manageable subset of paths through the tree, called *runs,* and statistically average the results of whatever calculations are to be performed over the given set of paths. Any two runs are completely independent, and each represents a different possible realization of the random model parameters over time. Each run plays out a self-contained scenario in time. For example, if we know the history of interest-rate levels at each step in time, we can determine path-dependent interest rate–contingent cash flows and, by appropriately discounting back (using the discounting rates generated at each step of our scenario), the current value of a security. Each run will generate a *different* price for such securities. Some of these runs may produce highly unlikely results, but the great majority, and hence the average, will tend toward the most likely outcome. The more runs are used, the more accurate will be the convergence of the simulation average to the true price of the security in question.

Conceptually, this methodology is *estimating* the *expected value* of some quantity, such as an option value, over all possible future scenarios, given some assumptions about how key variables will evolve through time. General statistical principles ensure that for a sufficiently large sample size (number of runs), the resulting estimate can be as stable and exact as we desire. More precisely, for a given number of steps N, tolerance ε, and probability p, we can find a number M such that the result of averaging M or more runs will be within ε of the true expected value with probability at least p. (Note that this is *not* a guarantee that the resulting value will be within ε of the real-world value of the security in question; this depends critically on other factors, such as the correctness of our assumptions about the evolution of key parameters and the accuracy of any initial inputs.)

In practice, this scheme is modified in several ways. Because we are no longer constrained to follow the branches in a binomial (or multinomial) lattice, the stochastic model variables are often allowed to evolve from step to step as *continuous* random variables, taking on any permissible value according to the probability distribution specifying their process. This allows for smoother modelling of the evolution of key parameters. Additional constraints may be placed on the allowable paths—negative or very large interest rates may be disallowed. For some applications, the parameter values generated for a given set of runs may be *normalized* to meet certain initial conditions or constraints. For example, the interest rates generated in a rate-driven simulation might be adjusted to ensure that the model properly prices certain benchmark securities, such as the current-issue Treasuries.

Simulation methods allow us to extract important additional information along with the primary output (usually a security price). For example, the variance of individual prices over the set of all runs gives a measure of reliability, or confidence interval, for the resulting price. Extreme values among the runs can be valuable as worst-case scenario analysis. Statistics can also be accumulated on the behavior of model parameters over the course of the runs. For example, we could get a sense of just how likely it is, given modelling assumptions, that interest rates will rise above, or fall below, some critical "outlying" levels (levels at which the user might begin to question the applicability of the modelling assumptions.)

Simulation models do have certain limitations. For example, they are not generally applicable for calculating the values of *American* options, which require a comparison of intrinsic value (value if exercised immediately) and option value (value if *not* exercised) at each step. To compute the value of the unexercised (American) option at step k, one would have to create a new simulation, rooted at this step, as the option value cannot be calculated based only on the known parameter values for the current run. The recursive nature of this bootstrapping process quickly makes the number of calculations prohibitively large.

Because each run of a simulation model is a straightforward calculation of option (or other) values, given certain hypothetical values of the parameters at each step, it can be simpler conceptually than many lattice-based models. However, because a large number (hundreds, often thousands) of runs are required to produce stable, reliable results, simulation models can be highly computation-intensive. For this reason, simulation models are sometimes most useful in confirming the accuracy and robustness of other, more approximate pricing models, or in quantifying the ways in which such models appear to deviate from exact values, rather than in day-to-day calculations.

Exotic Options

Some of the advanced techniques discussed in this section find special applicability in the valuation of certain so-called exotic options—options whose strike depends on factors other than the level of the underlying at a single point in time, often introducing path dependencies into the task of valuation.

One situation in which simulation techniques are appropriate is in the evaluation of *look-back* and *average-strike* options. A *look-back option* is a European option with an initially indeterminate strike; at expiration, the contract holder has the option to exercise at a strike price equal to *the minimum (for calls) or maximum (for puts) of the daily closing prices* of the underlying security over the life of the option. Clearly, the strike price, and hence the value of the option, is *path-dependent:* even on the expiration date, it is necessary to know the entire history of the security price over the life of the option in order to determine its value. A lattice-based approach would be inappropriate, as the lattice would not be *closed;* it would open out into a tree with 2^N nodes at the Nth level. A simulation approach is clearly more appropriate; at the end of each run we know the strike price, and hence the option value, which can then be discounted back at the appropriate rates to give a present value to be averaged with that from other runs.

An *average-strike option* is one for which the strike price is set to the *average* of all daily closing prices over the life of the option, rather than the maximum or minimum of these. Again, the strike, and hence the option value at expiration, are unavoidably path-dependent, and a simulation approach is indicated.

Valuation of Embedded Options

As noted above, option-like features may be found embedded in many financial instruments that are not themselves strictly options. The simplest example is the call feature of a callable bond. (There are also puttable bonds.) Another important example is the deliverability option embedded in a bond futures contract. There are actually a cluster of different deliverability options associated with a futures contract, and each of these carries different weight depending on specific market conditions. The seller has the option of which issue to deliver, the choice of delivery date, and even the so-called "afternoon option" of when to time delivery on the delivery date. For details, see Tang (1988).

Many interest-rate securities, such as caps, floors, and collars, can be viewed as composites of many options with different maturities and possibly other different features. Since such options are frequently long-term, or are "forward" options starting and ending at dates in the future at which prevailing interest rates are unknown, advanced option pricing techniques are frequently required for accurate theoretical valuation of these securities. Floating-rate bonds, bonds with sinking fund features, and many other complex securities also have embedded optionalities requiring special attention.

Optionality is also associated with the "prepay" feature of mortgage-backed securities. It should be noted, however, that the optionality of the prepay feature is somewhat different from that of other embedded options, as it is determined by a factor exogenous to the security itself—the prepay behavior of mortgage holders.

MODELS FOR EVALUATING MORTGAGE-BACKED SECURITIES

Mortgage-backed securities are, as the name suggests, securities backed by a pool of government agency–guaranteed mortgages. Principal and interest payments from the mortgages in the pool are "passed through" to the security holder. Mortgages themselves are very heterogeneous with respect to such factors as face amount, issue date, and terms of interest payments. Only by "pooling" many individual mortgages, and thus "homogenizing" them to some extent, can mortgage-backed securities with a definite coupon and maturity be created. Nevertheless, they remain more complex than U.S. Treasuries and many other securities in many respects. For background on mortgage-backed securities, including the uses of option-pricing techniques, see Fabozzi (1988).

Prepayment Effect

An important difference between mortgage-backed securities and other bonds is in their *prepayment risk.* This is the risk that, as interest rates fall, a significant proportion of homeowners will choose to refinance their mortgages, paying off existing mortgages at higher interest terms in exchange for lower current rates. This tendency can lead to sudden, unexpectedly large cash flows to the holders of mortgage-backed securities at precisely the wrong time for profitable reinvestment (as rates have fallen). Thus, prepayment risk is a form of reinvestment risk.

Prepayment risk can be viewed as a kind of *option:* the homeowner has the option to prepay the mortgage at any time. However, homeowners will sometimes exercise this option even when it is not advantageous, as, for example, when they must sell their home. The amount of principal prepayment to date is clearly a *path-dependent* feature of mortgage-backed securities—it will be sharply higher if interest rates dip significantly in the course of the security's life than if they remain flat.

Estimation of yields on mortgage-backed securities is thus complicated by uncertainty about future cash flows due to prepayment considerations. Static cash-flow yield calculations, based on coupon, remaining term, scheduled amortization, and prepay assumptions, are relatively straightforward, but exhibit extreme sensitivity to changes in prepay assumptions. Because of prepay uncertainty and other factors, mortgage instruments trade at a *yield spread* to Treasury instruments. Rather than calculating mortgage yields directly, one can seek to evaluate the yield spread to comparable Treasuries instead.

Descriptive Statistics

Weighted Average Coupon (WAC) and Weighted Average Maturity (WAM). Traditional measures of risk-return and sensitivity introduced in the context of U.S. Treasury notes and bonds, such as yield-to-maturity and duration, cannot be applied unmodified to mortgage-backed securities. For one thing, principal is paid over time, rather than being received in a lump sum at maturity. More critical is the prepayment effect described in the previous section, which makes the actual life of mortgage-backed securities *contingent* on the behavior of interest rates. A number of new descriptive statistics and analytical measures have been introduced to deal with these peculiarities of the MBS market.

As noted in Chapter 2, pass-through (asset-backed) securities are backed by a *pool* of actual mortgages, with a specified range of coupon, maturity, and seasoning characteristics. It is standard practice to calculate a **weighted average coupon (WAC)** and **weighted average maturity (WAM)** for such mortgage pools, using as weights the principal amount outstanding for each individual mortgage (which will naturally be less for more seasoned mortgages). These measures give a reasonably accurate projection of cash flows from the pool, depending on how wide a range of coupons, maturities, and seasonings are permitted. When dealing with the mortgage-backed security itself, rather than the underlying pool, it is necessary to adjust the WAC for servicing fees and delays. Also note that because servicing fees are calculated as a percentage of outstanding principal, which declines with time, the actual cash flows to pass-through holders will grow slightly over the term of the security. Because original maturities may often vary by as much as twenty years for thirty-year mortgage-backed securities, WAC and WAM alone are inadequate to accurately estimate the degree of seasoning of the underlying mortgages.

Weighted Average Life (WAL). Since future cash flows from a mortgage-backed security are only contingent, the traditional measures of effective life, such as duration (the present value weighted average of time to cash flows), have limited utility. **Weighted average life (WAL)**, the average time to receipt of principal, is considered a good proxy for the effective maturity of an MBS, and is also sometimes used as an indicator of interest-rate sensitivity. In general, securities with longer WALs will exhibit greater interest-rate sensitivity, although there can be exceptions.

Static Cash Flow Yield (SCFY). The **static cash flow yield (SCFY)** of an MBS is the discounting rate (IRR) making the present value of future cash flows equal to its market price, *assuming a constant prepayment rate corresponding to current interest rate levels.* The spread of SCFY to average life or duration-matched Treasury securities is a standard measure of value in the mortgage market. Such spreads can be compared with historical highs and lows to measure the richness or cheapness of the mortgage market relative to Treasuries. Such spreads have varied widely over the years, depending on many factors, including the volatility level of the Treasury market. In general, greater volatility in interest rates will be associated with lower MBS prices and higher spreads to Treasuries because the implied prepay option takes on greater value during such periods of higher interest-rate volatility. However, all such measures are highly sensitive to any change in prepayment assumptions.

Prepayment Models

More sophisticated MBS analytics depend on how assumptions about prepayment are modelled. A number of standard models and conventions are in use; most firms trading seriously in MBS securities also have developed their own proprietary prepayment models, which can be quite complex. In this section we review the most common conventional models and some of the considerations taken into account by most proprietary models.

Fixed Life. The *fixed-life* prepayment model assumes that principal will be paid up to some fixed date, at which time the borrower prepays in full. The conventional assumption is that a 30-year MBS has a fixed life of 12 years and a 15-year MBS a fixed life of 7 years. Yields calculated to the fixed life of a security are sometimes called *quoted yields*.

FHA Experience. The FHA model is based on detailed statistics compiled by the Federal Housing Administration indicating the proportion of mortgage loans prepaying (or defaulting) each year. The *FHA Experience factor* is the proportion of loans remaining insured at the end of each year. These factors are often interpreted as the *probability of survival* to a certain maturity for the class of mortgages concerned. FHA Experience certainly represents an advance over fixed life or flat prepay assumptions. It incorporates empirical data on prepayment rates for actual mortgages. However, because FHA statistics correlate only with mortgage age and don't take into account other mortgage characteristics such as coupon levels and historic interest rate patterns, they are of limited value.

Conditional Prepayment Rate (CPR). The prepayment models in widest use in the mortgage market are Conditional Prepayment Rate (CPR) models. A *conditional prepayment rate* represents the amount of all unscheduled principal payments made between two dates as an annualized percentage of the outstanding balance at the starting date for the period in question. Any prepayment model can be cast in terms of CPRs; *straight-line* CPR models, in which principal prepayments are assumed to take place at a constant annualized rate, are particularly simple and are widely used in the industry. Historical CPRs for actual mortgage pools can be calculated from data on mortgage pool factors (survival rates) published regularly in *The Bond Buyer,* for example, but caution should be exercised in estimating projected CPRs for the future from such historical data.

Public Securities Association (PSA) Standard Prepayment Model.   The Public Securities Association (PSA) Standard Prepayment Model was introduced in 1985 for use in the CMO market. This model assumes that a security will prepay at a 0.2 percent annual rate for the first month, with this rate increasing by 0.2 percent each month for the first 30 payments; after payment 30, it is assumed that there will be a constant 6 percent annual prepayment rate for the remainder of the security's life. The PSA model can be "scaled" by multiplying all its CPRs by a common factor; thus "200 percent PSA" would refer to a regime in which all the CPRs would be twice that of the standard PSA model. This model incorporates some of the effects of aging shown by empirical data with the simplicity of a straight-line CPR model. It is now widely used in the industry, especially with CMOs.

Proprietary Prepayment Models.   Although these conventional models are important to understand, as they are frequently the *lingua franca* of the mortgage market, many more sophisticated models exist, taking into account regional and seasonal factors in prepayment; general econometric variables such as inflation, unemployment, and housing starts; security-specific factors including seasoning and coupon level; and other factors such as the postulated "dumbo effect" (the fact that a certain proportion of borrowers will be late in refinancing, or will not refinance at all, even when interest rates fall by several percentage points). Prepayment modelling at this level is both an art and a science, and can become as complex and subtle as its practitioners desire. (For a model of prepayments on fixed-rate mortgage-backed securities, see Richard and Roll, 1989.)

One interesting model that differs in important ways from the straight-line CPR or PSA approaches as well as from the OAS approach to mortgage valuation is the so-called **Refinancing Threshold Pricing (RTP) Model.** This model posits a *heterogenous* population of borrowers, each with his or her own interest-rate threshold for refinancing. Using market data, the RTP model determines the proportions of borrowers in the different threshold classes and the presumed refinancing costs to each class. Assumptions are made about the way interest rates evolve through time — assumptions similar to those in some of the term structure–driven option-pricing models. Given a specified pool composition and interest rate process, the MBS in question can be valued by taking a weighted average of the expected present values of projected cash flows for each class of borrowers. Pool composition and interest rate process parameters can thus be *fitted* to existing market data; they are then used to perform theoretical valuations on other MBS securities. For more details, see Davidson and Herskovitz (1992).

OAS Models

An important measure for evaluating the yield spread between mortgage-backed securities and comparable Treasury issues is the so-called **Option Adjusted Spread (OAS)**. To calculate the OAS, one has to simulate the evolution of the term structure of interest rates, driven by the current Treasury yield curve. For example, the short rate might be assumed to obey a random process given by

$$r_{t+1} = r_t + \sigma_1 x \tag{4.26}$$

where r_t = short rate at step t
      σ_1 = short rate volatility
      x = a normally or lognormally distributed random variable

The spread of the long rate to the short rate might be modelled by a mean-reverting process given by

$$s_{t+1} = s_t + \sigma_2 y - \alpha(s_t - s_0) \tag{4.27}$$

where s_t = spread from long to short rate at step t
      σ_2 = volatility of this spread
      α = severity of mean-reversion
      s_0 = mean to which the spread reverts
      y = a normally or lognormally distributed random variable

Rates determined by such a process for a set of simulation runs can be normalized to the discount function implied by the current Treasury yield curve in much the same way as is done in the term structure–based option-pricing models.

Prepay assumptions can then be applied with considerable precision *at each step* of the simulation, as current interest rates are assumed to be known. This allows us to incorporate the *path-dependency* of the prepayment effect. The resulting cash flows in each simulation run are then discounted back to give a hypothetical price for the mortgage-backed security at the initial step, and these hypothetical prices are averaged over all simulation runs, giving a theoretical (model) price for the security in question. The resulting theoretical price will usually differ from the observed market price. The theoretical price can be brought in line with the market price by adding an appropriate *spread* to the rates used in discounting the cash flows back at each step. This spread is solved for iteratively in a fashion similar to that used to solve for the "additive drift" values in Dattatreya and Fabozzi's option-pricing model, although the calculations involved here are more intricate. Because it is determined by option-like features of the mortgage, such as the prepayment risk, this spread is known as the *option adjusted spread* for the security. This process can be calibrated so that for securities without embedded optionality features it gives values comparable to standard yield spreads, so the OAS of mortgage-backed securities can be compared meaningfully with the yield spreads of straight bonds.

(Some readers may wonder why simulation techniques can be applied to an option that, on the face of it, looks American in character. Objections to the use of such techniques do not apply here because the prepay function, which specifies the expected level of prepayments at a given level of interest rates, is given *exogenously;* it is not calculated as part of the modelling process.)

It should be observed that an actual *option price* is not computed in the process of calculating the OAS; instead, a yield spread corresponding to an embedded option-related feature of the given mortgage-backed security is calculated. Details of parameter estimation, normalization, and the like have been omitted; this example illustrates the wide applicability of option-pricing techniques to the related issue of valuing interest rate–contingent features of many securities, and the importance of OAS analysis as a tool in relative-value trading. For more details on OAS modeling, see Waldman and Gordon (1986), Askin, Hoffman and Meyer (1987), or Fabozzi (1988).

REFERENCES

Askin, David J., Hoffman, Woodward C., and Meyer, Stephen D. (1987). *The Drexel Burnham Mortgage Pricing Model: The Complete Evaluation of the Option Component of Mortgage Securities,* New York: Drexel Burnham Lambert Mortgage-Backed Securities Research.

Barone-Adesi, Giovanni and Whaley, Robert E. (1987). "Efficient Analytic Approximation of American Option Values," *The Journal of Finance,* Vol. XLII, No. 2 (June), 301–320.

Black, Fischer, and Scholes, Myron (1973). "The Pricing of Options and Corporate Liabilities," *Journal of Political Economy,* 81 (May-June), 637–659.

Bookstaber, R. (1989). *Simulation Methods for the Evaluation of Option Models,* New York: Morgan Stanley.

Bookstaber, R., Jacob, D., and Langsam, J. (1986). *Pitfalls in Debt Option Models,* New York: Morgan Stanley.

Cox, J., Ross, S., and Rubinstein, M. (1979). "Options Pricing: A Simplified Approach," *The Journal of Financial Economics,* 7 (September), 229–263.

Cox, John C., and Rubinstein, Mark (1985). *Options Markets*, Englewood Cliffs, NJ: Prentice Hall.

Dattatreya, R. E., and Fabozzi, Frank (1989). "A Simplified Model for Valuing Debt Options," *The Journal of Portfolio Management*, (Spring), 64–72.

Davidson, Andrew S., and Herskovitz, M. D. (1992). "A Comparison of Methods for Analyzing Mortgage-Backed Securities," in *The Handbook of Mortgage-Backed Securities* (third edition), (F. J. Fabozzi, ed.), Chicago: Probus Publishing Company.

Fabozzi, Frank J., ed. (1988). *The Handbook of Mortgage-Backed Securities (Revised Edition)*, Chicago: Probus Publishing Company.

Fong, H. Gifford, and Fabozzi, Frank (1985). *Fixed Income Portfolio Management*, Homewood, IL: Dow-Jones Irwin.

Ho, T., and Abrahamson, A. (1988). "Interest Rate Options," in *Financial Options: From Theory to Practice*, Proceedings of a conference at the Salomon Brothers Center, New York University, December 1988.

Ho, T., and Lee, S. B. (1986). "Term Structure Movements and Pricing Interest Rate Contingent Claims," *The Journal of Finance*, (December), 1011–1029.

Hull, J. (1989). *Options, Futures, and Other Derivative Securities*, Englewood Cliffs, NJ: Prentice-Hall.

Leibowitz, Martin L. (1980). *Cash Flow Characteristics of Mortgage Securities*, New York: Salomon Brothers Bond Portfolio Analysis Group.

MacMillan, L. W. (1986). "Analytic Approximation for the American Put Option," *Advances in Futures and Options Research* 1 (1986), 119–139.

Merton, Robert (1973). "Theory of Rational Option Pricing," *Bell Journal of Economics and Management Science*, 4 (Spring 1973), 141–183.

Natenberg, Sheldon (1988). *Option Volatility and Pricing Strategies: Advanced Trading Techniques for Professionals*, Chicago: Probus Publishing Company.

Richard, S. F., and Roll, R. (1989). "Prepayments on Fixed-Rate Mortgage-Backed Securities," *The Journal of Portfolio Management*, (Spring 1989), 73–81.

Ritchken, Peter (1987). *Options: Theory, Strategy and Applications*, Glenview, IL: Scott, Foresman and Co.

Sharpe, W. (1979). *Investments*, Englewood Cliffs, NJ: Prentice-Hall.

Tang, E. M. (1988). *The Effect of Delivery Options on Interest Rate Futures and Option Contracts*, San Francisco: Portfolio Management Technology.

Vasicek, O. A., and Fong, H. G. (1982). "Term Structure Modeling Using Exponential Splines," *The Journal of Finance,* Vol. XXXVII, No. 2 (May), 339–348.

Waldman, Michael, and Gordon, Mark (1986). *Evaluating the Option Features of Mortgage Securities,* New York: Salomon Brothers Mortgage Research.

Wong, A. (1991). *Trading and Investing in Bond Options,* New York: John Wiley & Sons.

5
Fixed-Income Analytics on the Trading Floor

The wide availability of trader workstations has had a dramatic impact on the amount of data that can be analyzed by traders in search of profit opportunities. This chapter presents three approaches by which systems administrators can provide fixed-income analytics to the trading floor producers including traders, sales representatives, and financial engineers and deal makers. A case study is included to illustrate the interaction of these design principles with practical constraints.

OVERVIEW OF ANALYTICS AND TECHNOLOGY ISSUES

Fixed-income securities trading requires in-depth knowledge of financial instruments, markets, and financial analytics. It also requires ready access to real-time and historical market data in forms appropriate to making timely intra- and inter-market comparisons and weighing the risk factors inherent in various trading and hedging strategies. Most successful traders seek to take maximum advantage of the full range of technological support available on the modern trading floor. This includes real-time market data feeds, customized analytics packages implementing both industry standard and proprietary models for valuation and sensitivity analysis, historical databases and appropriate user interfaces for viewing such data, and a range of decision support tools designed to meet the needs of individual traders and risk managers.

Trader Workstation

Many of the strategies discussed in this book would be far more difficult, if not impossible, without the benefits of modern technology, particularly the wide availability of a network of powerful multi-tasking computers on every trading floor. The growth in power and sophistication of desktop workstations during the 1980s has revolutionized the way in which fixed-income arbitrageurs operate. Coinciding with the rise of a massive, liquid bond market driven by the growth in government, corporate, and consumer debt and the greater volatility of interest rates during the 1980s, this revolution has sometimes been obscured by the earlier revolution brought about by the universal availability of personal computers.

Modern workstations differ from personal computers in several key ways. Their sheer *processing power* is much greater, surpassing that of mini- and even mainframe computers of an earlier generation. Indeed, even the super-computers of an earlier era have been surpassed by workstations alone or in networks. Cray Computers announced in early 1992 that it had entered into an agreement with SUN Microsystems, one of the leading producers of worksta-tions for both scientific and financial applications, to use their proprietary Sparc microprocessor, which is at the heart of the current top-of-the-line Sun Work-stations, as the motor for a new series of $1–3 million supercomputers (New York Times, January 24, 1992). Workstations are also *multi-tasking* computer environments, key to the arbitrageur who must often perform a variety of tasks simultaneously. Personal computers are only now beginning to break the bar-rier of single-tasking operation systems. Furthermore, most high-performance workstations are designed to operate in extensive *networks,* giving the arbi-trageur access to far greater resources than a single, stand-alone computer system could provide. This is the key to integration of firm-wide databases, real-time market data feeds, satellite connections with international markets, and dedicated computational servers.

Real-Time Data Feeds

Timeliness is often a critical success factor in fixed-income trading. As a mar-ket becomes more efficient and commodity-like, profit opportunities occupy windows of ever shorter duration, frequently measured in minutes. Only ready access to real-time market data can allow the trader to exploit such profit op-portunities.

The role of real-time data feeds in the fixed-income market is accentuated by the peculiar structure of the U.S. Treasury market. As described in Chapter 2, the primary dealers trade bonds "blindly" with each other only through a handful of *inter-dealer brokers,* whose screens provide full access to the details of bid and offer in that market, on a trade-by-trade basis. Data on the U.S. Treasury market, and on the broader fixed-income markets, including futures and options, are available from a number of **market data vendors.** Firms subscribe to these vendors to obtain real-time market data for their traders, but that is far from the end of the story. To take full advantage of profit opportunities, traders must be able to *compare* the prices of related securities across multiple market data sources; thus, during most of the hectic 1980s, fixed-income traders' desk spaces grew to resemble airline cockpits, with rows and stacks of electronic monitors competing with the traders' own PCs and workstations—a financial Tower of Babel!

One of the powerful trends in trading technology of the 1990s has been the *integration* of real-time data feeds on a *single* trader workstation, either in the form of *multiple display windows* or in the often more efficient form of *composite pages,* where market data from multiple vendors is combined in a single display.

Because most data vendors in the fixed-income market distribute their data in the form of video pages, creating composite pages poses some interesting technological challenges. The simplest solution is to "cut and paste" the actual video displays, so a trader can customize his or her view of the market to see data for selected groups of securities from specified vendors, but this loses much of the potential added value of data composition. More powerful, but technically more challenging, is the creation of *true* composite displays, wherein vendors' data is *digitized* (or "shredded," as the process of parsing individual quotes and other market data out of the stream of data is called) and combined to show, for example, *best bid and offer* across all available vendors for a given market. Such digitized data also lends itself to market-minding functions. The growing availability of such market data composition techniques, including third-party vendors providing relatively robust and user-friendly interfaces to vendor data streams for the workstations platform, is sure to change the very structure of the market in fixed-income market data over the coming decade.

Using Analytics and Technology

All this may give the incorrect impression that a fixed-income trader also has to be a computer expert to succeed. Of course, a certain level of analytic and computer skills can indeed be helpful, but perhaps the most valuable skill a trader can acquire is a *functional* understanding of how to acquire and manage the *appropriate technology* for his or her needs. A good working relationship with knowledgeable technicians and analytical specialists can be as important to a trader as his or her relationship with other traders and investors.

Different traders and firms have found different solutions to the problem of assembling appropriate technological resources, but all have certain factors in common. Rather than recommending a single, rigid formula, this chapter presents three somewhat different approaches, each drawn from industry experience, and each with features suitable for the needs of certain firms or individual traders. This is not a book about technology, so it does not include highly technical discussions; specific technical details are likely to be out of date within six months or a year in any case. Rather, it seeks to convey a *qualitative* sense of appropriate technological requirements for successful fixed-income trading, emphasizing how the various components of a technological solution should fit smoothly with each other and the needs of particular traders and institutions. Much of what is discussed here applies more widely to the entire fixed-income securities industry, but the focus is on the specific needs of the trader rather than, say, a structured-investment portfolio manager or a firm's back-office operations.

As an illustration, the Appendix to this chapter includes a case study of the actual development of a fixed-income proprietary trading system. The experience documented in this study combines elements from two of the approaches described in this chapter, and illustrates how real-world time and resource constraints help shape the development process.

THE ANALYTICAL ENGINE: A GENERAL PURPOSE SOLVER

System Integration

One approach to providing technological support for fixed-income trading is what is best described as the **analytical engine** approach. This is the most *tightly integrated* approach to the problem, and is used by many trading firms (or divisions of larger firms) where operations, and often trading strategies, are closely coordinated. Properly implemented, this approach can provide a firm with tremendously powerful tools for all its analytic needs. It automatically provides a common analytical framework for all participants, including risk managers, who may find that this approach gives them the most coherent overview of a firm's (or group's) exposure and performance. Like any monolithic approach, however, it has its drawbacks. It typically requires a large, long-term commitment of resources to a single technological complex, it provides less flexibility for individual users who may have idiosyncratic requirements, and it can be cumbersome when it comes to shifting gears and introducing new techniques and new technology.

Typically, this approach includes a major commitment to one or two hardware vendors, perhaps including mainframe or even supercomputing facilities. It takes an all-inclusive approach to a firm's analytic and technological needs, seeking to meet the needs of all users within a given firm or department. It involves a major commitment to software development and maintenance. It incorporates firmwide proprietary analytics — in some cases, its design may be driven by the nature of such proprietary analytics and the related trading strategies. And it often tends to shape the kind of trading strategies available, or convenient, to system users. The following is *one* version of what such a system might look like.

The Solver

The core of the system will be a complex of techniques for solving all the firm's analytical problems, including such standard calculations as price-yield functional relationships, Black-Scholes option-pricing models and related algorithms, and option-adjusted spread (OAS) modelling for mortgage securities. It will also provide the capability of solving more general classes of problems such as linear, quadratic and integer programming optimization problems, stochastic differential equations, Monte Carlo simulations, and time series regressions. The techniques emphasized will depend to some extent on the specific needs of the firm and the theoretical preferences of the system designers, but some versions of all of these techniques are almost certain to be included. Another important feature will be the careful implementation of a suite of *proprietary analytics,* perhaps including mortgage prepayment models, long-term option-pricing models, models of the term structure of interest rates and volatilities, and other econometric models. Firms with a commitment to such a large, centralized analytical engine are also likely to have a long-term commitment to a variety of powerful, detailed proprietary analytics, which may in turn provide the *rationale* for some of the analytical engine's special features.

Specification Language/User Interface

The "solver" or "engine" of the system may not be directly accessible to all users; while this feature will vary widely with system design, it is likely that many problems, particularly those related to proprietary analytics, may require access through a specialized interface, or specification language. In firms committed to a centralized analytical engine, many or most users acquire common skills and a common language for dealing with the firm's analytics through a common, firmwide user interface. The design and implementation of an interface can be a critical feature of such a system, for the interface largely determines the usability and flexibility of the system.

Ideally, a specification language should help the user to formulate problems precisely enough to generate useful solutions. Many of the more powerful commercially available packages for solving differential equations or linear programming problems have their own specification languages, but these are rarely designed for or ideally suited to the financial world, and they tend to be complex and demanding, like any powerful language. An appropriate interface should *help* users think about problems in terms that make sense to them and to the firm; it should be clear and consistent throughout, and it should never be an *obstacle* to visualization of scenarios and trading strategies. A proper specification language should take into account the needs and skills of its intended users; if many of them are used to working with spreadsheets, for example, it might take the form of a modified spreadsheet.

Report Generation/Presentation Interface

The *solutions* to problems should also be presented in an appropriate, immediately useful form. The trader typically has little time to translate obscure expressions or separate out key data from background noise; the purpose of technology is to extract and focus on the *relevant* analytic results. Reporting should, accordingly, be in a format familiar and immediately usable by the trader; if this means a spread-sheet format, or simple graphics, then that should be the design adopted. Of course, if one asks the wrong questions, one seldom gets the right answers; thus, the design of a *presentation* interface cannot be separated from the design of the *specification* interface, and ideally the two will have a common syntax and format. This may come more naturally in a centralized analytical engine approach than in more loosely coupled approaches. Nevertheless, it can be surprising how often these simple principles are ignored.

THE FIXED-INCOME ANALYTICS TOOLKIT: A MODULAR APPROACH

Modularity

A second approach to solving traders' and firms' analytic needs is the "toolkit" approach. This approach is less tightly coupled and centralized than the analytical engine approach, and tends to be found in smaller and more entrepreneurial firms. It is characterized by a *modular* approach to technology and analytic techniques; it recognizes that different traders and groups may have different needs and preferences, and attempts to incorporate the flexibility necessary to meet these needs.

Such an approach tends to take full advantage of the inherent flexibility of the networked workstation environment, although it may also incorporate larger computers as computational servers or for other specialized tasks (such as back-office reporting). By its nature, a toolkit approach is more eclectic than the analytical engine approach, but it by no means ignores the importance of standards. Indeed, in an environment where individuals and groups may have customized applications and technological configurations, standards become crucial. Firms taking this approach are frequently strong believers in the "open-standards" approach to hardware and software—that is, they will select particular vendors, technologies, and software packages based on their use of common open design standards and their ability to communicate freely with other systems. Similarly, they will enforce their own standards for hardware deployment and software development within the firm; the essence of modularity is the ability of systems to communicate with each other, and of components to be reused in many combinations.

Object-Oriented Approach

The toolkit approach leads naturally to the adoption of an *object-oriented* approach to software engineering by such firms. While there are exceptions, one expects to see a commitment to the C and C++ programming languages, probably in a UNIX™ operating system environment, rather than to FORTRAN or COBOL in an IBM mainframe (or PC) environment. An object-oriented approach implies that common objects, such as securities, curves or schedules, or markets can be defined and used throughout the firm in a variety of customized applications. As securities and markets evolve, the structures implementing them can, with proper design, evolve relatively painlessly. This may require a higher *general* level of sophistication on the part of the programming staff than does the centralized approach, but it can also lead to greater versatility and productivity, and to less dependence on a few individual programmers.

Generic Analytics

The toolkit approach almost always depends on the availability of a firmwide set of standard analytical routines—many separate routines, rather than one integrated solver or engine. Such analytics would include industry standard models, probably in a form very similar to that underlying a centralized engine or any other approach. It can also incorporate a potentially endless collection of specialized routines including proprietary models, the use of which can be limited to individual traders or groups (emphasizing the entrepreneurial orientation of this approach to system design). While common, basic analytics are essential for back-office and risk management purposes, much of the development of trading strategy rests on the continual refinement of techniques for measuring relative value, implied volatilities, and various intra- and intermarket spreads, and it would not be surprising to find various groups and traders within a single firm with different, perhaps incompatible approaches to these areas. The ability to combine standardized generic analytics with customized proprietary routines is one of the strengths of this approach to systems design.

Customized Applications

A modular approach to system design can also provide greater flexibility in developing customized applications for individual traders and groups, especially in *scenario analysis,* which can be of great importance to the arbitrage trader and risk manager. It is possible to design a system based on the combination of generic and proprietary analytics in which a trader can define one or many "universes"—each with its own specifications of such features as the evolution of the term structure of interest rates, the presumed spread between certain key securities and their derivatives, and the variability of volatilities and their dependence on other parameters—and then to study the behavior of various securities and portfolios in such environments. It is also possible to allow users to define *generic securities,* such as options on futures on underlying securities that may not yet even be traded in existing financial markets, but may be anticipated (or planned by market makers who need to study how such instruments would trade if they *were* introduced).

In general, a modular approach to system development allows users greater freedom in customizing their support environment—in regard to the kind of analytics available, the kinds of user interfaces and reporting they enjoy, and the kinds of scenario analysis, simulations, and historical studies they employ. It also imposes greater responsibilities on both the users and the system developers: freedom to choose always implies freedom to choose unwisely! Such an approach not only presupposes an *entrepreneurial* environment, but an *imaginative* one, in which both traders and technical support personnel are prepared to make best use of the toolkits at their disposal.

THE TRADER'S ASSISTANT: A DECISION SUPPORT ENVIRONMENT

A third approach to analytic and technological support for traders is what is called the "trader's assistant," but could almost be termed the "sorcerer's apprentice." This approach is likely to be most suitable for an individual trader or small group operating with some autonomy, whether within the context of a larger firm or not. It takes into account the fact that traders need to monitor a wide range of sometimes complex conditions in a spectrum of markets. It also emphasizes the need for *scenario analysis*. It is an approach likely to be implemented today by specialized technology and software developers or consultants, perhaps along with one of the other approaches described above, rather than by traditional MIS departments. As the industry continues to mature and technology advances, this is unlikely to remain true for long.

Flexibility

This approach emphasizes the trader's need for *flexibility* in analytic and technological support. Most traders, if asked for a wish list of their ideal on-line trading support system, would talk about the need for real-time market data, historical comparisons, spreadsheet and time-series analysis, and instant theoretical pricing and hedging calculations. Many would probably also cite a desire for yield curve modelling and the ability to compare price and/or yield spreads, converted and adjusted in appropriate fashions among a wide range of markets. The ability to derive certain standard scenario-related information, such as total return to a horizon date or worst-case exposure for a hedged position, is essential. Beyond this, more detailed requests would depend greatly on traders' individual strategies and techniques, and the specific markets in which they specialize. This is where flexibility and customization have a big role to play.

Trading is an art as well as a science, and we live in an era when technology makes important contributions to the arts. By providing a customized environment allowing a trader to *zero in* on the data of greatest significance, a "trader's assistant" environment can leverage the trader's experience, natural skills, and talents, making him or her many times more productive. If a particular trader is partial to three-dimensional, color graphic renderings of the performance characteristics of CMOs, and if these tools will enhance productivity, why are such graphics not provided? The three reasons usually given are (1) cost; (2) technical feasibility; (3) tradition/politics. The first two can in many cases be overcome if the proper technological groundwork is laid in advance—that is, if the *generic* hardware and software techniques required for such support are put in place, and staff are trained in their use. The last is the real obstacle, and often leads to arguments about "how things are done around here," or why one individual can't have a customized system because "everyone else would want one." The best counter-argument to this is obviously the increased productivity brought about the appropriate use of available technology. Those who take advantage of such opportunities will eventually outcompete those who do not. Let us look at just a few aspects of what might be accomplished with currently available technology.

Graphics-Based Scenario Analysis

It is often said that a picture is worth a thousand words. In the fixed-income securities industry, there are times when a picture can be worth more than a few thousand dollars. Arbitrage, for example, is the art of finding *relative value,* and the emphasis is on *price and yield spreads* rather than on absolute prices or yields. A tool that enables a relative value trader to view the spreads between selected families of securities over a range of maturities, yield levels, volatilities, or other parameters, would certainly be very helpful. For a trader "working the yield curve," a flexible graphic view of the yield curve and related features (such as currents, off-the runs, and implied forward rates) would be a vital resource. Such tools should, of course, present the data in *either* tabular (numerical) or graphic format at the click of a mouse. (Many traders find a graphic view vital to getting an overview of the range and scope of trading opportunities that exist within the targeted markets, but will only feel comfortable when they can see the actual numbers, which are what make the trade real to them.)

Creative use of graphics can also highlight the key features of the scenario analysis arbitrage traders perform. Whether the question is what range of interest rate movements would make a particular options spread trade profitable, or which non-parallel yield curve shifts would lead to the worst-case exposure for a given hedge position, the ability to see the answer at a glance, perhaps highlighted in green or red, gives the arbitrageur that much more speed and confidence in trading activity.

Real-Time Data Feeds

As discussed earlier, real-time data feeds are becoming an essential component of the fixed-income securities market. Profit opportunities can be fleeting; the proper technological tools can make the difference between spotting a trade and never even knowing it was there. Integrated with the kind of tools for graphic and scenario analysis described above, real-time data feeds can further enhance the productivity of an arbitrage trader.

User-Specifiable Market-Minding Functions

By integrating real-time market data feeds with sophisticated customized analytics, it is possible to build a true "trader's apprentice"—a system that will monitor specified markets for conditions *specified by the individual trader,* alerting the trader or triggering some other specific action, such as the automatic generation of a report, when such conditions arise. The development of an interface flexible enough to satisfy the requirements of a range of aggressive users is well within the scope of current technology, and there have been substantial steps in this direction in recent years.

Historical Analysis

As will be emphasized time and again in this book, *arbitrage trading should be called relative-value trading*. To detect and evaluate opportunities to lock in relative value trades, an arbitrageur will frequently wish to compare a given spread, volatility, or repo rate implied by the market with *historical* spreads, volatilities, or repo rates for that market. This comparison will often tell the trader whether to seize a trading opportunity or let it pass. If spreads or implied volatilities for a given market are approaching or have passed specified "trigger points," it is often a clear signal of an arbitrage opportunity. Most traders cannot hold the entire market history in their memories; as markets grow increasingly complex, they depend more and more on technological support to track and display such historical data.

What Are the Relevant Variables?   The first question one must ask is, "*What* historical data should be saved and displayed?" To a large extent, this is a question the individual trader, trading group, or firm has to answer. But some generalizations may be made. Because spreads are a simple difference of two terms, save the actual prices or rates, and calculate spreads as required. Because volatilities are statistical constructs requiring greater computational effort, it may be worthwhile to save key (7-day, 30-day) volatilities and only calculate special cases on demand. The same applies to any derived data that is likely to be referenced frequently and cannot be reconstructed with minimal computational effort.

What Is the Appropriate Presentation Format?   At least as important as ready access to the relevant variables is the ability to present data in a format familiar and useful to the user. Traders will have their own preferred presentation formats, but guidelines include the ability to convert rapidly between common formats (such as discount versus bond-equivalent rates; quoted versus invoice price), and the ability to provide both graphic and tabular displays of data. The ability to display relationships between data in more than one dimension (historical spreads to the yield curve by date and maturity or duration, for example) can also be valuable, as can the ability to perform basic statistical manipulations with the data (regressions and other time-series analysis) for those users comfortable with such analytical tools.

Database Issues. Fixed-income markets are complex, active, and numerous. To save every market tick in every security would tax the capacity of even the most powerful database servicer. Traders and firms should make judicious decisions as to what market data is likely to be of use to them. (Some historical data is also available from vendors, so decisions about some markets in which a trader or firm is not currently active may be safely postponed.) Careful attention should be paid to the choice of an appropriate database *and database design* responsive enough to meet the traders' needs and flexible enough to meet the changes in market structure and conventions sure to come with time.

BEYOND WORKSTATIONS: LEVERAGING TECHNOLOGICAL ADVANTAGE

Just as workstations represented a technological revolution for traders in the 1980s and as PCs did before them, new technological innovations are already beckoning from over the horizon. Which of these will be the keys to increased trader productivity in the 1990s and beyond remains to be determined, but there is no doubt that those quick to take advantage of appropriate new technologies will reap the juiciest rewards. In this section, we take a brief, speculative glance into the future.

Networking

Workstations alone are a powerful trading tool, but together their power is multiplied. Networking is likely to be one of the keys to leveraging the technological advantage of future systems *and to increasing the productivity of firms' currently installed technological bases*. It is already commonplace for network administrators to arrange for "batch" jobs to take advantage of the slack capacity of hundreds of workstations during non-trading hours. Even with 'round-the-clock trading encroaching on these slack hours, increasingly sophisticated tools for network management and "load balancing" allow skilled administrators to turn existing networks of workstations into the equivalent of multiple mainframes or supercomputers.

Networking can also give traders and support personnel instant access to firm resources anywhere in the world: distributed databases, shared supercomputing resources, or even the human skills of financial analysts and modelers at remote sites, via e-mail and multi-media communications. We will see traders and other industry professionals treating their workstations more as gateways to a host of resources than as stand-alone productivity tools.

Supercomputers as Computational Servers

As financial instruments and markets grow more complex, so do analytical modelling techniques. The increasing demand for intensive computing power required by Monte Carlo simulation techniques in mortgage modelling or sophisticated lattice-based finite-difference methods in option valuation have led to the introduction of *computational servers* as network resources. These may be dedicated, high-performance nodes of the workstation network or full-blown supercomputers. The high end of the computer industry is changing so rapidly that it's hard to predict whether the "supercomputer" of the mid-1990s will be a separate machine or simply a configuration of dedicated nodes, but in either case the result is a tremendous enhancement of the user's *effective* computational capacity, and hence an extension of the analytical tools readily available.

Market Minding and Pattern Matching Using Artificial Intelligence

Trader's assistant programs, capable of performing key market minding functions (filtering data and alerting the trader to potentially profitable market opportunities based on specified formulas) are a newly emerging technology. But much more is possible in this regard, even with currently existing technology.

Using techniques from artificial intelligence and expert systems, one can design programs capable of filtering market data for *generalized patterns*— theoretically, for any combination of securities and prices that might constitute a profitable trade. One can also create programs capable of monitoring a trader's activities and *learning to identify the patterns the trader considers arbitrage opportunities;* in effect, a true trader's apprentice, capable of learning and growing along with the trader. Similar programs could be designed to pore over detailed historical data seeking instances of particular qualitative relationships, either to test hypothetical trading strategies by "paper trading" against the historical record, or to help formulate new potential trading strategies. "Risk demons" could constantly monitor the positions of a trading group or desk for exposure to various kinds of market risk, balancing firm-specified criteria against perceived market trends based on monitoring of real-time market data. The long-term potential for such intelligent, market-minding, trader's apprentice systems is open-ended.

Virtual Reality in the Trading Room

In recent years, flight simulators and tools for medical research allowing real-time three-dimensional imaging of the living body have brought so-called virtual reality within the realm of the practical and even commercial. It is not beyond belief that by the early 21st century our most sophisticated traders will "plug in" to their trading systems, with relevant market data displayed to them in a constantly updated, graphic, and even kinesthetic format, filtered and shaped by customized "intelligent" subsystems.

APPENDIX 5A:
A CASE STUDY IN THE DEVELOPMENT
OF A TRADING SYSTEM

This appendix describes the actual implementation of a network of trader workstations on a fixed-income trading desk. Non-proprietary details of the hardware and software configuration will be described, as well as an overview of the design and implementation process.

The group to be supported was small, consisting of a relative-value trader, an options specialist, and a trading assistant/analyst, but potential was seen for growth and diversification, so the approach taken was guided by a combination of the latter two design philosophies outlined in Chapter 5. However, no development team ever has the luxury of operating on a *tabula rasa,* with infinite time and resources for ideal development. Time pressures and resource limitations (an implementation team consisting of two full-time programmers and one part-time assistant) led to a number of compromises and shortcuts in the design process. The team was nevertheless successful in adhering to the spirit of its design philosophy, and readers should gain from reflecting on the kinds of real-life constraints that inevitably shape the system development process.

Environment

The facilities present at project start included a network of IBM PS/2 computers controlling the switching of installed vendor price-feed monitors and supporting a range of spread-sheet applications, reports, and a variety of third-party financial software packages. Back-office facilities consisted of one minicomputer running a trade accounting package and another running a third-party general accounting software package. No in-house applications existed beyond the level of spreadsheet applications.

Platform

The choice of implementation platform conformed to the designers' desire to have a modular system that would take advantage of industry standards while allowing for flexible application development and future system growth. The choice of platform was also strongly influenced by the need to bring up a skeleton applications system as quickly as possible, and by the desire to minimize learning-curve delays and new technology exposure by using established technologies familiar to the development team. It is possible that other hardware and software choices would have been given serious consideration if time and project team resources had not been limited.

The platform consisted of four major components:

1. **Hardware**

   A UNIX-based workstation with built-in networking and high-resolution color graphics capabilities was chosen as the trader workstation. A larger and more powerful version of the same machine was selected as the server for network file system, price feed, and database. The vendor chosen was familiar to the senior user and the programming team; alternatives were not seriously investigated.

   The initial network configuration consisted of five desktop workstations, one deskside file server, a printer with PostScript™ capabilities, a 330 MB hard disk drive, a high speed modem for remote file transfer, and an 8mm cartridge tape backup system.

2. **Software Development Environment**

   The C programming language was adopted because it was familiar to the programming team and fully supported by a development environment of the chosen hardware with its UNIX operating system. It was also viewed as a *de facto* standard in the financial workstation programming community. The windowing system used was the proprietary graphic user interface (GUI) provided by the workstation manufacturer. A different, more standardized and portable GUI might have been used had the team not faced the time pressures it did.

3. **Database**

   The database management system chosen was a relational database with built-in networking capabilities, data integrity and security features, and a structured query language (SQL) that would interface well with our application development language. The system chosen also had the advantages of being well established in the industry, and of being familiar to the senior programmer, again cutting startup time.

4. **Digital Price Feed**

   The digital price feed was chose primarily because of its convenient interface with the C programming language and because of the specific pricing feeds it provided. This feed provided two price access modes: "polling" and "question and answer." This choice of options gave the application designer the important opportunity to optimize network load under some common circumstances.

Priorities

The critical applications development path was dictated by the need to get the trading desk running on the new system as soon as possible. The potential applications were therefore divided into two classes: starter applications and full function applications. The starter set consisted of three key applications: (1) a Treasury yield-spread calculator, (2) an options pricing calculator, and (3) a trade entry/position summary system.

Database Access. Each of these key applications required database access and a set of standard financial functions. Because none of these components were initially in place, these applications were designed as stand-alone modules, but in such a way that calls to database and financial functions could easily be replaced by standard Data Base Management Systems (DBMS) and financial library calls when those modules were in place.

Database access was initially implemented using the generic UNIX system database utility package ("ndbm"). Financial functions were written as needed in a form that could ultimately be compiled into a shared financial library. Once these applications were in place, the traders were able to begin using the new production system.

The next priority was the database. This module could be broken down into three sections or phases:

- **Database Design:** The database was designed to meet the trading needs of the group, but also to model data in a way allowing useful abstraction of the relationships between individual elements, so that the *meaning* of each data element was clear, allowing for anticipated future growth and change with minimal frustration.
- **General Purpose DB Access Routines:** A layer of software was designed and written to handle all general purpose DB access calls; this feature was intended to isolate and simplify the most used functionality of DBMS, easing the task of application development and maintenance and providing at least a degree of portability should the DBMS be changed or replaced.
- **Special Purpose DB Access Routines:** A set of special routines was designed and written, taking into account the specific data model developed for the securities database and known special applications requirements.

This set included the ability to group securities according to various criteria and to access trader portfolio information.

Once the DBMS module was in place, the existing stand-alone applications had to be retrofitted to make use of the DBMS and its support software. Because both the stand-alone applications and DBMS modules had been written modularly with this in mind, this task took less than a week, with most of the time devoted to testing new functionality.

Price Feed Access.   The real-time price feed was installed on the system by the vendors just as the DBMS modules were completed. The vendor's software did not provide access to price data in a format usable by the application software, however, because firm conventions for security identifiers and some price display formats differed. More significantly, the vendor's package did not include network access to the price feed. A symbol filter and network distribution software for the price feed had to be written in-house.

Symbol Filter.   This was a set of pattern-matching and string manipulation functions capable of translating to and from the vendor format. This module was written so that all lower-level routines could be accessed via two "wrapper" functions, which could be used flexibly to perform symbol translation to or from the vendor format for any security. This made it easy to isolate modifications in the underlying translations of particular symbol types.

Network Distribution Software.   This module was written in such a way as to relieve application program developers of the need to handle network communication with the real-time feeds. It provided a standard, flexible application interface to the real-time price feeds, using either polling or question-and-answer interrupts. This software was designed in three parts:

1. A network distribution mechanism
2. A workstation distribution mechanism
3. An application interface

The network and workstation distribution mechanisms ensured that each trader application could deal with a price feed as if it were purely local to that trader's workstation. The application interface insulated applications (and programmers responsible for them) from any knowledge of the specific network distribution or real-time price feed protocols, so that in principle the price feed and the network protocols could be changed without affecting the applications.

Once this module was in place, it was a matter of integrating this functionality into the existing applications; there was no need to replace a previous stand-alone interface, so this process was accomplished in a matter of days.

Applications

At this point, the project team had provided full support for the key applications. The next step was to design a toolkit of application development libraries that could be used to rapidly develop a wider family of full function applications.

The importance of designing and building a modular software infrastructure before progressing to application development cannot be overemphasized. If common functionality is confirmed to separately maintained libraries, global changes in design can be implemented by making changes only to the relevant libraries, and without rewriting specific applications. Making use of standardized routines dramatically reduces the costs of application maintenance as well, insulating the application programmer from knowledge of many specialized modules and ensuring a common underlying architecture and design for all applications.

At this point in the project, application development began in earnest. The toolkit eventually developed by the project team included the following functional areas:

- Option Tools
  (1) Options pricing analysis
  (2) Real-time exchange-traded options monitor
  (3) Option portfolio scenario analysis tools
- Cash/Futures Tools
  (1) Treasury spread analytics and display
  (2) Treasury current yield analytics and display
  (3) Basis analytics and display
- Accounting Tools
  (1) Trade entry
  (2) Mark to market
  (3) Net position
  (4) Account manager
- Graphic Tools
  (1) Historical price/yield analysis and display
  (2) Real-time multiple tick analysis and display

Option Tools. This package was designed to provide application support for relative-value options traders. An options pricing calculator ("optcalc") allowed the rapid calculation of option prices and risk values for any given set of parameters. It displayed the effects of variations in one or two option parameters at a time, for example in a matrix varying underlying price on one axis and implied volatility on the other.

The real-time options monitor ("opttrk") tracked exchange-traded options prices and risk parameters on a continuously updated trade-by-trade basis. With each trade of a given underlying or option on it, the price and risk parameters for that group of options was updated, and the relevant display line highlighted for the trader.

The option portfolio scenario application ("scenario") calculated the response of a mixed portfolio to changes in the prices of any of its component securities, as well as to changes in overall volatility, time-to-expiration, or repo rates. The trader was shown the portfolio's profit and loss statement (P&L), net position (net delta), and net gamma for each such scenario, in either graphic or tabular form.

Cash/Futures Tools. These tools were designed as decision support tools for a variety of possible relative value trading strategies involving cash U.S. Treasuries and/or futures.

The spread monitor ("sprd") monitored the yield spreads within a group of securities, usually defined by maturity range. One security was designated the benchmark or "driver," with other securities spread to it. Holding spreads constant, the entire group could be repriced based on a change in the benchmark yield or price. As off-the-run Treasury issues trade less frequently than the benchmark "current" issue, this application was designed to request new price information from the price feed once a minute, using the "question-and-answer" interrupt protocol, thus reducing network load and improving performance.

The current yield spread matrix ("cmatrix") allowed users to monitor the overall shape of the yield curve and view its change from the previous day. This application, too, requested updates from the real-time price data feed only once a minute or so.

The basis monitor ("basmon") monitored the relationship between U.S. Treasury bond and note futures and their basket of deliverable issues. Gross and net basis were displayed, and the issues were arranged in order of decreasing implied repo rate so the cheapest-to-deliver was always at the top of the trader's screen.

The maturity sector net position calculator ("sector") was seen as an adjunct to the options scenario application, which did not provide very useful information for portfolios without large options components. This application grouped securities within a portfolio by maturity, and calculated the exposure of each component to that sector of the yield curve, allowing for the simulation of non-parallel as well as parallel yield-curve shifts.

Accounting Tools. The accounting tools developed were very simple, and primarily designed to provide support for trader management of their portfolio positions. They were not designed as a replacement for the firm's existing trade accounting software package, although an interface between the two was contemplated.

Trade entry ("trade") allowed entry of tables into the database by portfolio; in addition to allowing input of trades, the application displayed total current position in securities traded in that portfolio.

Mark-to-market ("mtm") was used by traders to calculate their daily P&L. Current prices for securities in the selected portfolio were obtained either from the database or from the live price feeds, depending on availability and currency. Interest and commissions were handled manually. The display was designed to resemble the firm's daily portfolio summary sheets.

Net positions ("netpos") performed the standard net position calculation for a given portfolio with respect to a specified benchmark security.

The account manager application ("accmgr") allowed a manager to combine trader portfolios for aggregate performance and risk exposure analysis.

Graphic Tools. Several of the applications described above had graphic display capabilities, and a library of routines was developed to support certain applications requiring more extensive graphic display and data analysis capabilities.

The historical price/yield display ("cspread") gave the user a means of displaying historical price and yield spreads for any of the instruments for which daily price and yield histories were maintained. A "reference" security was entered, followed by a list of the securities for which spreads should be displayed. Both graphic and tabular output were supported.

The real-time multiple tick display ("prdis") allowed the user to monitor each trade for an arbitrary group of securities. The display included quotes and changes from the previous trading day, as well as user-specified high and low "alert" levels that would trigger a message display. Its main use was the continuous, real-time display of tick charts for up to five securities simultaneously.

Remarks

With the design philosophy and resources described above, the development team was able to put in place a full function fixed-income trading system in less than one year. It is important to note that the design and development process, and the determination priorities, involved active interaction between traders and developers. This interaction was key to both the rapid development and deployment of the system, and to the fact that most of the applications were immediately heavily used by the traders. The system's logic and design remained relatively clean with a clear path toward growth and enhancement, and system maintenance promised to be a manageable task.

Without close communication between traders and developers, such a system can take much longer to deliver and yet fail to satisfy the users' key needs, leading to a vicious cycle of revisions, enhancements, and work-arounds. Maintenance of such a system can become a nightmare, and productivity of both end users and developers is likely to suffer.

6
Relative-Value Trading in Short-Maturity Instruments

Short-term interest rate instruments in the United States are driven by the federal fund and discount rate set by the Federal Reserve Bank Board. As market participants have different and ever-changing outlooks on the economy, these interest-rate instruments fluctuate widely in response to new releases of economic data, global political events, sizable moves in the stock markets, the Fed's open-market operations, and perceived changes in prevailing Fed policies. This volatility invariably destabilizes the relationships among the various short-term instruments including Treasury bills and coupons, T-bill and Eurodollar future contracts (and options thereon), swaps, and short-maturity mortgage derivative products, thereby generating profitable trading opportunities. Using specific examples, this chapter illustrates how such opportunities can be identified and exploited.

SHORT-END BASIS TRADING

Actively traded Treasury bill instruments in the secondary market include (1) cash bills with maturities ranging from three months to one year, (2) the "when issued" three-month and six-month bills, and (3) the first three T-bill future contracts. To determine relative value among these instruments, a trader must consider each cash bill's overnight and term repo rates. Instead of speculating on forthcoming interest-rate direction and major shifts in the Treasury bill

173

yield curve, statistical arbitrageurs spot profit opportunities by determining whether the T-bill future contracts are mispriced relative to their respective deliverable cash bills, and identifying the best cash bill to go long (or short) should the shape of the Treasury bill yield curve remain unchanged.

T-Bill Future Versus Its Deliverable Bill

The price of a Treasury bill (T-bill) future contract and that of the only "cash" Treasury bill deliverable against the contract will always converge on the last trading day of the future contract (contract date). A profit opportunity arises when a significant price (or yield) difference exists between a future contract and its underlying cash bill, after adjusting for the cash bill's carrying cost (the difference between its market yield and its repo rated-based financing cost) from today's settlement date to the contract date. If a trader *buys long the bill basis* by simultaneously selling short a T-bill contract and buying long the deliverable bill, the resulting trade is mathematically equivalent to being **long the cash bill's implied (or embedded) repo rate from today's settlement date to the contract date.** Consequently, this basis trade is an arbitrage if the cash bill's **actual repo rate** for the same time period is *lower than* the cash bill's **implied repo rate** embedded in the trade. Conversely, an arbitrageur will *sell short the bill basis* by simultaneously buying long a T-bill contract and selling short the deliverable bill if it is determined that the contract is excessively cheap *relative* to its deliverable cash bill, which happens when the cash bill's actual repo rate from today's settlement date to the contract date is *higher than* the cash bill's implied repo rate for the same period. If the future contract is fairly priced against its deliverable cash bill, then going short (or long) the bill basis is mathematically equivalent to betting that the cash bill's implied repo rate, which is a measure of short-term interest rate, is going up (or down); the bill basis trade can therefore be viewed as a synthetic money market instrument.

Example 6.1

On September 14, 1989, the December 1989 T-bill future contract, TBZ89, traded at 93.00, while its deliverable bill, the 3/15/90 maturity bill, was trading at 7.46 percent discount. A trader had to pay $962,492.78, which is equal to $1,000,000 \times [1 - [(0.0746 \times 181)/360]]$, to buy $1 million face value of the cash bill, which had 181 days left to maturity counting from the 9/15/89 settlement date. If the trader also sold one TBZ89 contract at 93.00, then he or she had "pre-sold" the deliverable bill on December 15, 1989 (the contract's last trading day, or its "contract date") at a discount price of 7.00 percent, or equivalently at a price of $982,500.00, which is equal to $1,000,000 × [1 − [(0.07 × 90)/360]]. The trader had effectively bought a synthetic instrument that cost $962,492.78 on 9/15/89 and paid back $982,500.00 on 12/15/89, thereby generating a money market yield return of 8.223 percent for the 91-day investment period. This 8.223 percent return was the T-bill contract's **implied repo rate** on September 14, 1989. An arbitrage trader would have compared the computed implied repo rate to the deliverable bill's actual term repo rate for the same investment period. Any significant discrepancy between these two repo rates would have constituted an arbitrage opportunity because the two instruments have the same credit quality as well.

∎

Example 6.2

On December 10, 1990, the March 1991 T-bill future contract, TBH91, traded at 93.64, while its deliverable bill, the 6/6/91 maturity bill, was trading at 6.75 percent discount. TBH91's *implied* repo rate was, therefore, trading at 7.41 percent. The *actual* term repo rate for the 6/6/91 bill for the 12/11/90 to 3/7/91 period was quoted at 7.45 percent bid and 7.35 percent offer, and as usual, the implied repo rate was not sufficiently different from the actual term repo rate to trigger an arbitrage trade.

The federal funds rate prevailing on 12/10/90 was 7.25 percent. If this federal funds rate were to remain at the 7.25 percent level, a trader could finance the purchase of the 6/6/91 bill by rolling overnight repo transactions for the 12/11/90 to 3/7/91 period, and the expected resulting *effective* term repo rate would be about 7.25 percent, which is significantly lower than the 7.41 percent implied repo rate. The risk was that the Federal Reserve Bank would tighten monetary policy during this period, and the resulting effective term repo rate could be much higher than 7.41 percent. With a 16 basis-point cushion, however, a statistical arbitrageur could consider this trade to be low-risk, especially since the Federal Reserve Bank cut the federal funds rate by 25 basis points in the previous week; moreover, if the Federal Reserve were to cut the rate again, there could be a windfall profit.

The Federal Reserve cut the discount rate by 50 basis points, and the federal fund rate by 25 basis ponts, on December 18, 1990; it cut the federal fund rate by another 25 basis points on January 8, 1991. If a relative-value trader had bought the implied repo rate of 7.41 percent on December 10, 1990, the trade would have made over 50 basis points (in "3-month bill equivalent") of profit in one month, with a conceivable risk of less than 10 basis points. On January 6, 1991, the 6/6/91 bill traded at 6.20 percent discount, a 55 basis point drop from December 10, 1990, while TBH91 traded at 94.02, which was only 38 basis points higher than its previous level.

Remarks

The bill basis is a financing trade. If the term repo rate is locked-up for the duration of the trade, it is a riskless arbitrage; otherwise, the trade is exposed to financing risks due to daily fluctuations in the overnight repo rate.

The bill future contracts often trade as a component of the so-called TED spread to the corresponding ultra-liquid Eurodollar future contracts. Historically, whenever the TED spread has widened drastically as a result of a big stock market drop, a major bank failure, or a war, the bill future contract has tended to be overpriced relative to its (less liquid) deliverable bill. Conversely, for accounting reasons, the "off-the-run" deliverable bills usually are relatively cheap right before the year end, when investment managers are cleaning up their portfolios.

Two-Year Note Basis

Although a handful of Treasury notes are deliverable against each two-year note future contract, the cheapest-to-deliver issue for short-sellers of the future contract can be readily identified by an arbitrageur's proprietary relative-value analytics. The distinctive feature of the two-year note basis trade is that the cheapest-to-deliver issue usually remains unchanged throughout a future contract's active trading life, even if the market prices (or yields) and volatilities of the deliverable Treasury notes change drastically. Consequently, as in bill-basis trading, a profit opportunity exists when there is a significant price (or yield) difference between the future contract and its cheapest-to-deliver issue, after adjusting for the issue's carrying costs to the expected delivery date in the contract month. Again, the arbitrageur will buy long the excessively cheap instrument (a future contract, for example) and simultaneously sell short the relatively rich instrument (the cheapest-to-deliver note, for example). Similar to the bill basis, the two-year note basis trade can be used as a synthetic money market instrument to make a directional bet on short-term interest rate.

It is difficult to spot a riskless bill-basis arbitrage, and a two-year note basis arbitrage is tricky to execute even when the opportunity exists. However, by continuously monitoring a combination of these two basis trades, which are different synthetic money market instruments, and other short-term interest rate investments, executable arbitrage trades can often be identified.

Example 6.3

On July 2, 1991, the September two-year note future contract traded at a price of 101 $\frac{1}{64}$. With a positively sloped yield curve, the expected delivery

Table 6.1 Price, Yield, Conversion Factor, and
Implied Repo Rate for Five Treasury Notes

Coupon (%)	Maturity Date	Price (in decimal)	Yield (in %)	Conversion Factor	Implied Repo Rate (in %)
8.750	8/15/93	103.0859	7.148	1.0130	5.348
8.000	8/15/93	101.6914	7.119	0.9999	4.979
8.250	9/30/93	102.2070	7.158	1.0045	4.916
8.125	6/30/93	102.0352	7.011	1.0018	4.460
7.000	6/30/93	100.0156	6.991	0.9838	4.269

date against this contract was September 30, 1991, the last day of the delivery
month. There were five Treasury notes deliverable against this future contract,
and each issue's price, yield, conversion factor, and implied repo rate from
7/3/91 to 9/30/91 are shown in Table 6.1.

The cheapest-to-deliver issue was UST 8.750 percent of 8/15/93. With federal fund rate targeted at 5.75 percent and the overnight repo rate trading around
6.05 percent, the two-year note basis trade's 5.348 percent implied repo rate
was an excellent short for the relative-value trader. Moreover, on the same day,
the September 1991 T-bill contract, TBU91, traded at an implied repo rate of
5.920 percent, which was 57 basis points higher than that of the two-year note
contract.

Remarks

Supply and demand imbalance in the repo market is the principal reason for
the existence of profit opportunities in implied repo rate trades. Two-year note
futures, however, often become relatively cheap when speculators in the futures
market bet heavily on the yield curve to flatten beyond the two-year maturity
sector.

■

LOCAL YIELD-CURVE ARBITRAGE

Rolling-Down-the-Yield-Curve Strategies

Determining relative value in a cash-versus-future basis trade in the short-
maturity sector is rather straightforward because a future contract and its deliverable issue are directly related instruments. Yield-curve arbitrage, on the other
hand, requires comparisons among issues with different coupons and maturities
along the Treasury yield curve. To determine relative value in this situation,
certain assumptions must first be made. The most common assumption adopted

by relative-value traders is that the *shape* of the yield curve remains unchanged from today's "trade date" to a specified "horizon date." To yield-spread traders, this assumption is equivalent to assuming that the trade date's yield curve and the horizon's yield curve are parallel. Under this assumption, for example, the relatively optimal Treasury coupon issue (among those with maturity less than two years) to go long (or short) from today's trade date to the horizon date, which is one month from the trade date, can routinely be determined.

Example 6.4

To identify the best relative value among Treasury issues with maturity less than two years, an arbitrageur must first determine each coupon's **30-day net rolling yield value**, as follows:

Step 1: For each coupon issue, using its 30-day term repo rate, compute its forward price to be settled on the horizon date, which is 30 days from the current trade date.

Forward price = Spot price − (Coupon income − Repo interest)

Step 2: Using standard price-to-yield calculations, determine each coupon's forward yield on the horizon date, which again is 30 days from the trade date.

Step 3: For each coupon issue, identify the Treasury note whose maturity is shorter by approximately 30 days. This shorter-maturity note's spot yield becomes the given coupon issue's yield in 30 days if the yield curve remains unchanged. Subtracting this expected yield from the coupon issue's forward yield on the horizon date (computed in Step 2) will produce the issue's **30-day net rolling yield value.**

Step 4: The best coupon issue to long (or short) in a yield curve trade is the one with the maximum (or minimum) 30-day net rolling yield value.

On April 30, 1991, the 30-day net rolling yield values for a selection of Treasury coupon issues are given in Table 6.2.

The 7.750 percent of 10/31/92 issue was, therefore, the best coupon to buy long in, while the 7.000 percent of 4/30/93 issue was the best short for a yield curve trade among the eight issues included in this analysis. A value-of-a-basis-point weighted trade involving these two issues only, however, would be exposed to the flattening of the yield curve in this maturity sector. To reduce this exposure, short-end arbitrageurs often employ butterfly spread trades (an example of which is given in the case study shown later in this chapter), whose optimal components are identified by the net rolling yield value analysis. ∎

Table 6.2 30-Day Net Rolling Yield Values for Selected Treasury Coupon Issues

Coupon	Maturity	Price (in decimal)	Yield (in %)	30-day Repo (in %)	Forward Yield (in %)	Expected Yield (in %)	Net Rolling Yield Value (in basis points)
8.125	9/30/92	102.0039	6.612	6.05	6.637	6.567	7.0
7.750	10/31/92	101.4883	6.689	6.05	6.714	6.612	10.2
7.375	11/30/92	100.9688	6.713	6.05	6.744	6.689	5.5
7.250	12/31/92	100.7500	6.757	6.05	6.790	6.713	7.7
7.000	1/31/93	100.3281	6.789	6.05	6.822	6.757	6.5
6.750	2/28/93	99.8906	6.807	6.05	6.834	6.789	4.5
7.125	3/31/93	100.5313	6.819	5.80	6.859	6.807	5.2
7.000	4/30/93	100.3750	6.795	6.05	6.819	6.819	0.0

Cash Treasuries Versus Future Contracts

Example 6.5

The purpose of this trade was to capture the cheapness of the front T-bill contract relative to the cash bills in the six-month maturity sector.

Putting on the Trade

The following trade was executed on 3/21/89 (trade date). Ratios of the values-of-a-basis-point were used to weight the trade:

1. Long 1.88 June T-bill Future (TBM89) at 90.54, which has a 9.690 percent forward Money Market ("MMkt") Yield on 6/1/89.
2. Short 1.00 9/21/89 T-bill (182 day) at 9.09 percent discount, which has a spot 9.541 percent MMkt yield on 3/21/89.

On Thursday 3/23/89, the short position 6-month bill was rolled into the next when-issued (WI) 6-month T-bill, and this position was rolled continually every week to keep the maturity of the short position at 182 days.

Trade Analysis: Risk, Return, and Breakeven Analysis

Why was TBM 89 cheap on 3/21/89? The 8/31/89 T-bill was the issue deliverable to the TBM89 on the delivery date (6/1/89). This bill was trading at 9.08 percent discount with a MMkt yield of 9.468 percent. The contract itself was trading at a MMkt yield of 9.690 percent, which implied that the forward MMkt yield of the 8/31/89 bill on 6/1/89 (with a then 3-month maturity) was 22.2 basis points higher than the cash (five-month+) bill's spot yield. These yield relationships would not seem unreasonable if the current 3-month bill is trading at or around the 9.690 percent yield level. However, on 3/21/89, the 6/22/89 T-bill was trading at 9.09 percent discount with a MMkt yield of 9.306 percent, which was 38.4 basis points lower than the forward MMkt yield of the three-month bill on 6/1/89 reflected by TBM89's low price of 90.54.

Why short the 6-month bill? On 3/21/89, with the spot six-month bill (9/21/89 maturity) trading at a 9.10 percent discount with a MMkt yield of 9.541 percent, the spot six-month/three-month yield spread was trading at 23.5 basis points (9.541 percent − 9.306 percent). Let us now examine how much this spread would have to change between 3/21/89 and 6/1/89 for the trade to be at risk, under various yield curve assumptions.

• Assume that the TBM89 and the generic six-month T-bill's yield both stay the same. On 6/1/89, under this assumption, the trade would break even and the trading portfolio would have the following components (1) long 1.88 TBM89's deliverable bill, the 8/31/89 T-bill, which would be the then three-month bill, at a 9.460 percent discount with a MMkt yield of 9.690 percent; (2) short 1.00 the six-month bill, with a 11/31/89 maturity, at 9.100 percent discount with a MMkt yield of 9.541 percent. In other words, the trade would be long 1.88 three-month bill and short 1.00 six-month bill on 6/1/89 at a yield spread of −14.9 basis points (9.541 percent − 9.690 percent). Recall that the spot six-month/three-month yield spread was at +23.5 basis points on 3/21/89. Therefore, the trade would still break even should this yield spread invert by 38.4 basis points (23.5 + 14.9) from 3/21/89 to 6/1/89. Since such inversion was unlikely to happen, the trade was expected to be profitable with high probability. (In options terminology, the trade was equivalent to selling extremely high implied volatility.)

• Assume TBM89's price stays the same but the six-month T-bill rolls to the market implied forward yield. By going long on TBM89, the trade had essentially locked in a forward yield of 9.690 percent for the three-month bill on 6/1/89. However, the trade did not lock in the forward yield of the six-month bill on 6/1/89. In the previous scenario analysis, by assuming the six-month yield stays the same, the trade has artificially locked up a forward yield of 9.541 percent for the six-month bill on 6/1/89. In the present scenario, this simplistic assumption is relaxed. Using a proprietary yield-curve model, it could be determined that the current market implied that the six-month bill should yield 9.617 percent on 6/21/89, and therefore, the six-month bill would have an expected positive roll from 3/21/89 to 6/1/89 of about 7.6 basis points (9.617 percent − 9.541 percent). As a result, on 6/1/89, the trade portfolio would be long 1.88 three-month bill and short 1.00 six-month bill at a yield spread of −7.3 basis points (9.617 percent − 9.690 percent). Therefore, under this more conservative assumption, our trade would still break even should the six-month/three-month yield spread invert by 30.8 basis points (23.5 + 7.3) from 3/21/89 to 6/1/89. Again, our analysis indicated that this trade would be profitable with high probability.

Results

The trade was taken off on 4/21/89 because, as suggested by relative-value analysis, TBM89 outperformed the six-month bill by 37 basis points since 3/21/89. On that day, TBM89 traded at 91.43 with an 8.760 percent MMkt yield, which reflected a drop of 89 basis points in discount or 93 basis points in MMkt yield from 3/21/89. During the same period, the 182-day T-bill had a 56 basis-point drop in MMkt yield from 9.541 percent to 8.981 percent. The profit of the trade per 1.88 TBM contract was $1,355:

1. Gain in TBM89 = 1.88 × 89 basis points (due to discount yield change) × $25 per basis points = $4,183
2. Loss in 182-day cash T-Bill = 1.00 × 56 basis points (due to MMkt yield change) × $50.50 per basis points = −$2,828

Note that each discount yield basis point for the TBM is $25, and the value-of-a-basis-point of the 182-day T-bill is approximately $50.50.

Remarks

This type of relative-value trading opportunity exists because cash bills generally lag behind the highly liquid front T-bill contract when the market makes a strong move up or down, due to either a developing trend or excessive speculation.

Financing cost consideration is often the critical component of this type of trade. Special attention must be paid to the technical nature of certain "special" cash bills in the repo market. For example, the size of the weekly "roll in" six-month T-bills is a function of the financing cost.

■

YIELD SPREADS AMONG THE SHORT-END YIELD CURVES

Treasury Bills Versus Coupon Issues

Consider the yield difference between a Treasury note and a similar duration Treasury bill in the 9- to 12-month maturity sector. The Treasury note usually trades at a higher yield than the comparable bill because of the bill's greater liquidity and higher convexity. For the relative-value trader, a statistical arbitrage opportunity arises when the spread is trading at or beyond its historical limits; the premise that this yield spread's movement follows a mean-reverting process can be empirically validated.

Example 6.6

As shown in Figure 6.1a, the yield curve for the Treasury bills and coupons in the 6- to 12-month maturity sector nearly coincided on January 3, 1989. There was a profit opportunity because Treasury bills usually trade at much lower yields than coupons with similar maturity. The most profitable trade to execute

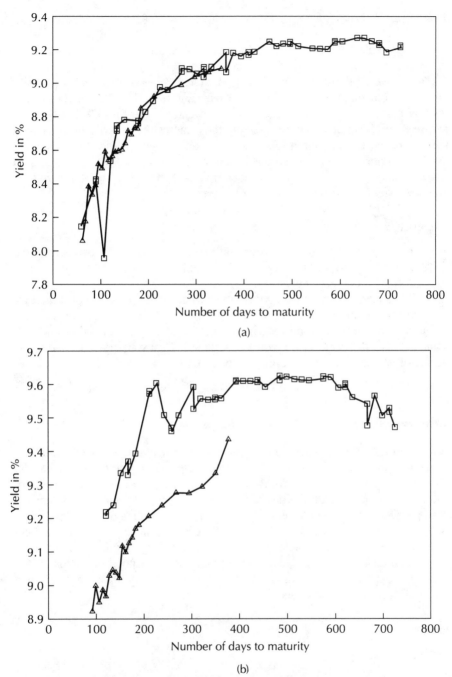

Figure 6.1 Yield curve for treasury bills (in triangles) and coupons (in squares): (a) on January 3, 1989; (b) on March 3, 1989.

on 1/3/89 would have been buying long the 12-month bill and selling short the 12-month coupon.

The *shape* of the two yield curves on March 3, 1989, was not drastically different from that on January 3, 1989 (see Figure 6.1b). But relative to the coupon curve, the bill curve had moved lower by more than 28 basis points in the 8- to 10-month maturity sector. It is interesting to note that between the two dates, the 12-month bill rode down the bill curve a lot more than the 12-month note rode down the coupon curve. Therefore, in bill-versus-coupon trades, traders must take into consideration both the *yield spread and roll-down-the-yield-curve effects*.

Remarks

Treasury bills are very much in demand when there is credit concern in the debt markets; therefore, the bill-to-coupon yield spread often moves in tandem with other credit spread indicators.

Treasury coupon issues have reinvestment risk while bills do not; this reinvestment risk premium is often reflected in the yield spread.

Supply and demand imbalance in specific Treasury bill issues has a significant impact on the bill-to-coupon yield spread. Cost-of-carry considerations, again, often demonstrate the profitability of such spread trades.

∎

Treasury Coupons Against Eurodollar Strips

Aside from the yield curve for Treasury bills and notes, short-end relative-value traders also monitor the "Eurodollar strip" yield curve, which can be constructed mathematically from the prices of the strip of Eurodollar future contracts. Eurodollar future contracts are the most liquid financial instruments in the world, and a contract's ending value on its last trading day (contract date) is the same as the prevailing 90-day LIBOR rate. Since LIBOR rates reflect interbank credit risks and therefore contain some risk premium, the Eurodollar strip curve has yields consistently higher than the corresponding yields on the Treasury coupon curve. A statistical arbitrage opportunity arises, again, when the credit spreads trade beyond their normal trading range.

Example 6.7

Profit Opportunity

During the first two weeks in March 1989, the strip consisting of the front three Eurodollar contracts traded excessively cheap to the Treasury coupon curve. This was caused primarily by a series of economic indicators suggesting that the U.S. economy might be facing significant inflationary pressure; there were also a few large leveraged buyout deals, including the RJR Nabisco transaction, to be financed during that month, adding upward pressure on short-term interest rates. The highly liquid Eurodollar contracts, especially the front strip, went down much further than other money market instruments, creating the profit opportunity.

Strategies

A number of strategies could have been employed to exploit the relative cheapness of the individual Eurodollar contracts. Instead of using a combination strategy whose risk/reward characteristics might be difficult to pinpoint, a trader might execute this easy-to-understand trade whose risks could be identified with a high degree of accuracy and whose trading position would be easy to manage.

This strategy would capture the first three Eurodollar contracts' cheapness to the Treasury coupon curve and their cheapness to the following strip of four Eurodollar contracts. It was designed specifically to exploit the fact that the one-year credit spread, between the Eurodollar strip curve and the Treasury coupon curve, was trading at 119.3 basis points (bond equivalent yield) while the two-year credit spread was trading at only 90 basis points. In the process, the tightness of the prevailing two-year note in the repo market was also captured.

The Trade

The trade executed on 3/13/89 (for 3/14/89 settlement) is illustrated in Table 6.3.

Remarks

There are actually two components in this trade:

(a) Short Two 1-Year Credit Spread	(b) Long One 2-Year Credit Spread
Short (2) 7.375% of 3/31/90	Long (1) 9.375% of 2/28/91
Long (2) cash LIBOR	Short (1) cash LIBOR
(3/14/89-EDM89's contract date)	(3/14/89-EDM89's contract date)
Long (2) EDM89	Short (1) EDM89
Long (2) EDU89	Short (1) EDU89
Long (2) EDZ89	Short (1) EDZ89
	Short (1) EDH90
	Short (1) EDM90
	Short (1) EDU90
	Short (1) EDZ90

Table 6.3 Trade of Example 6.7 on March 13, 1989

Long/Short	Issue/Contract	Price	Yield	Value (01)	Weighting
Long	EDM89	89.26		$25.00	1.5
Long	EDU89	89.27		$25.00	1.0
Long	EDZ89	89.41		$25.00	1.0
Short	7.375% of 3/31/90*	97.7031	9.677%*	$95.68	2.0
Long	9.375% of 2/28/91	99.5469	9.630%	$174.58	1.0
Short	EDH90	89.90		$25.00	1.0
Short	EDM90	90.05		$25.00	1.0
Short	EDU90	90.22		$25.00	1.0
Short	EDZ90	90.23		$25.00	1.0

*Actual maturity on 4/2/90; yield shown is for the actual settlement date.

Netting out the two components of this trade would give back the trade itself. One minor adjustment, however, has to be made. Since the required cash LIBOR instrument and the one-month LIBOR contract were not available at the time, an extra 0.5 EDM89 was used instead, although the trade was taking on some basis risks between cash LIBOR and the EDM89 contract. The trade, as noted, should be weighted such that the aggregate position has a value-of-a-basis point close to zero.

Trade Analytics

On 3/14/89, the bond equivalent yield of the one-year and two-year Eurodollar strip curve was 10.87 percent and 10.53 percent, respectively. Because the one-year note (7.375 percent of 3/31/90) traded at 9.677 percent and the two-year note (9.375 percent of 2/28/91) at 9.630 percent, the one-year TED was at 119.3 basis points and the two-year TED at 90 basis points. These results strongly suggested going short the one-year credit spread and long the two-year credit spread. Moreover, the one-year cash LIBOR-to-coupon yield spread prevailing on 3/13/89 was 101.5 basis points, providing another indication that the one-year Eurodollar strip-to-coupon spread was relatively expensive.

Another verification could be obtained by computing the 1-year forward 1-year credit spread. First, the one-year forward bond equivalent yield of the one-year Eurodollar strip curve was computed to be 9.161 percent, using the prices of EDH90, EDM90, EDU90, and EDZ90 only. Then the one-year forward bond-equivalent yield of the then one-year note was found to be 8.67 percent, using the discount curve derived from the empirical Treasury yield curve. These results, when combined, gave a 1-year forward 1-year credit spread of 49 basis points, clearly indicating that the four contracts in 1990 should be sold short against the one-year forward one-year Treasury yield.

There was also an opportunity to take advantage of the repo rate discrepancy between the one-year and two-year notes. The three-month term repo rate on the two-year note was 8.5 percent and the three-month term reverse RP on the one-year note was 9.4 percent; this gave rise to a profit of $1,580.54 (per million) in carrying the cash position (long one two-year note and short two one-year notes) for three months.

Actual Results

On 4/17/89, the trade could be unwound at the prices given in Table 6.4. Here is the method for doing the costs of carry calculations. For a long position,

Net cost of carry = Coupon income − Repo interest + Amortization

Table 6.4 Trade of Example 6.7 on April 17, 1989

Long/Short	Issue/Contract	Price (yield)	Change Since 3/13/91 Price (yield)	Weights (VBP)	P&L (in $) Due to Yield Change	P&L (in $) Due to Amortization
Long	EDM89	89.76 (10.24%)	+0.50 (−50.0)	1.5 ($25.00)	+1,875.00	0.00
Long	EDU89	89.68 (10.32%)	+0.41 (−41.0)	1.0 ($25.00)	+1,025.00	0.00
Long	EDZ89	89.66 (10.34%)	+0.25 (−25.0)	1.0 ($25.00)	+625.00	0.00
Short	7.375% of 3/31/90	98.0156 (9.550%)	+0.3125 (−12.7)	2.0 ($87.56)	−2,224.02	−4,025.98
Long	9.375% of 2/28/91	99.7813 (9.493%)	+0.2344 (−13.7)	1.0 ($167.47)	+2,294.34	+49.41
Short	EDH90	89.96 (10.04%)	+0.16 (−16.0)	1.0 ($25.00)	−400.00	0.00
Short	EDM90	90.12 (9.88%)	+0.07 (−7.0)	1.0 ($25.00)	−175.00	0.00
Short	EDU90	90.23 (9.77%)	+0.01 (−1.0)	1.0 ($25.00)	−25.00	0.00
Short	EDZ90	90.20 (9.80%)	−0.03 (+3.0)	1.0 ($25.00)	+75.00	0.00
				Total:	+3,070.32	−3,976.57

1. Short two 7.375% of 3/31/90

Period One: (3/14/89 to 3/31/89 settlement):

Coupon Income = ($73,750/2) × (17/181) = $3,463.40

Repo interests = ($980,156.25 + $33,411.60)
× (17/360) × 0.094 = $4,499.12

Period Two: (3/31/89 to 4/18/89 settlement):

Coupon income = ($73,750/2) × (18/184) = $3,607.34

Repo interests = $980,156.25* × (18/360) × 0.094 = $4,606.73*

Total cost of carry = 2 × (−$3,463.40 + $4,499.12
−$3,607.34 + $4,606.73) = $4,070.22

Net cost of carry = $4,070.22 − $4,025.98 = $44.24

2. Long one 9.375% of 2/28/91

Coupon income = ($93,750/2) × (35/184) = $8,916.44

Repo interests = ($997,812.50 + $3,311.82)
× (35/360) × 0.085 = $8,273.18

Net cost of carry = $8,916.44 − $8,273.18 + $49.41 = $692.67

Net total carry = $44.24 + $692.67 = $736.91

Total profit (per $ million) = Profit & loss
due to yield change
+ net total carry
= $3,070.32 + $736.91 = $3,807.23

Remarks

Besides the Treasury bill, Treasury coupon, and the Eurodollar strip yield curve, there are also yield curves for mortgage-backed derivatives and utility bonds. The yield spread curves constructed from the differences between pairs of curves within this short-maturity family are often kinked, indicating good risk/reward spread trading opportunities.

Intermarket yield spreads generally depend on the debt market's perception of credit risk level, excessive speculative behavior of future contract traders, and supply and demand imbalance of debt issues in the repo market. Consequently, intercurve spread trades are risky because their profit-and-loss swings can be extreme. ∎

*Approximation

A CASE STUDY: THE 1991 TWO-YEAR NOTE SQUEEZE

"DID SOMEONE SQUEEZE TREASURY NOTES?" was the headline of a July 1, 1991, *Business Week* article by Gary Weiss and Dean Foust. This was the first of many articles that reported on how the 6.750 percent of 5/31/93 May two-year notes were "cornered" at the May 22, 1991, auction and how this note's short-sellers were squeezed for many weeks. Ignored by most reporters, however, was the simultaneous "short squeeze" of the 7.000 percent of 4/30/93 April two-year notes; this under-publicized squeeze was actually the more severe one and it lasted for more than three months. Because of the lack of precedence, this "back-to-back" two-year short squeeze was extremely effective (the short sellers had no place to hide) and many arbitrageurs lost millions of dollars.

To understand why so many arbitrageurs were trapped and lost money in this episode, consider also the 8.625 percent of 5/15/93 Treasury note. This "old" note has a maturity 15 days longer than the April two-year note and 16 days shorter than the May two-year note. Because of liquidity premium and coupon rate differences, the 8.625 percent of 5/15/93 note was expected to trade at a yield only **slightly** higher than the average of the April and May two-year notes. Instead, on July 2, 1991, this "old" note traded at a yield that was more than 30 basis points higher than each of the squeezed notes (see Table 6.5). The yield spreads between this "old" note and each of the two-year issues, during the period 5/28/91 to 9/13/91, are shown in Table 6.5; the unusual yield spreads prevailing during this period clearly indicate the presence of a **double squeeze**. The following hypothetical case study is included to show how arbitrageurs lost a significant amount of money due to this short squeeze.

Act I: A Two-Year Note Basis Trade

On May 6, 1991, the June 1991 two-year note future contract TUM91 traded at a price of 101.6406. The cheapest-to-deliver issue for this contract was the 8.625 percent of 5/15/93, which was trading at 103.2188 and had an implied repo rate of 4.950 percent for the period 5/7/91 to 6/28/91 (the contract's expected delivery date). With federal funds rate at 5.75 percent and 30-day term repo rate trading around 5.50 percent, this two-year implied repo trade offered a rare, low-risk profit opportunity. The trader therefore sold short $100 million face value of the 8.625 percent of 5/15/93 at 103.2188 and went long 500 TUM91 contracts (each contract has $200,000 face value) at 101.6406.

On June 3, 1991, with TUM91 trading at 101.7348 and the 8.625 percent of 5/15/93 at 102.9844, the implied repo rate had moved to 5.894 percent, from the 4.950 percent rate prevailing on May 6, 1991. The trader could have, and should have, taken profits on that day. Instead, the trader spotted an eye-catching yield-curve arbitrage opportunity.

Table 6.5 The Back-to-Back Two-Year Note Squeeze

Date	(1) 3 p.m. Yield for 7.000% of 4/30/93	(2) 3 p.m. Yield for 8.625% of 5/31/93	(3) 3 p.m. Yield for 6.750% of 5/31/93	Yield Spreads (b.p.)	
				(2)−(1)	(3)−(2)
05/28/91	6.678	6.788	6.657	11.0	(13.1)
05/29/91	6.625	6.802	6.614	17.7	(18.8)
05/30/91	6.606	6.769	6.588	16.3	(18.1)
05/31/91	6.729	6.861	6.681	13.2	(18.0)
06/03/91	6.799	6.952	6.775	15.3	(17.7)
06/04/91	6.781	6.959	6.783	17.8	(17.6)
06/05/91	6.807	6.982	6.809	17.5	(17.3)
06/06/91	6.860	7.036	6.860	17.6	(17.6)
06/07/91	6.985	7.155	6.981	17.0	(17.4)
06/10/91	6.985	7.153	6.981	16.8	(17.2)
06/11/91	6.985	7.142	6.973	15.7	(16.9)
06/12/91	7.057	7.201	7.042	14.4	(15.9)
06/13/91	7.066	7.186	7.052	12.0	(13.4)
06/14/91	7.002	7.123	6.991	12.1	(13.2)
06/17/91	7.002	7.120	6.991	11.8	(12.9)
06/18/91	6.984	7.136	6.965	15.2	(17.1)
06/19/91	6.929	7.081	6.913	15.2	(16.8)
06/20/91	6.865	7.022	6.843	15.7	(17.9)
06/21/91	6.919	7.081	6.895	16.2	(18.6)
06/24/91	6.947	7.114	6.931	16.7	(18.3)
06/25/91	6.937	7.121	6.904	18.4	(21.7)
06/27/91	6.817	7.033	6.799	21.6	(23.4)
06/28/91	6.697	6.933	6.675	23.6	(25.8)
07/01/91	6.734	7.019	6.710	28.5	(30.9)
07/02/91	6.631	7.050	6.745	41.9	(30.5)
07/05/91	6.777	7.122	6.816	34.5	(30.6)
07/08/91	6.786	7.048	6.861	26.2	(18.7)
07/09/91	6.740	7.055	6.861	31.5	(19.4)
07/10/91	6.730	7.026	6.870	29.6	(15.6)
07/11/91	6.672	6.983	6.861	31.1	(12.2)
07/12/91	6.625	6.944	6.816	31.9	(12.8)
07/15/91	6.615	6.951	6.825	33.6	(12.6)
07/16/91	6.690	6.958	6.834	26.8	(12.4)
07/17/91	6.746	6.992	6.879	24.6	(11.3)
07/19/91	6.716	6.928	6.834	21.2	(9.4)
07/22/91	6.725	6.971	6.853	24.6	(11.8)
07/23/91	6.762	7.005	6.889	24.3	(11.6)
07/24/91	6.695	6.930	6.834	23.5	(9.6)
07/25/91	6.685	6.904	6.825	21.9	(7.9)
08/08/91	6.252	6.448	6.453	19.6	0.5
08/09/91	6.231	6.436	6.434	20.5	(0.2)
08/12/91	6.230	6.423	6.424	19.3	0.1

(continued)

Table 6.5 (continued)

| | (1) 3 p.m. Yield for 7.000% | (2) 3 p.m. Yield for 8.625% | (3) 3 p.m. Yield for 6.750% | Yield Spreads (b.p.) | |
Date	of 4/30/93	of 5/31/93	of 5/31/93	(2)−(1)	(3)−(2)
08/13/91	6.190	6.402	6.405	21.2	0.3
08/14/91	6.083	6.296	6.302	21.3	0.6
08/15/91	6.040	6.248	6.263	20.8	1.5
08/16/91	6.048	6.226	6.215	17.8	(1.1)
08/19/91	5.959	6.147	6.139	18.8	(0.8)
08/20/91	5.890	6.097	6.073	20.7	(2.4)
08/21/91	5.995	6.206	6.185	21.1	(2.1)
08/22/91	5.991	6.205	6.182	21.4	(2.3)
08/23/91	6.156	6.372	6.342	21.6	(3.0)
08/26/91	6.195	6.407	6.379	21.2	(2.8)
08/27/91	6.164	6.356	6.331	19.2	(2.5)
08/28/91	6.054	6.248	6.226	19.4	(2.2)
08/29/91	5.999	6.186	6.185	18.7	(0.1)
08/30/91	6.087	6.269	6.270	18.2	0.1
09/03/91	6.065	6.246	6.241	18.1	(0.5)
09/04/91	6.044	6.233	6.221	18.9	(1.2)
09/05/91	6.050	6.252	6.228	20.2	(2.4)
09/06/91	5.978	6.190	6.189	21.2	(0.1)
09/09/91	5.956	6.158	6.159	20.2	0.1
09/10/91	5.945	6.154	6.148	20.9	(0.6)
09/11/91	5.963	6.170	6.177	20.7	0.7
09/12/91	6.030	6.120	6.135	9.0	1.5
09/13/91	6.059	6.116	6.125	5.7	0.9

Act II: A Phenomenal Arbitrage Opportunity

Also on June 3, 1991, the May two-year note, the 6.750 percent of 5/31/93, traded at a yield of 6.775 percent while the 8.625 percent of 5/15/93 (the cheapest-to-deliver issue for TUM91) was trading at 6.952 percent. A yield "pick-up" of 17.7 basis points could be obtained by buying long the 8.625 percent of 5/15/93 and selling short the 6.75 percent of 5/31/93, and the trader took the plunge and did $100 million face value of this coupon swap.

As a result of this coupon swap, the two-year implied repo rate trade had changed into a trading position that was (1) long 500 TUM91 contracts, and (2) short $100 million face value of the 6.750 percent of 5/31/92. To avoid a possible squeeze in the repo market, term financing to June 28, 1991, for the May two-year note was arranged at a repo rate of 4.494 percent. Based on this term repo rate, the trader effectively sold short the May two-year note at a forward yield of 6.858 percent for settlement on June 28, 1991. At the same time, TUM91 was trading at 101.7344 and the 8.625 percent of 5/15/93 had a conversion factor of 1.0108 for TUM91. The deliverable note's corresponding forward yield on June 28, 1991, was 6.984 percent, which was 12.6 basis points higher than the May two-year's forward yield.

In other words, forward yield analysis indicated that, after adjusting for carrying costs, the trade had a forward yield "pick-up" of 12.6 basis points for settlement on June 28, 1991. Since the two component issues of this trade had a maturity difference of only 16 days, this spread was significantly wide by any historical standard. As the May two-year squeeze was not expected to last beyond June 28, 1991, (when it would become the "old" two-year note), the trader decided it was a good statistical bet that this yield spread would trade back down to the 5 basis points level.

Unfortunately, on June 24, 1991, this yield spread traded at 18.3 basis points (see Table 6.5) and the "two-year basis plus yield-curve arbitrage" trade was losing 6 basis points. Because the May two-year note's value-of-a-basis-point was about $175, the $100 million trade position was losing $105,000.

To make matters worse, the April two-year note was trading at a yield of 16.7 basis points lower than that of the 8.625 percent of 5/15/93. Instead of taking a loss, the trader completed a yield-curve butterfly trade. Not expecting that both the April and May two-year notes would be squeezed at the same time, the trader sold short $100 million face value of the April two-year note and bought long $100 million of the 8.625 percent of 5/15/93.

Again, to avoid being squeezed in the repo market, term financing for the short positions to July 29, 1992, were arranged at repo rates of 5.55 percent (April two-year) and 4.944 percent (May two-year). Performing a similar forward yield analysis as before, the trader had a butterfly trade where the 8.625 percent of 5/15/93 would pick up 13.4 and 13.7 basis points, respectively, against the April and May two-year notes. Since the components of this trade had maturity differences of 15 and 16 days, this forward yield spread pick-up was phenomenal and unprecedented in the two-year maturity sector. Moreover, because both two-year issues would become "old, old" two-year notes on July 29, 1991, the trader again decided that this butterfly trade was an excellent statistical bet, whose only risk was its exposure to supply and demand imbalance in the April and May two-year notes.

Act III: A Disaster

On July 1, 1991, the butterfly spread traded at a spot yield pick-up of 59.4 basis points, 24.4 basis points higher than its level on June 24, 1991. At this point, the combined trade position was losing 30.4 basis points in two-year note equivalents ($175 per basis point per million), or $532,000. The trader was ready to take a loss, but decided to wait one more day.

During a 30-minute stretch in the morning of July 2, 1991, the April two-year note's price moved up by $\frac{1}{32}$ a minute while the 30-year bond traded in a narrow range. What happened was that many of the short sellers in the April two-year notes were getting out that morning, creating a run on the issue. The trader got out of the butterfly trade at around 70 basis points and lost $717,500 (41 basis points in two-year note equivalents) on a $100 million face value yield-curve *arbitrage* trade!

EPILOGUE

1. In August 1991, Salomon Brothers admitted that it had violated Treasury procedures in the May two-year note auction, and many traders who lost money during the squeeze have since filed lawsuits against the firm for damage compensation.
2. The May two-year note squeeze ended during the first week of August.
3. As shown in Table 6.5, the April two-year remained "special" until September 12, 1991. No one expected that!
4. With regulators keeping their keen eyes on the Treasury securities repo markets, short squeezes have been rare since August, 1991. The recent short squeezes did not last long, even when they occurred. The surprising beneficiaries of this consequence are the arbitrageurs, who generally have little control over or effective hedge against financing risks manifested in the past by nightmarish short squeezes like the 1991 episode.

7

Yield Spreads in the Intermediate- and Long-Maturity Sectors

Arbitrage trading in the intermediate- and long-maturity sectors also focuses on identifying excessively mispriced yield spreads. T-bond and T-note basis traders exploit price spreads between future contracts and their deliverable issues, after adjusting for the deliverables' carrying costs and their prevailing volatility premium. While rolling-down-the-yield-curve strategies are also useful in these maturity sectors, yield-curve traders prefer to bet on forthcoming yield-curve movements, using their knowledge of Treasuries' supply/demand imbalance and other seasonal effects. Domestic agency bonds, mortgage-backed securities, corporate debts, interest-rate swaps, and foreign government bonds all have their own yield curves. Excessive spreads among these yield curves, including the Treasuries', sometimes provide genuine arbitrage opportunities to the alert trader. An example of an intermarket trade involving Treasuries, options, and mortgage-backed securities is presented. The various risk factors that must be considered in evaluating cross-market yield spreads are also discussed.

CASH/FUTURES BASIS TRADING

Treasury note and bond future contracts are traded on the Chicago Board of Trade (CBT) with a face value of $100,000 and settlement dates in the months of March, June, September, and December. Ten-year note contracts call for the delivery of Treasury issues with maturities of 6.5–10 years from the delivery date. Contracts can be traded through the next 8 delivery months, but contracts beyond the nearest 3 are typically very illiquid. T-bond future contracts call for the delivery of Treasury issues with maturity or call date no less than 15 years from the delivery date, and deliverable issues against the 5-year note contract must have 4.25–5.25 years left to maturity on delivery date.

A future contract holder taking delivery does not know in advance which bond will be delivered and exactly how much has to be paid until just before delivery. Moreover, although there is no trading in the contracts during the delivery month's last seven business days, delivery can take place on *any* business day in that month, at the discretion of the contract seller who is delivering against the contract. Because they determine which issues will eventually be delivered, and on what day deliveries will occur, short sellers have significant advantages over the contract holders. The various advantages enjoyed (or options held) by the contract sellers will be discussed.

Options Embedded in the Future Contracts

Each of the delivery-related embedded options has its own terms and value. They are (1) the *quality* option, (2) the *end-of-month* option, (3) the *afternoon* or *wild card* option, (4) the *timing* option, and (5) the *new issue* option.

The Quality Option. The full invoice price (IP) actually paid on delivery is determined by the future contract's settlement price (FSP) times the contract size ($100,000) and the deliverable issue's conversion factor (CF), plus the issue's accrued interest (ACCRUED) on the delivery date: IP = (FSP × $100,000 × CF) + ACCRUED.

A deliverable issue's "gross basis" (BASIS) is defined as the difference between its cash price (CBP) and the product of its CF and the contract's FSP: BASIS = CBP − (CF × FSP). When it is necessary to deliver against a future contract, the contract seller will seek to deliver the issue that has the *highest* invoice price relative to its cash price, which is the issue with the *smallest* basis. Basis traders continually monitor each deliverable issue's basis movement toward the contract's delivery month, especially those that are most likely to be the cheapest-to-deliver issue.

The quality option is the contract seller's option as to which Treasury issue to deliver during the delivery month. Under the current contract specification, it can be shown that longer duration issues tend to become cheaper to deliver as interest rates rise above 8 percent, and the shorter duration ones become cheaper to deliver as rates fall below 8 percent. The quality option's value is *highest* when the prevailing rate is 8 percent because even a small increase (or decrease) in this rate makes a longer (or shorter) duration issue cheaper to deliver than the current cheapest-to-deliver issue. On the other hand, if the prevailing rate is much higher (or lower) than 8 percent, the cheapest-to-deliver issue is almost surely the deliverable Treasury with the longest (or shortest) duration, and there is little chance that other issues with drastically different durations would become the cheapest-to-deliver issue (unless the prevailing rate jumps back toward 8 percent). Accordingly, the value of the quality option increases with the *anticipated interest rate volatility* for the time period to the contract's delivery date.

The value of the quality option is actually the *maximum* of a bundle of option values, one for each potentially deliverable issue. Moreover, the strike prices of these options are not fixed; they vary as interest rates and the yield spreads among the deliverables issues change. Since Black-Scholes models are applicable only to the pricing of a single option with a fixed strike price, they are not the appropriate tools for evaluation this delivery option. (See Tang, 1988.)

The End-of-Month Option. This is the contract seller's option as to which issue to deliver *after the contract has stopped trading*. At this point, the settlement price for the future contract has already been set; small changes in interest rates can thus effect a switch in the cheapest-to-deliver issue. This is a short-term but potentially very volatile American option; very often, this end-of-month option has a greater value than the quality option despite its shorter life span, because of its higher sensitivity to interest-rate volatility. Consequently, evaluating the end-of-month option requires an approach different from the one used for the quality option.

The Afternoon or Wildcard Option. This is the seller's option to declare intent to deliver at any time prior to 8 P.M. eastern time during the first 15 business days of the delivery month. Since the future markets close at 3 P.M. eastern time while the cash bond market trades actively until 5 P.M. eastern time, there is a "window of opportunity" for the seller to take advantage of favorable interest-rate movements. To evaluate this option, traders must bear in mind that its strike priced is reset each day with the repricing of the future contract.

The Timing Option.   This is the seller's option to deliver on any day of the delivery month; the emphasis here is not on *which issue* is delivered, but rather on considerations of *carrying costs.* In an environment of positive carry (upward-sloping yield curve), ignoring the possible effects of the other delivery-related options, delivery is normally deferred to the last business day. Conversely, in an inverted yield-curve environment, early delivery is advantageous. The value of this option is thus contingent on the likelihood of a yield-curve inversion, and its value is the highest when the yield curve is flat.

The New Issue Option.   This is the value associated with the possibility that a new Treasury issue may turn out to be the cheapest-to-deliver against the future contract. While rarely of much value in the T-bond contract, this option can play a role in environments of high but falling yields, where new issues are likely to have both the lowest coupon and the longest maturity among the deliverable issues, factors that combine to give them the longest duration and make them good candidates for the cheapest-to-deliver issue. The option, however, is of significant value in the five-year note contract because there are monthly auctions of new five-year notes.

Remark

The diversity of characteristics of these options, and the fact, for example, that they must generally be considered European prior to the delivery period, but American thereafter (but possibly with varying strikes) makes clear that the basis trader should have access to some of the more sophisticated option-pricing methodologies described in Chapter 4.

Example 7.1

On July 18, 1991, the September 1991 five-year note future contract settles at a price of $99\,{}^{23}/_{32}$. The cheapest-to-deliver issue was the 7.625 percent of 5/31/96, which had a closing price of $98\,{}^{23}/_{32}$. With a conversion factor of 0.9855, this issue's gross basis was worth about ${}^{14.25}/_{32}$. Assuming a term repo rate of 5.870 percent to the expected September 30, 1991, delivery date in the then upward-sloping yield-curve environment, this cheapest-to-deliver issue had (1) a remaining carrying cost of ${}^{10.50}/_{32}$, (2) a net basis (gross basis − carry) of ${}^{3.75}/_{32}$, and (3) a forward price of $98\,{}^{12.50}/_{32}$ for settlement on September 30, 1991. The cheapest-to-deliver issue's net basis would be zero on the delivery date, but the ${}^{3.75}/_{32}$ profit suggested by this analysis for the basis short seller did not take into effect the value of the delivery options.

Using an 8.5 percent yield volatility, the five-year note contract's delivery options were found to have a combined value of $2.875/_{32}$, which included (1) quality option: $0.625/_{32}$, (2) end-of-month option: $0.625/_{32}$, (3) wildcard option: $0.000/_{32}$, (4) timing option: $0.375/_{32}$, and (5) new issue option: $1.250/_{32}$. Moreover, because the 7.625 percent of 5/31/96's conversion factor–adjusted forward price for September 30, 1991, settlement was $99\,26.825/_{32}$, the fair value of the five-year contract on July 17, 1991, was $99\,23.95/_{32}$. This embedded option analysis indicated that the contract was relatively cheap by $0.95/_{32}$; therefore, the $3.75/_{32}$ profit suggested by traditional net basis analysis for the basis short seller was off by the contract's option value because this optionality was ignored.

■

Example 7.2

On July 18, 1991, the September 1991 10-year note contract settled at a price of $97\,12/_{32}$. The cheapest-to-deliver issue was the 8.500 percent of 11/15/00, which had a closing price of 101. With a conversion factor of 1.0316, this issue's gross basis was trading at $17.5/_{32}$. Assuming a term repo rate of 5.870 percent to the expected September 30, 1991, delivery date, this cheapest-to-deliver issue had (1) a remaining carrying cost of $14.875/_{32}$, (2) a net basis of $2.625/_{32}$, and (3) a forward price of $100\,17.125/_{32}$ for settlement on September 30, 1991.

The 10-year note contract's delivery options were found to have a combined value of $3.125/_{32}$, using a yield volatility of 8.5 percent. Because the 8.500 percent of 11/15/00's conversion-factor-adjusted forward price for September 30, 1991, settlement was $97\,14.578/_{32}$, the fair value of this T-note contract on July 18, 1991, was $97\,11.453/_{32}$. The T-note contract was actually relatively rich by about $0.5/_{32}$, and selling the cheapest-to-deliver issue's basis to capture its $2.625/_{32}$ net basis is a mistake that an arbitrageur would not have made.

■

Example 7.3

On July 18, 1991, the September T-bond contract settled at a price of $93\,10/_{32}$. The cheapest-to-deliver issue was the 7.500 percent of 11/15/16, which had (1) a closing price of $88\,26/_{32}$, (2) a conversion factor of 0.9463, (3) a gross basis of $16.375/_{32}$, (4) a carrying cost of $13.250/_{32}$ to the September 30, 1991, delivery date, and (5) a forward price of $88\,12.750/_{32}$ for settlement on September 30, 1991, based on a 5.870 percent term repo rate.

Again, using a rate volatility of 8.5 percent, the T-bond contract's delivery options were valued as follows: (1) quality option: $^{1.375}/_{32}$, (2) end-of-month option: $^{2.000}/_{32}$, (3) wild card option: 0.000, (4) timing option: $^{0.625}/_{32}$, and (5) new issue option: 0.000. Subtracting the total option value of $^{4.000}/_{32}$ from the 7.500 percent of 11/15/16's conversion-factor-adjusted forward price of $93^{13.274}/_{32}$ for settlement on September 30, 1991, the contract's fair value was determined to be $93^{9.274}/_{32}$. Since the contract settled at $93^{10}/_{32}$ on July 18, 1991, it was relatively rich by $^{0.726}/_{32}$.

∎

Basis Trading

Basis trading was one of the bread-and-butter strategies for U.S. fixed-income arbitrageurs in the early 1980s, when few market participants knew how to properly evaluate the future contract's various embedded options. In the late 1980s, basis trading also proved profitable for arbitrageurs operating in the French, German, and Japanese bond markets.

A T-bond basis trade consists of four component bets: (1) bond yield level, (2) local yield-curve configuration (or yield spreads among the deliverable issues), (3) forthcoming bond market volatility, and (4) the costs of carrying the deliverable issues to the expected delivery date in the contract month. Profit opportunities arise when one or more of these components are excessively mispriced. An arbitrageur will buy a deliverable issue's basis (that is, buy the cash issue and sell a weighted amount of the future contract), if it is determined that this basis is underpriced, after adjusting for the prevailing market volatility level and for the issue's carrying cost to the expected delivery date. If the "market volatility" component of the bond basis is mispriced, the arbitrageur will also use bond options to exploit this profit potential. Opportunities in the five- and ten-year note basis trades are similarly identified, using the arbitrageur's proprietary models for (1) evaluating the various options embedded in the delivery process, (2) ranking the deliverable issues in the order of their "cheapness" on the trade date, and (3) examining the deliverability of the issues on any future date, including the expected delivery date, for a wide range of interest-rate scenarios.

Example 7.4

On April 11, 1991, the June 1991 T-bond contract had a settlement price of $95^{3}/_{32}$. The cheapest-to-deliver issue was the 9.250 percent of 2/15/16, which had (1) a closing price of $108^{21}/_{32}$ (8.412 percent yield), (2) a conversion factor of 1.1334, and (3) a gross basis of $^{28.125}/_{32}$. Using a 5.800 percent term repo rate, this issue's carrying cost to the June 28, 1991, delivery date was approximately $^{18.519}/_{32}$, and its net basis on April 11, 1991, was $^{9.606}/_{32}$. However, embedded option analysis indicated that the delivery option was worth $^{8.250}/_{32}$ based on a yield volatility of 11.3 percent, and the contract was found to be fairly priced relative to its cheapest-to-deliver issue.

The prevailing 30-year cash bond was the 7.875 percent of 2/15/21. It had (1) a closing price of $95\,^{17}/_{32}$ (8.279 percent yield), (2) a conversion factor of 0.9859, and (3) a gross basis of $^{56.875}/_{32}$. Because of its special condition in the repo market, its term repo rate to June 28, 1991, was 5.000 percent, its daily carrying cost was therefore approximately $^{0.256}/_{32}$, and its net basis on April 11, 1991, was $^{37.138}/_{32}$. A basis trader decided to sell this 30-year bond's basis at $^{56.875}/_{32}$ by (1) selling short $100 million face value of the 7.875 percent of 2/15/21 at $95\,^{17}/_{32}$, and (2) buying long 986 June 1991 T-bond contract at $95\,^{3}/_{32}$.

On May 8, 1991, 27 days later, the June 1991 T-bond contract had a settlement price of $96\,^{1}/_{32}$, reflecting a $^{30}/_{32}$ gain from April 11, and the basis trade had a capital gain of $924,375.00 (986 × 30 × $31.25) from this future contract component. Meanwhile, the 7.875 percent of 2/15/21 had a closing price of $95\,^{31}/_{32}$ on that same day, reflecting only a $^{14}/_{32}$ gain from April 11, and the basis trade had a capital gain of $437,500 (100 × 14 × $312.50) by being short $100 million face value of the 30-year bond. With a 5.000 percent special repo rate, carrying the short position in the cash 30-year bond for those 27 days cost $216,277.69. The basis trade, therefore, was making $270,597.31 on May 8, 1991.

As indicated by the embedded option analysis, the T-bond contract was fairly priced on April 11, 1991. This trade worked because the 30-year bond was relatively rich on that day and then became much cheaper (by about 3 basis points) relative to the cheapest-to-deliver issue on May 8, 1991. This happened because a new 30-year bond was scheduled to be auctioned in May, at which time the 7.875 percent of 2/15/21 would become the "old" 30-year bond and would lose much of its liquidity premium.

This basis trade, however, was exposed to some significant risks. The 30-year bond could have been squeezed in the repo market, because many arbitrageurs would sell it short in the weeks before the May 30-year bond auction; a prudent basis trader would try to lock up a reasonable term repo rate for the cash bond to the upcoming auction date.

Another risk was that bond prices might jump to much higher levels, causing a much shorter duration bond to become the cheapest-to-deliver issue. In this scenario, the T-bond contract, which would be tied to the prevailing cheapest-to-deliver issue, would lag far behind the cash 30-year bond in the market rally and the bond basis would increase in value. If the yield spreads among the deliverable issues were to remain unchanged, then short sellers of the

30-year bond basis were effectively selling synthetic call options on the cash bond; therefore, they could expect this basis trade to be profitable as long as the cash bond's price did not increase significantly.

However, short sellers of the 30-year bond basis were anticipating the realization that the 30-year bond would become cheaper relative to the cheapest-to-deliver issue, after adjusting for differences in carrying costs. This was the real bet embedded in the bond basis trade; this was the reason why the trade in this example made money, despite the fact that the T-bond contract's price went up by almost one point in 27 days.

To hedge away the unwanted "market yield level" risk, an arbitrage purist would have bought some call options on the cash bond (OTC options) or on the T-bond contract (CBT options), especially if these options were trading at implied volatilities much lower than the 11.3 percent yield volatility used in the embedded option analysis, to protect against any big drop in the bond yield. This "volatility hedge" would have contributed additional profits to the trade in this example, because of the $30/32$ price increase in the T-bond contract, and to an increase in yield volatility from 11.3 percent on April 11 to 12.0 percent on May 8, 1991.

■

YIELD-CURVE ARBITRAGE

Instead of focusing of cash/futures relationships, yield-curve arbitrageurs try to exploit mispriced yield spreads among Treasury issues with maturities ranging from 3 months to 30 years. Yield-curve traders prefer to bet on forthcoming yield-curve movements using only the "current" coupon issues, which include the most recently issued 30-year bond, 10-year, 7-year, 5-year, 3-year, and 2-year notes. On the other hand, statistical arbitrageurs operating within certain maturity sectors of the Treasury yield curve often employ rolling-down-the-yield-curve strategies to take advantage of any irregularity in the local yield-curve configuration. The determinants driving the profit opportunities in these yield-curve arbitrage trades will be discussed.

Local Yield-Curve Arbitrage

To determine relative value in local yield-curve arbitrage, traders often assume that the shape of the yield curve will remain unchanged from today's trade date to a specified horizon date. To yield spread traders, this assumption is equivalent to assuming that the trade date's yield curve and the horizon's yield curve are parallel. Under this assumption as shown in Chapter 6, the relatively optimal Treasury coupon issue within a maturity sector to go long or short from today's trade date to the horizon date can routinely be determined. No profit opportunity will be evident from this rolling-down-the-curve analysis if the local yield curve resembles a straight line with no kinks or cusps, and if no issue in the sector trades special in the repo market.

There is, however, *almost always* a dent in every maturity sector of the Treasury yield curve. Because of its higher liquidity, each maturity sector's current coupon usually commands a yield or price premium, and it normally trades a few basis points rich to comparable-maturity, off-the-run issues. An extremely bearish environment for Treasuries provides the rare exception; during such a disaster scenario, the current issue actually has to trade cheaper than the off-the-run issues to attract buyers. Divide the yield spread between the current coupon and a similar duration off-the-run issue by the current coupon's yield, and a measure of the current issue's liquidity premium can be obtained. For five-year notes, for example, the liquidity premium has a historical range of 0 percent to 6 percent. It was 0 percent at the end of the Treasuries' bear market in 1984, and then peaked at around 6 percent in 1986. The current five-year coupon's liquidity premium has been trading in a narrower range since the beginning of 1991, when five-year note auctions became monthly, instead of quarterly, affairs.

Most yield-curve arbitrageurs are also aware of the fact that off-the-run issues that do not have a current coupon in their maturity sector tend to trade cheap against other off-the-run issues. For example, Treasury issues in the eight- to nine-year maturity sector usually trade poorly until their maturities approach the seven-year area. Meanwhile, off-the-run issues in the six- and four-year maturity areas will begin to trade better only when their maturities get closer, respectively, to the five- and three-year areas. Without the sponsorship of a current coupon within their sector, off-the-run issues effectively trade cheap by an illiquidity premium. Once they move into a maturity sector with a current issue, however, these off-the-run coupons will attract the attention of various market participants, and they will eventually trade off the current issue by only the current coupon's liquidity premium if they have coupons and maturities similar to that of the current issue.

Treasury issues within the same maturity sector often have substantially different coupon rates. In a bull market environment, premium-priced issues (priced above 100) with high coupon rates usually trade at higher yields than discount-priced issues (priced below 100) with lower coupon rates because the premium-priced issues' additional coupon interests will have to reinvested at lower interest rates in the future. To exploit such kinks in the local yield curve, relative-value traders must know how to identify excessive yield differences caused by the disparity in coupon rates alone. Whereas mathematical traders use duration and convexity measures to compare similar maturity issues, other traders use statistical procedures to determine how the market had historically priced a premium issue's coupon rate effect, based on the difference between the coupon rate and the current interest rate (see Breaks, 1987). Some total return investors, on the other hand, use scenario analysis to decide whether one issue "dominates" another issue with similar maturity; this happens when one issue outperforms another, in terms of investment return to the maturity date, for a wide range of conceivable reinvestment rate patterns.

Remarks

Arbitrage traders are perpetually short the current issues. This is a critical component of their bread-and-butter trades. For example, the erosion of the 2- and 5-year notes' liquidity premium amounts to about 2–3 basis points each per month. Of course, they are exposed to the risk of being occasionally short-squeezed in the repo market.

The 30-year bond-basis trade described in Example 7.4 is actually an example of local yield-curve arbitrage. The basis short seller was banking on the erosion of the bond's liquidity premium when it became an "off-the-run" bond after the May 1991 refunding auction.

Arbitrageurs generally prefer to hold long positions in off-the-run issues whose maturities are approaching a current coupon area; the usual favorites are issues with maturities between (1) 1–1.25 years, (2) 2–2.25 years, (3) 3–3.5 years, (4) 5–5.5 years, and (5) 7–7.5 years. Very often, these issues are found to have the highest *net rolling yield values* within their maturity sectors by using the traditional rolling-down-the-yield-curve analysis (see Chapter 6).

Traders prefer discount-priced (or premium priced) issues in a bull (or bear) market because of reinvestment rate considerations. Since the effect of coupon disparities on yield spreads often varies erratically with market environments, much patience and discipline is required to spot and exploit any excessively mispriced yield spread caused by this persistent factor.

In the Japanese government securities market, bonds with high coupons always trade at a higher price than those with similar maturity but lower coupon rates because the former bonds are preferred by insurance companies and other major institutional investors.

Betting on Yield-Curve Movements

Yield-curve traders focus their attention on the yield spreads among the current coupon Treasury issues. For example, on October 8, 1991, the current coupon yield curve was as follows:

1. 2-year note (6.125% of 9/30/93):
   yield: 5.894%; value-of-a-basis-point (VBP): $184.20;
   overnight (O/N) repo rate: 5.20%; term repo rate: 5.00% to 10/31/91
2. 3-year note (6.875% of 8/15/94):
   yield: 6.143%; VBP: $260.80;
   O/N repo: 4.600%; term repo: 4.600% to 11/15/91
3. 5-year note (7.000% of 9/30/96):
   yield: 6.811%; VBP: $417.90;
   O/N repo: 4.900%; term repo: 4.600% to 10/31/91
4. 7-year note (8.250% of 7/15/98):
   yield: 7.171%; VBP: $547.40:
   O/N repo: 3.500%; term repo: 3.90% to 10/15/91
5. 10-year note (7.875% of 8/15/01):
   yield: 7.424%; VBP: $703.90;
   O/N repo: 4.625%; term repo: 4.30% to 11/15/91
6. 30-year bond (8.125% of 8/15/21):
   yield: 7.819%; VBP: $1183.10;
   O/N repo: 4.800%; term repo: 4.375% to 11/15/91

It should be noted that all the current issues were special on that day, with general overnight repo rate trading at 5.25%. For each current coupon, the term repo rate shown was for the period from October 8, 1991, to the "date," which was the day on which the next current issue in its maturity sector would be issued.

Suppose that a yield-curve trader decided that the yield spread between the 2-year and 10-year notes would continue to increase from 153 basis points. To bet and profit from this anticipated yield-curve movement, the trader could *buy the yield curve* by buying long $100 million face value for the 2-year note and simultaneously selling short $26.2 million face value of the 10-year note. By using the ratio between the two issues' value-of-a-basis-point to weigh the trade, and selling $0.262 million (equal to $184.20/$703.90) 10-year notes against buying $1 million two-year notes, the trader made sure that the hedged position was a bet *only* on the yield spread between the two issues. The difference in carrying costs between the two issues, however, was also a critical component of the yield-curve bet; in this trade, note that the long position was much bigger than the short position.

On October 30, 1991, the Federal Reserve Bank Board cut the federal funds rate by 25 basis points to 5.00 percent. The 2-year to 10-year yield spread traded at 173.6 basis points on that day, picking up 20.6 basis points in 22 days when compared with the October 8, 1991 level. The trader would have made, excluding carrying costs, approximately $379,040, which is equal to $100 million (2-year note) × 20.6 basis points (profit) × $184 (2 year's VBP).

This type of yield-curve trading, however, is very risky. The two components of the trade are only marginally related to one another, and neither provides an effective hedge of the other. The yield spreads among the current coupon Treasury issues are often significantly affected by various political and economic events. These include (1) monetary policy change executed or expected to be executed by the Federal Reserve Bank Board and other central banks, (2) announcement and deliberation of the federal government's fiscal policy proposals, (3) state of the economy and price stability reflected in the latest releases of statistical data, (4) bank failure, wars, and other international political crises that may drastically affect the country's economic growth and the market's inflation expectations, (5) supply and demand imbalance in Treasury issues caused by upcoming auctions and extraordinary behavior of some influential market participants.

Many risk managers, therefore, consider yield-curve trading as speculative bets; indeed, some yield-curve traders use technical charts, which are standard tools for speculators, to support their trading decisions. Experienced and disciplined yield-curve arbitrageurs, however, do enjoy substantial competitive advantage because they have acquired in-depth knowledge of market irregularities and seasonalities.

Yield-Curve Butterfly Spreads. On October 8, 1991, instead of betting on the 2-year to 10-year note yield spread to increase, a statistical arbitrageur decided to buy the 5-year, 7-year, and 10-year note butterfly spread. With a new 7-year note to be issued on October 15, the trader wanted to take advantage of the pending erosion in the 7-year note's liquidity premium without significant exposure to yield-curve risks. Because the 5-year to 7-year yield spread was at 36.0 basis points and the 7-year to 10-year spread was at 25.3 basis points, the trader bought the butterfly at a spread of 10.7 basis points by buying 1.31 5-year notes and 0.78 10-year notes against selling 2.00 7-year notes.

Butterfly spread trades are less risky because one "wing" bets that the curve will steepen in a particular maturity sector, while the other bets that the curve will flatten in a different sector. Statistical arbitrageurs have been studying the historical behavior of these yield spreads intensively to establish trading ranges and seasonal patterns, and many of them stand ready to exploit any consistently recurring pattern and any significant deviations from established yield-spread boundaries.

TREASURIES VERSUS MORTGAGE-BACKED SECURITIES

Fixed-income arbitrageurs in the intermediate maturity sector have been actively monitoring and trading the yield spreads between the current coupon mortgage pass-through securities and the 7- and 10-year Treasury notes. The following trade, involving a current coupon GNMA, an on-the-run 7-year Treasury note, and OTC options on the Treasury note, is included to illustrate the various risk components embedded in such an intermarket arbitrage.

Background

With interest rates decreasing steadily and rapidly in the first four months of 1986, many homeowners refinanced their mortgage debts that spring. This trend led to a dramatic increase in the prepayment of mortgage loans backing the GNMA, FNMA, and FHLMC pass-through securities, and to a concentrated new supply of current coupon securities. Moreover, many fixed-income portfolio managers swapped out of their mortgage securities holdings into comparable Treasury issues. In the summer of 1986, because of the market's excessive prepayment fear and the supply and demand inbalance in the mortgage securities markets, current coupon GNMAs, FNMAs and FHLMCs traded at yield levels more than 200 basis points higher than the yields of Treasury issues in the 7- to 10-year maturity sector.

Profit Opportunity

On October 30, 1986, the current coupon 7-year note, the 7.125 percent of 10/15/93, had a 3 P.M. price of $100 \frac{9}{32}$ (yield = 7.074 percent). This 7-year note's 3-month carrying costs, for the period between October 30, 1986, and January 30, 1987, was $\frac{10}{32}$. Moreover, the 7-year note's 4-month at-the-money call option (strike price = $100 \frac{9}{32}$; expiration date: March 2, 1987) had a price of $\frac{47}{32}$, and a corresponding implied volatility of 7.20 percent (which was high by historical standards).

On that same day, GNMA 9.00 percent was the current coupon and its November 1986 and February 1987 forward settlement price was, respectively, $99 \frac{28}{32}$ and $98 \frac{21}{32}$. The 3-month "dollar roll" from November 1986 to February 1987 was, therefore, trading at $\frac{39}{32}$, which was $\frac{29}{32}$ *higher* than the 3-month carrying costs for the current 7-year note. Moreover, assuming a 7.70 percent constant prepayment rate, the GNMA 9.00 percent coupon's November forward yield was estimated to be 9.114 percent (note that a current coupon's yield is insensitive to the assumed prepayment rate), which was 204 basis points *higher* than the 7-year note's spot yield on October 30, 1986.

To exploit (1) an attractively high GNMA dollar-roll, (2) a current coupon 7-year note that would lose its liquidity premium in 2.5 months, and (3) excessively underpriced GNMA securities, even after adjusting by the value of the embedded prepayment options, an arbitrageur made the following trade on October 30, 1986.

The Trade

1. Go long $100 million February 1987 GNMA 9.00% coupon at $98\,21/32$.
2. Sell short $100 million 7.125 percent of 10/15/93 at $99\,31/32$ for January 30, 1987, settlement. (This is equivalent to selling the 7-year note at $100\,9/32$ on October 30, 1986 and then "locking in" a 3-month carrying cost of $10/32$.)
3. Buy $60 million OTC call options, with a strike price of $100\,9/32$ and expiring on March 2, 1987, on the 7-year note at a price of $47/32$. (The option's implied volatility was 7.20 percent.)

Remarks

The trade's horizon date was January 30, 1987, making it a 3-month trade to exploit the excessively mispriced spread between the GNMA 9.00 percent coupon and the 7-year note in the forward market.

By going long the February GNMA 9.00 percent coupon, the trade took full advantage of the 3-month roll of $39/32$, in addition to its relative cheapness to the 7-year note.

The trader could have sold the 10-year note, or a combination of 7- and 10-year notes and the T-note contract, instead of selling only the 7-year note; the simplest case is presented here.

Because of its short position in the 7-year note, the trade would have been exposed to repo rate risks if term financing to the horizon date had not been arranged immediately.

Because homeowners control the prepayment option, GNMA securities holders must hedge against this specific risk by buying some interest-rate options. The trader could have bought options on a variety of cash or future Treasury instruments, or on interest-rate caps, floors, or swaps. Again, the simplest case is presented here.

In this example, the trader actually paid a very high implied volatility for the option protection; however, by going long the GNMA 9.00 percent coupon, the trader effectively sold the embedded prepayment options at much higher volatility levels.

To examine the trade's exposure to market parameters including (1) the 7-year Treasury's yield-to-maturity, (2) the GNMA 9.00 percent coupon's prepayment rate estimate, and (3) the Treasury note options' implied volatility level, scenario analysis was performed to evaluate the trade's profit-and-loss status for a wide range of parameter combinations and on multiple horizon dates. The trade's expected risk and reward were also computed, using various probability assumptions on the possible outcomes.

Results

On January 30, 1987, the February GNMA 9.00 percent coupon traded at a price of 103 when the 7.125 percent of 10/15/93 was trading at $100\,^{19}/_{32}$ (yield = 7.010 percent). In other words, the February GNMA 9.00 percent's price went up by $^{139}/_{32}$, while the 7-year note's forward price went up by only $^{20}/_{32}$ (there was a $^{10}/_{32}$ carrying cost). Ignoring the call option component for the time being, the $100 million face value trade made $^{129}/_{32}$, or $4,031,250. The trader paid $^{47}/_{32}$ for the call option, which was worth $^{29.5}/_{32}$ on January 30, 1987 (the 30-day option was trading at an implied volatility of 3.68 percent on that day). The $60 million face value option component, therefore, lost $^{17.5}/_{32}$ or $328,125. In total, the trade made a $3,703,125 profit.

On January 30, 1987, the 7-year note's yield of 7.010 percent was only 6 basis points lower than its October 30, 1986, level. However, when the market's excessive prepayment fear subsided, accompanied by a steady drop in the supply of current-coupon mortgage securities and a marked decrease in bond market volatility, GNMAs, FNMAs, and FHLMCs become attractive to fixed-income investors again by the end of 1986. The current coupon GNMA 8.00 percent traded at a yield level only 126 basis points higher than the yield of the 7-year current coupon on January 30, 1987.

Other Intermarket Trades

Aside from the highly liquid Treasuries and mortgage-backed securites, domestic agency bonds, corporate debts (including junk bonds), interest-rate swaps, and foreign government bonds all have their own yield curves. While basis and yield-curve trading have already become standard arbitrage in the French, German, and Japanese bond markets (and are spreading to other evolving markets), excessive spreads *among* these yield curves also provide profit opportunities to alert and enterprising traders.

There have been many occasions on which the JGB future contract traded at a yield level much higher than the corresponding fixed-side yield of a 10-year Japanese yen-based interest-rate swap (see Chapter 1), and similar opportunities occurred in other capital markets. Arbitrageurs specializing in credit-spread arbitrage continually monitor (1) the government securities and related future contracts, (2) the corporate bonds, and (3) the interest-rate swap markets in the major financial centers around the world, to search for and capture such profit opportunities.

Intercountry yield-spread trades have become increasingly popular in the past few years, especially among traders who base their decisions on the fundamental analysis of international economies. Trades in this category are often done within the same currency blocks to reduce any unnecessary risk. Examples include (1) buying 10-year Canadian government bonds against selling 10-year U.S. Treasuries, and (2) buying Italian Treasuries and funding them with German marks. Unlike basis and yield-curve trading within each government securities market, intercountry trades are exposed to the sometimes significant and often volatile "country risk."

REFERENCES

Breaks, Jackson D. (1987). "Yield Curve Arbitrage and Trading," in *The Handbook of Treasury Securities* (F. J. Fabozzi, ed.), Chicago: Probus Publishing Company.

Burghardt, G., Lane, M., and Papa, J. (1989). *The Treasury Bond Basis,* Chicago: Probus Publishing Company.

Tang, Eric M. (1988). *The Effect of Delivery Options on Interest Rate Futures and Options Contracts,* San Francisco: Portfolio Management Technology.

8

Relative-Volatility Trading in Bond Options

Riskless arbitrage opportunities now rarely appear in the options markets. Arbitrage traders have come to depend on strategies that are based on relative-volatility analysis. This chapter presents some of the classic options arbitrage strategies such as conversion and reversion. A discussion of relative-value analysis in bond options follows, with its application in listed options trading illustrated by an example. The important role that options play as hedging tools in *all* fixed-income arbitrage trading is then addressed, linking cash and futures trading with options strategies through relative-volatility analysis.

CLASSIC OPTIONS ARBITRAGE STRATEGIES

What Is Put-Call Parity?

Options market makers often use the **put-call parity** relationship in determining what bid-ask spread they will quote for a given option. Specific examples are provided to illustrate how market makers quote prices of options on bond futures using put-call parity. These illustrations also show how *arbitrageurs* can use the put-call parity relationship to take advantage of temporarily mispriced options. The reasons for using listed options in the following examples include easy trade execution and low transaction costs, because both futures and options on them are very liquid and they both trade on the CBT. The other consideration is that, as examples in the previous chapters clearly demonstrate, leveraged trades involving cash bonds must take carrying costs into account, and such treatment would make these simple examples tedious.

The put-call parity principle asserts that there is a *necessary relationship* between the prices of put and call options struck at the same price K and the price S of the underlying bond future

$$P = C - DF(S - K) \qquad (8.1)$$

where P = price of a put option
   C = price of a call option
   S = price of the underlying bond future
   K = strike price
   $DF(.)$ = discounting function giving the net present value of the variable in parentheses at expiration

Put-call parity is *independent of any particular pricing model*. It is a general consequence of the payoff behavior at expiration of puts and calls with the same strike price.

Put-call parity can be expressed in many different forms; the two approximate forms that are most often used by market makers to help make market quotes are:

1. Buying a call on a bond future is almost equivalent to buying a put (same strike and expiration as call) and simultaneously buying long the future at the strike price.
2. Buying a put on a bond future is almost equivalent to buying a call (same strike and expiration as put) and simultaneously selling short the future at the strike price.

On August 15, 1988, the December 1988 T-Bond future had a closing price of $83\,^{30}/_{32}$. The three-month risk-free rate on this date was 7.225 percent. The closing prices of options on this contract were as shown in Table 8.1.

Example 8.1: Making Quotes on a Thinly Traded Option

Minutes before the close of trading, when the December T-bond contract is trading at $83\,^{30}/_{32}$, an options market maker is asked to make a market for a December call with a strike price of 82 (December 82 call). Since the calls have not traded all day, the market maker is not able to give quotes based on order flow information. The December 82 puts, however, have been very active and are trading at $1\,^{23}/_{64}$ bid and $1\,^{27}/_{64}$ offer. Based on this market information, how can the market maker make a market for the December 82 call?

Table 8.1   Price Information
for Examples 8.1 and 8.2

Strike Price	Call Price	Put Price
80	$4\,^{40}/_{64}$	$0\,^{54}/_{64}$
82	$3\,^{18}/_{64}$	$1\,^{25}/_{64}$
84	$2\,^{8}/_{64}$	$2\,^{13}/_{64}$
86	$1\,^{18}/_{64}$	$3\,^{20}/_{64}$
88	$0\,^{46}/_{64}$	$4\,^{46}/_{64}$
90	$0\,^{25}/_{64}$	$6\,^{24}/_{64}$

Using Put-Call Parity

From the given information, the market maker is willing to do the following trades:

December 82 put:	Buy at $1\,^{23}/_{64}$	Sell at $1\,^{27}/_{64}$
December T-bond:	Buy at $83\,^{30}/_{32}$	Sell at $83\,^{30}/_{32}$

Using put-call parity, the market maker is therefore willing to buy a synthetic December 82 call by:

1. Buying a December 82 put at $1\,^{23}/_{64}$, and
2. Buying long the T-bond contract at $83\,^{30}/_{32}$.

This synthetic call has a payoff diagram almost equivalent to that of a December 82 call purchased at $3\,^{19}/_{64}$, which is obtained by taking $1\,^{23}/_{64}$ + ($83\,^{30}/_{32}$ − 82). This does not mean that the market maker is willing to bid for the December 82 call, because the synthetic call the market maker is willing to buy has an initial cash payment of $1\,^{23}/_{64}$, which is $1\,^{60}/_{64}$ less than $3\,^{19}/_{64}$. Because the 3-month risk-free interest rate on August 15, 1988, is 7.225 percent, the interest cost from this day to option expiration (November 18, 1988) for the $1\,^{60}/_{64}$ difference is approximately $^{2}/_{64}$. The market maker will therefore make a bid of only $3\,^{17}/_{64}$, which is $3\,^{19}/_{64}$ − $^{2}/_{64}$, for the December 82 call. This bid of $3\,^{17}/_{64}$ can be obtained directly by using Equation (8.1), which states that

$$C = P + \mathrm{DF}(S - K)$$
$$= 1\,^{23}/_{64} + \mathrm{DF}\,(83\,^{30}/_{32} - 82)$$
$$= 1\,^{23}/_{64} + 1\,^{60}/_{64} \times \left(1 - \frac{0.07225}{4}\right) = 3\,^{17}/_{64}.$$

Similarly, the market maker is willing to sell a synthetic December 82 call by:

1. Selling a December 82 put at $1\,^{27}/_{64}$, and
2. Shorting the T-bond contract at $83\,^{30}/_{32}$,

which has a payoff diagram almost equivalent to that of a December 82 call sold at $3\,^{23}/_{64}$. ($3\,^{23}/_{64} = 1\,^{27}/_{64} + (83\,^{30}/_{32} - 82)$.) Taking into account the $^{2}/_{64}$ 3-month interest on the difference between $3\,^{23}/_{64}$ and $1\,^{27}/_{64}$, and because the market maker takes in more cash up front from the actual call, the market maker should be willing to offer the December 82 call at $3\,^{21}/_{64}$. Again, this offer of $3\,^{12}/_{64}$ can be obtained directly by applying Equation (8.1).

(Note that the financing cost for the futures margin is assumed to be negligible.)

The Quotes

The market maker has to consider that the December T-bond contract may trade at a price different from $83\,^{30}/_{32}$. The expected quote for this December 1982 call is $3\,^{16}/_{64}$ bid and $3\,^{22}/_{64}$ offer. The $^{6}/_{64}$ bid-ask spread is really not that wide, considering that the call has not traded all day.

The previous example shows how market makers can use put-call price relationships to help them make markets. As demonstrated in the following example, the actual profit they can expect to make in such trades is far less than the bid-ask spread.

■

Example 8.2: Profit Margin if Quote Is Hit/Lifted

Suppose that the $3\,^{16}/_{64}$ bid made on the December 82 call by the market maker in Example 8.1 was hit by a customer. To make a $^{2}/_{64}$ profit, the market maker can reduce the offer from $3\,^{22}/_{64}$ to $3\,^{18}/_{64}$, hoping for a quick sale to completely offset the position. Suppose that there is no buyer of the December 82 call even at $3\,^{18}/_{64}$. This market maker will have missed a profit-making opportunity, in spite of the superior offer, which is a direct result of the transaction flow. Based on the information given in the previous example, what follow-up trades should the market maker do to hedge risk or to lock up profits?

Using Put-Call Parity

The market maker just bought a December 82 call at a price of $3\,^{16}/_{64}$. From the given information, the current price quotes are:

December 82 put: $1^{23}/_{64}$ bid; $1^{27}/_{64}$ offer
December T-bond: Trading at $83^{30}/_{22}$

To offset this position, the market maker has to sell a synthetic December 82 call. From the put-call relationship, this can be done by:

1. Selling a December put at the current bid of $1^{23}/_{64}$, and
2. Selling short the T-bond contract at $83^{30}/_{32}$.

(Note that the put is sold on the **bid,** not on the offer side.)

The combined position, including the bought call, is called a **reverse conversion.** This position has a riskless profit of about $^1/_{64}$, calculated as follows:

The 3-month interest cost of the initial cash payout of $1^{51}/_{64}$, based on the 7.225 percent risk-free rate, is about $^2/_{64}$. The combined position, excluding the interest cost, gives a payout of $^3/_{64}$ no matter what the December T-bond price is at the close of trading on November 18, 1988. For example, if the December T-Bond closes at 82,

1. T-bond contract will bring in a $1^{60}/_{64}$ gain
2. December 82 call will expire worthless and bring a $3^{16}/_{64}$ loss
3. December 82 put will expire worthless and bring a $1^{23}/_{64}$ gain

The net gain is $^3/_{64}$. The result of this analysis stays the same no matter what the closing December T-bond price is.

Remark

If the market maker has instead sold a December 82 call at $3^{22}/_{64}$, and follows that up by:

1. Buying a December 82 put at $1^{27}/_{64}$, and
2. Buying long the T-bond contract at $83^{30}/_{32}$,

the combined **conversion** position has a riskless profit of about $^1/_{64}$, which is made up of $^2/_{64}$ interest gain and a $^1/_{64}$ net loss for this position on November 18, 1988.

■

Riskless Arbitrage

1. By combining (1) the sale of a call option, (2) the purchase of a put option with the same strike price and identical expiration date, and (3) the purchase of the underlying cash or future instrument for the call and put options, a trader is said to have done a **conversion** trade.

2. A **reverse conversion** trade, on the other hand, involves (1) the purchase of call, (2) the sale of a put with the same strike and expiration date, and (3) the sale of the underlying cash or future instrument for the options.

3. Riskless arbitrage opportunities occur when an option (for example, long a call) and its synthetic equivalent (for example, short a put and short the underlying instrument) are trading at different prices, after adjusting for any difference in interest costs.

4. Opportunities in mispriced conversions and reverse conversions, when they occur, are usually not readily exploitable by most off-the-exchange or non-dealer traders. Proprietary arbitrage traders, equipped with advanced computer technology, continuously monitor, identify, and make money by eliminating such opportunities. In the United States, several hedge fund (private investment pool) operators made handsome profits in the early 1980s by doing this type of arbitrage in the *equity* options markets, while mostly market makers have successfully employed these strategies in the bond options market.

5. Arbitrage opportunities can often be found in the emerging options markets. When JGB options began trading in 1988, sophisticated traders often found mispriced options that did not follow the put-call parity relationships. Similar opportunities can now be identified in the fast-growing European debt option markets.

6. Profit margin, by definition, is very low in these arbitrage trades. High leverage, low transaction costs, and excellent execution are key to successful arbitrage trading. The $1/64$ "riskless" profit in the above example is much smaller than the market maker's $6/64$ bid-ask spread; if transaction costs (including commissions and executions slippage) and financing costs of the futures' margin are not neglected, there may not be any profit at all. Unlike most arbitrageurs doing conversion or reverse conversion trades, market makers often go after bigger profits by trying to put the offsetting synthetic option position on a better level, knowing full well that they are taking market risk on the inventory.

RELATIVE-VALUE ANALYSIS IN BOND OPTIONS

Role of Implied Volatilities

As pointed out in Chapter 4, the only unobservable input to an option pricing model is the bond's volatility between the current and expiration dates. For a selected model, and with the values of all other input parameters completely specified, the price of an option can be computed given the underlying bond's volatility; inversely, the bond's implied volatility can be found given the option's price. The future volatility of a bond, and hence the fair value of its option, is unknown and can only be estimated. Options traders often track a bond's past volatilities, but historical volatility is normally not a good indicator of future volatility because a bond's volatility varies erratically over time. Options dealers and relative-value traders focus their attention on implied volatilities, not because they necessarily provide accurate estimates of future bond volatilities, but because they can be used to judge the *relative* cheapness or richness of an option, either against other options on the same underlying bond, or against options on other related bond instruments.

Remark

Implied volatilities computed from different options pricing models are generally different. While the most commonly used models will give reasonably close values, traders should be wary of comparing implied volatilities based on different models too freely, especially if the models are based on significantly different assumptions.

Relationships Between Implied Volatilities

Relative-value options traders pay special attention to significant deviations from the following *implied volatilities* relationships:

1. *Consider put and call options with the same strike, expiration date, and underlying bond. Their implied volatilities should be the same.*
    This is a direct consequence of the put-call parity described in Chapter 4. For example, the December 12, 1988, closing prices and the corresponding implied volatilities of options on the March 1989 T-bond contract are shown in Table 8.2. Although the implied volatilities of puts and calls with the same strike are different, these differences are very small. The biggest discrepancy occurs at the 94 strike; the 94 put (call)

Table 8.2 December 12, 1988, Data
on March 1989 T-Bond Contract

Strike Price	Call	Implied Volatility (%)	Delta	Put	Implied Volatility (%)	Delta
86	$3\,^{56}/_{64}$	12.018	0.759	$^{39}/_{64}$	12.255	−0.228
88	$2\,^{26}/_{64}$	11.449	0.614	$1\,^{9}/_{64}$	11.771	−0.373
90	$1\,^{21}/_{64}$	11.126	0.430	$2\,^{1}/_{64}$	11.449	−0.552
92	$^{42}/_{64}$	11.288	0.259	$3\,^{20}/_{64}$	11.610	−0.719
94	$^{20}/_{64}$	11.771	0.141	$4\,^{60}/_{64}$	12.255	−0.833

has an implied volatility of 12.255 percent (11.771 percent). As pointed out in the last section, relative-value traders, with the help of advanced computer technology, continually monitor, identify, and profit from the riskless arbitrage opportunities that occur when option prices deviate from put-call parity. Consequently, as with the December 12, 1988, data, quoted prices always have implied volatilities that are in line with the put-call relationships.

The closing price of the March 1989 T-bond contract was $89^{11}/_{32}$. The implied volatility, price, and delta of the five nearest-to-the-money options are given in Table 8.2.

Note that these options have 66 days to expiration.

2. *Consider put (or call) options with the same expiration date and underlying security. Their implied volatilities should have a structured pattern across strike prices.*

Another interesting characteristic of the implied volatilities shown in Table 8.2 is that the volatilities differ across strike prices for both calls and puts. Specifically, implied volatilities increase as strike prices get further and further away from the current March 1989 T-bond contract price of $89^{11}/_{32}$. Out-of-the-money options are much more actively traded than deep-in-the-money ones. The observed pattern indicates that out-of-the-money options have higher implied volatilities than near-the-money ones; however, because of put-call parity, the thinly traded deep-in-the-money options also have higher implied volatilities than near-the-money ones. From a dealer's perspective, as long as the *structure* of implied volatilities across strike prices (relative to the current price of the underlying security) is stable from day to day, that pattern should be used as a guideline for making market quotes. From a relative-value trader's perspective, any deviation from such a *structure* reflects a profit opportunity. In such situations, options with implied volatilities higher (lower) than that of a known structure are considered to be relatively rich (cheap). The relative-value trader would simultaneously buy a relatively cheap option and sell a relatively rich one, hedge away all other risk exposures, and wait for the implied volatilities to get back in line with the known *structure*. A specific example will be given below to show how relative-value traders use this approach to make money.

From a conceptual perspective, all market participants would question why such a pattern for implied volatilities persists. Since all the options in Table 8.2 are on the same underlying bond future contract and have the same expiration date, their implied volatilities reflect different estimates of the **same** actual volatility of the T-bond contract during the life of these options. How can the estimates be so different? And why do near-the-money options have lower implied volatilities?

The option-pricing models described in Chapter 4 assume that the bond market is continuous and prices evolve smoothly over time. These models are not appropriate if prices are expected to make sudden drastic changes, and the bond market has sometimes exhibited such discontinuous movements in the past. (The bond market was extremely volatile during the first week of April 1987 and also during the week of October 19, 1987.) Buyers of the way-out-of-the-money options are speculators who clearly expect the market to be discontinuous during the life of the option; otherwise, their investments would be wasted as their options would expire worthless with high probability. At the same time, knowledgeable sellers are reluctant to price these out-of-the-money options using models that assume a continuous market. Moreover, even with delta-neutral hedging (see Chapter 4), these sellers still face significant gamma and vega risks in such *short-volatility* option positions. To compensate for their risks, sellers will push up the price of these options.

In summary, there are two major reasons for way-out-of-the-money options to have higher implied volatilities than near-the-money ones. First, buyers of way-out-of-the-money options are speculators who expect the market to be discontinuous and are therefore willing to pay a slightly higher price consistent with such expectations. (This price will give a higher implied volatility if this volatility is computed from a model using a "continuous market" assumption.) Second, even after hedging away their delta risks, sellers of these options still have gamma and vega risks that can be especially significant if the market is discontinuous. Consequently, they will only sell such options if the corresponding implied volatilities are high enough to compensate for their risks.

3. *Consider put (or call) options with the same strike and underlying security. Their implied volatilities across expiration dates should not be significantly different.*

Options with different times to expiration *can* have very different volatilities. For example, a 7-day option can be expected to have a significantly higher volatility than a 30-day one if important political and economic events are expected to happen within the next 7 days and no such major events are to occur in the subsequent 23 days. Conversely, if no significant events are expected in the next 7 days, and this period is to be followed by 23 eventful days, then the 7-day option should have a much lower implied volatility than the 30-day one. Some traders, however, argue that the 7-day volatility is a subset of the 30-day one, and that therefore these two volatilities should not be significantly different. Consequently, traders and investors sometimes like to put on "time spreads" when at-the-money options with different expiration dates have drastically different implied volatilities; however, the risks involved in such a trade cannot be ignored.

4. *Consider at-the-money options, with the same expiration date, on two different underlying securities. The ratio of their implied volatilities should be close to the ratio of their values-of-a-basis-point.*

A bond's value-of-a-basis-point (VBP) is its price change if its yield is changed by one basis point (see Chapter 3). Assuming that the yield curves of the two underlying bonds are parallel, the ratio of their VBPs reflects the relative volatility of the two bonds. Bond yields, of course, do not always move in parallel; however, for any two bonds, the ratio of their at-the-money implied volatilities is generally very close to the ratio of their VBPs. The relationship between the implied volatilities of a cash bond and a bond futures contract can be similarly established. Because a future contract does not have a VBP, approximations have to be used. One suggestion is to identify a few bond issues that are most likely to be delivered against the contract and use the average VBPs of these issues as the contract's own VBP. A more precise approach is given in Tang (1988), where the contract's VBP is explicitly evaluated.

A Relative-Value Trade Using Listed Options

Consider a relative-value trader whose job is to consistently make money trading listed options on T-bond future contracts. The trader has a workstation that shows continuously, in real time, the last traded prices and the corresponding implied volatilities of all these options. Based on experience, the trader knows that, most the time, the implied volatilities of the five nearest-to-the-money options of the March T-bond have followed the December 12, 1988, closing pattern shown in Table 8.2. Specifically, implied volatilities increase as strike prices get further away from the current contract price. These relationships among the put implied volatilities are quantified and summarized in Table 8.3.

Suppose that on the morning of December 13, 1988, the March 1989 T-bond contract was trading at $89\,11/32$, the previous day's closing price. The trader noticed that the 88 put was trading at an implied volatility of 12.578 percent while the 90 put was still trading at 11.449 percent.

Table 8.3   Structure of Puts' Implied Volatilities Across Strike Prices

Strike Price	Strike Minus $89\,11/32$	Put Price	Implied Volatility (%)	Relative (to 90 put) Implied Volatility
86	$-3\,11/32$	$39/64$	12.255	1.070
88	$-1\,11/32$	$1\ 9/64$	11.771	1.028
90	$21/32$	$2\ 1/64$	11.449	1.000
92	$2\,21/32$	$3\,20/64$	11.610	1.014
94	$4\,21/32$	$4\,60/64$	12.255	1.070

Table 8.4 A Snapshot of March
T-Bond Options Prices on 12/13/1988

Strike Price	Put Price	Implied Volatility (%)	"Expected" Implied Volatility (%)	Put Delta
86	$^{39}/_{64}$	12.255	12.255	−0.228
88	$1\,^{16}/_{64}$	12.578	11.771	−0.381
90	$2\,^{1}/_{64}$	11.449	11.449	−0.552
92	$3\,^{20}/_{64}$	11.610	11.610	−0.719
94	$4\,^{60}/_{64}$	12.255	12.255	−0.833

From Table 8.4, it is clear that the 88 put option was relatively overpriced. This window of opportunity might last only a few moments. Either the implied volatility of this 88 put would decrease and get back in line with the other puts, or the other implied volatilities would increase as well. In either case, the relative-value trader must take action quickly.

STEP 1: Sell ten 88 puts on the March 1989 T-bond contract.

Hedging away Unwanted Risks. The trader found that the 88 put was a *relatively overpriced* option and quickly sold ten such puts at a price of $1\,^{16}/_{64}$. (Note that each contract has a $100,000 face value.) If the trader did not hedge the *short option* position, which had a delta (in $millions) of 0.381 ($= -1 \times -0.381$), the trader would lose a lot of money should the price of the March T-bond contract take a big fall. The option was only *relatively* overpriced; a short position in it would still have significant market risk.

Delta-Neutral Hedging Using the Underlying Bond Contract. The 88 put has a delta of −0.381. Because the trader was short ten such puts, the unhedged position delta (in $millions) was 0.381. Theoretically, this option position could be delta-hedged by selling short 3.81 March T-bond contracts at $89\,^{11}/_{32}$. The trader would hedge by selling short 4 contracts, and the resulting hedged position has the following risk parameters:

1. Delta $= -0.019$
   With a slightly negative delta, this position would have a small loss (gain) in value if the contract price moved up (down).
2. Gamma $= -0.079$
   With a negative gamma, this position would lose money if the T-bond contract moved up or down significantly. Specifically, this position would lose about $^{4.6}/_{64}$ (computed from actual option price changes, not directly from the gamma value) if the contract price went up by one point.

3. Theta = 5.70

With a positive theta, this position would have a daily increase of $^{5.7}/_{365}$ points or $^1/_{64}$ in value should other factors stay the same.

4. Vega = 0.14

Suppose the implied volatility dropped from the traded 12.578 percent to the *expected* volatility of 11.771 percent (see Table 8.4), a decrease of 0.807 percent. This position should make a $^7/_{64}$ (= $^9/_{64}$ × 0.807) profit.

This hedged position would therefore make the *expected* $^7/_{64}$ profit should the 88 put's implied volatility get back to 11.771 percent. Unfortunately, there would not be any profit if, instead, the other implied volatilities eventually moved up to its level. Worse still, this position would lose money if the March contract's actual or implied volatility increased significantly.

Hedging With Other Put Options. From Table 8.4, the trader would decide that all other puts on the March 1989 T-bond contract were relatively well-priced. The relative-value trader would like to hedge away as many risks as possible, and could do this by hedging the 88 put position with the most similar options. In this case, the best hedge would be to buy five 86 puts and five 90 puts.

STEP 2: Buy five 86 puts and five 90 puts to hedge.

The risk characteristics of the individual options in this hedged position are summarized in Table 8.5. The position's risk parameters were:

1. Delta = −0.009
2. Gamma = −0.002
3. Theta = 0.000
4. Vega = −0.0156

This hedged position had negligible delta, gamma, and theta risks. It would decrease in value by 0.0156 points of $^1/_{64}$ if all three implied volatilities increase by 1 percent, and therefore its vega risk is also very small. Moreover, profits would be made should the implied volatilities return to the *expected* relative pattern. This will now be demonstrated using the following three scenarios:

Table 8.5 Hedged Position in March T-Bond Puts

Long or Short	Type	Strike Price	Option Price	Amt. ($MM)	Delta	Gamma	Theta	Vega
Long	put	86	$^{39}/_{64}$	0.5	−0.228	−0.063	−5.70	0.1094
Short	put	88	1 $^{16}/_{64}$	−1.0	+0.381	+0.079	+5.70	0.1406
Long	put	90	2 $^1/_{64}$	0.5	−0.552	−0.091	−5.70	0.1406

Scenario 1: If T-Bond Price Stayed the Same at $^{11}/_{32}$

1. *If the 88 put's implied volatility dropped back to 11.771 percent.*
   In this case, as the prices shown in Tables 8.3 and 8.4 would indicate, the price of the 88 put would drop from $1\,^{16}/_{64}$ back to $1\,^{9}/_{64}$. Because the trader was short ten (or $1 million) 88 puts, the trader would make a profit of $^{7}/_{64}$ or $1,093.75.

2. *If the implied volatilities of the 86 and 90 puts increased to levels that would be consistent with the expected pattern.*
   The implied volatility of the 88 put was trading at 12.578 percent. If the relative implied volatilities shown in Table 8.3 were to hold true, then the 86 put's implied volatility would be 13.092% (= 12.578% × 1.070/1.028), and the 90 put's implied volatility would be 12.235% (= 12.578% × 1.0/1.028). Using these implied volatilities, the 86 and 90 put, respectively, would be worth $^{45}/_{64}$ and $2\,^{8}/_{64}$. Since the trader was long five (or $0.5 million) 86 and 90 puts, he would make a profit of $^{6.5}/_{64}$, the sum of ($^{45}/_{64} - \,^{39}/_{64})/2 + (2\,^{8}/_{64} - 2\,^{1}/_{64})/2$, or $1,015.63.
   The only risk in this scenario was that the 88 put would get relatively more expensive, in spite of the *expected* pattern.

Scenario 2: If T-Bond Price Decreased by Two Points to $87\,^{11}/_{32}$.

1. *If all the implied volatilities stayed the same.*
   In this scenario, all three parts would go up in value because the T-bond contract price went down by two points. If all the implied volatilities stayed the same, then (1) the 86 put, with a 12.255 percent volatility, would increase in value from $^{39}/_{64}$ to $1\,^{11}/_{64}$ for the $^{36}/_{64}$ gain, (2) the 88 put, with a 12.578 percent volatility, would increase in value from $1\,^{16}/_{64}$ to $2\,^{9}/_{64}$ for a $^{57}/_{64}$ gain, and (3) the 90 put, with a 11.449 percent volatility, would increase in value from $2\,^{1}/_{64}$ to $3\,^{17}/_{64}$ for a $^{80}/_{64}$ gain. The trader would therefore make a profit of $^{1}/_{64}$, which is the sum of $(0.5 \times \,^{36}/_{64}) + (-1.0 \times \,^{57}/_{64}) + (0.5 \times \,^{80}/_{64})$. This result is not unexpected because the position had a very small negative delta. If the 88 put volatility eventually dropped back to 11.771 percent, its price would be $2\,^{1}/_{64}$ (instead of $2\,^{9}/_{64}$) and there would be an additional profit of $^{8}/_{64}$. This case, however, is unlikely to occur because it would imply that the 86 and 88 puts, closest to the money after the price of the T-bond contract had moved to $87\,^{11}/_{32}$, would end up having higher implied volatilities than the 90 and 92 puts. The following case is a more likely event.

2. *If all the implied volatilities, relative to the contract price, remained the same.*
   In this case, after the contract price had moved by exactly two points, the 86, 88, and 90 puts would, respectively, take on the "old" volatility of the 88, 90, and 92 puts. Consequently, (1) the 86 put, with the new 12.578 percent volatility, would increase in value from $^{34}/_{64}$ to $1\,^{13}/_{64}$ for

a $^{38}/_{64}$ gain, (2) the 88 put, with the new 11.449 percent volatility, would increase in value from $1^{16}/_{64}$ to $1^{62}/_{64}$ for a $^{46}/_{64}$ gain, and (3) the 90 put, with the new 11.610 percent volatility, would increase in value from $2^{1}/_{64}$ to $3^{18}/_{64}$ for a $^{81}/_{64}$ gain. The trader would therefore make a profit of $^{13.5}/_{64}$, which is the sum of $(0.5 \times \, ^{38}/_{64}) + (-1.0 \times \, ^{46}/_{64}) + (0.5 \times \, ^{81}/_{64})$. Even if the 86 put's (not the 88 put's) volatility dropped back to 11.771 percent, its price would be $1^{6}/_{64}$ (instead of $1^{13}/_{64}$) and there would still be a profit of $^{10}/_{64}$!

Scenario 3: If T-Bond Price Increased by Two Points to $91^{11}/_{32}$.

1. *If all the implied volatilities stayed the same.*

    In this scenario, all three puts would go down in value because the T-bond contract price went up by two points. If all the implied volatilities stayed the same, then (1) the 86 put, with a 12.255 percent volatility, would decrease in value from $^{39}/_{64}$ to $^{18}/_{64}$ for a $^{21}/_{64}$ loss, (2) the 88 put, with a 12.578 percent volatility, would decrease in value from $1^{16}/_{64}$ to $^{43}/_{64}$ for a $^{37}/_{64}$ loss, and (3) the 90 put, with a 11.449 percent volatility, would decrease in value from $2^{1}/_{64}$ to $1^{8}/_{64}$ for a $^{57}/_{64}$ loss. The trader would therefore have a loss of $^{2}/_{64}$, which is the sum of $(0.5 \times \, -^{21}/_{64}) + (-1.0 \times \, -^{37}/_{64}) + (0.5 \times \, -^{57}/_{64})$. This result is not un-expected because the position had a very small negative delta. If the 88 put volatility eventually dropped back to 11.771 percent, its price would be $^{37}/_{64}$ (instead of $^{43}/_{64}$), and the trader would make a profit of $^{4}/_{64}$!

2. *If all the implied volatilities, relative to the contract price, remained the same.*

    In this case, after the contract price had moved by exactly two points, the 86, 88, and 90 puts would, respectively, take on the "old" volatility of the 84, 86, and 88 puts (the 84 put's old volatility is assumed to be 12.255 percent in this analysis). Consequently, the 86 put, with the "new" 12.255 percent volatility, would decrease in value from $^{39}/_{64}$ to $^{18}/_{64}$ for a $^{21}/_{64}$ loss, (2) the 88 put, with the new 12.255 percent volatility, would decrease in value from $1^{16}/_{64}$ to $^{41}/_{64}$ for a $^{39}/_{64}$ loss, and (3) the 90 put, with the new 12.578 percent volatility, would decrease in value from $2^{1}/_{64}$ to $1^{18}/_{64}$ for a $^{47}/_{64}$ loss. The trader would therefore make a profit of $^{5}/_{64}$, which is the sum of $(0.5 \times \, -^{21}/_{64}) + (-1.0 \times \, -^{39}/_{64}) + (0.5 \times \, -^{47}/_{64})$. Even if the 90 put's (not the 88 put's) volatility dropped back to 11.771 percent, its price would be $1^{11}/_{64}$ (instead of $1^{18}/_{64}$) and there would still be a profit of $^{1.5}/_{64}$!

In summary, if the trader hedged the short ten 88 puts position with five 86 puts and five 90 puts, the overall position would have very small exposure to the various risk factors. The delta risk was small (delta = 0.009) and gamma and theta risks were almost zero. Meanwhile, the trader would make significant profits if the implied volatilities eventually get back to a *normal* pattern. However, the trader would lose 4/64 (the initial cost of the trade) should the 88 put remain relatively overpriced throughout the duration of the option contract.

Remarks

1. This example illustrates the approach taken by the relative-value traders to make steady profits in the options markets. Such profit opportunities tend to occur with some regularity, although the figures used in the example are exaggerated; a listed option (like the 88 put) mispriced by $7/64$ is difficult to find in real-life trading. As long as their analyses are correct, relative-value traders will make money while incurring very limited risks. However, they can expect to lose money when fundamental shifts occur, albeit infrequently, in the options markets. For example, if relative implied volatilities were to make a permanent structural change, all traders would think a profit opportunity existed; they would lose money when the relative volatilities did not reverse back to their "old" structure. Unlike outright speculators, relative-value traders have to work hard to get consistent, moderate profits, but they lose infrequently and their downside risks are limited.

2. Advanced computer technology also plays an important role in relative-value trading. Trader workstations with digital price feeds can be used to identify mispriced options in a timely fashion, which will increase the likelihood of profitable trades being executed. A scenario-driven performance system for evaluating actual and hypothetical trades is an essential tool for relative-value traders because they will be able to perform sophisticated "what if" analysis.

3. Relative-value traders want to take advantage of relatively mispriced options. They do not want any unnecessary market risk in their trade positions. As demonstrated in the above example, to hedge a position on an option, the best strategy is to use other options that are most similar to it. This way, traders can eliminate most, if not all, of the other risks, and can wait to make some profits when the relatively mispriced options become fairly priced. Moreover, if the identified option is relatively overpriced, traders should hedge with options that are relatively underpriced; if no underpriced options can be found, they should use fairly priced ones.

4. Relative-value traders always take profit immediately after the relatively mispriced option returns to a fair price. There is no reason to stay with the trade because it is not expected to make any more profit.

5. Most successful option traders make their money by consistently placing good risk/reward bets on forthcoming relative volatilities. Traders who were long "short-end volatilities" and short "long-end volatilities" in 1991 and 1992, for example, when the direction of the U.S. economy was very much in doubt, would have made some handsome profits.

IMPORTANCE OF OPTIONS
IN FIXED-INCOME ARBITRAGE

As seen in Chapter 7, optionality is an unavoidable component of many of the classic relative-value trades. For example, because of the delivery options embedded in the T-bond and T-note contracts, cash-versus-futures basis trading in Treasury notes and bonds combines the components of local yield-curve arbitrage, repo trading, interest-rate directional bet, and volatility analysis. Another example is mortgage-backed securities, with their cash flow characteristics largely dependent on the behavior of the homeowners who hold the prepayment options. Lesser known are the implicit optionalities of some of the standard arbitrage strategies.

Shorting Volatility via Yield-Curve Arbitrage

An important assumption in all classic yield-curve arbitrage strategies, including local rolling-down-the-yield-curve trades, is that the *shape of the yield curve remains unchanged* for the duration of the trade. This type of trade is therefore exposed to the risk that the shape of the yield curve might change drastically.

Diligent students of yield-curve arbitrage would, after careful examination and statistical analysis of historical data, know that the geometric shapes of local yield curves (yield curves for Treasuries within a two-year maturity range) generally remain very stable within any two-month period. There are obvious exceptions. For example, yield curve shapes often change dramatically during periods of significant market volatilities or uncertainties, such as when the Federal Reserve Bank is actively easing or tightening monetary policy, or during international political or economic events that may drastically affect global credit markets and intermarket capital flows. Similar to options traders who are consistently short volatilities in the option markets, traders who bank on rolling-down-the-yield-curve strategies occasionally lose money on these trades because of unforeseen, adverse market volatility. On the aggregate, however, these trades have historically been stellar performers, mostly because yield-curve arbitrageurs benefit significantly from the high *implied volatilities* embedded in these relative-value trades. Of course, users of this type of trade can hedge their exposure to the change in yield curve shape by buying options, especially when the options are trading at relatively low implied volatilities. The resulting combination trade would be a **relative implied volatilities trade**—buying low and selling high relative implied volatilities. For example, short-end arbitrageurs can use T-bill and Eurodollar options traded on the CME to hedge their rolling-down-the-yield-curve positions. The challenge to the interested trader is to identify the correct hedge ratio, or equivalently, the correct size of the option (long volatility) hedge.

The optionality embedded in cross-maturity-sector yield-curve trades like *selling the 3-year, 7-year, 10-year butterfly* is less obvious to the casual relative-value trader, who would often be distracted by the equally important "repo financing" component of this type of trade. There have been two independent attempts made toward the implicit evaluation of these embedded options. Instead of weighing each of the three components of such butterfly trades by its value-of-a-basis-point, several innovative primary dealers have suggested weighing schemes derived from thoughtful correlational analysis among the historical yield spreads of the two butterfly wings. Such weight adjustments can be viewed as indirect ways of hedging away some of the optionalities, and hence unwanted adverse volatilities, embedded in these classic yield-curve butterfly trades.

TED Spread as a Put Option

The TED spread, the price difference between the 91-day $1 million face value T-bill futures contract and the corresponding 90-day $1 million Eurodollar futures contract, has been adopted by many as the indicator of the market's perception on credit and political risk. Treasury bills are regarded as riskless investments because they are backed by the full faith and credit of the U.S. government. Meanwhile, Eurodollars are U.S. dollars on deposit in foreign financial institutions, and the LIBOR rate on which the Eurodollar futures contract is based reflects interbank credit risks. Consequently, the TED spread is always positive, and a very wide TED spread is historically associated with high political uncertainty (war), economic weakness (stock market crash), or low confidence in the financial system (bank failures).

In the absence of major political or economic events, the TED spread historically tends to widen as interest rates increase and narrow as interest rates decline. When interest rates are decreasing because of factors unrelated to credit and uncertainty concerns, investors are willing to take on extra risks to get higher yields than the riskless investments' low returns, contributing to the narrowing of the TED spread. On the other hand, if credit demand is high and interest rates are increasing, investors are more likely to opt for lower risk investments such as the Treasury bills.

The aforementioned qualitative behavior of the TED spread can be confirmed by examining its historical movements. Indeed, statistical analysis of TED spread movements would clearly indicated the following option-like characteristics:

1. TED spread has a floor limit; it has never traded below 20 basis points.
2. Like a Eurodollar put option, it generally decreases (increases) in value as the front Eurodollar contract's price goes up (down). Its value occasionally increases sharply due to the occurrence of political or economic events that may have significant impact on the credit markets.

3. Like any other option, its value decreases over time, and drastically so within the last month of its contract life.

Most relative-value traders do not want to be short the TED spread outright, because of its horrendous downside potential—TED spread has occasionally traded over 180 basis points historically. Unless the TED spread is already trading at extremely low levels by historical standards, adjusted for the time to expiration (contract date), buying long the TED spread more often than not is an unwise trade because of its decreasing time value. Patient traders who have been closely monitoring the "option-adjusted" spread, however, can often use relatively low TED spreads as effective cheap puts to hedge away their exposure to adverse rate movements in their yield-curve arbitrage trades or outright interest-rate bets.

Callable Bond Arbitrage

Interest-rate option markets have grown dramatically in the past 10 years, and many recently issued securities in the global capital markets contain option-like features. This example in callable bond arbitrage in the Treasury market will illustrate the opportunities that often exist in this and other similar markets.

[1.1] One of the earliest callable bonds issued by the U.S. Treasury is the UST 7 percent coupon issue with maturity date of May 15, 1998, and a call date of May 15, 1993 (strike price = 100).

[1.2] On February 4, 1992, when the then 5-year note with a maturity date of January 31, 1997, was trading at a yield of 6.454 percent, the callable UST 7 percent of 5/15/98 traded at a price of 101.19 with a yield-to-maturity of 6.762 percent and a yield-to-call date of 6.006 percent. As a comparative reference, the non-callable UST 9 percent of 5/15/98 traded at a price of 110.41 with a yield-to-maturity of 6.923 percent, the yield of the callable bond is lower than the non-callable note by 16.1 basis points because there is a high probability that the Treasury would call the UST 7 percent of 7/15/98 at par on 5/15/93.

[1.3] Meanwhile, the non-callable note with a maturity date identical to the callable bond's call date, the UST 7.625 percent coupon on 5/15/93, was trading at a price of 103.56 with a yield of 4.686 percent. The yield spread between the two issues (one callable and one non-callable) was, therefore, trading at a spread of 131 basis points, when the then 5-year note had a yield of 6.454 percent. With the Treasury expected to call in the UST 7 percent of 5/15/98 on 5/15/93, this yield spread appeared attractive to most relative-value traders and portfolio managers.

[1.4] A handful of sophisticated players took advantage of this and other similar profit opportunities. One reason for the occurrence of such opportunities is that Wall Street firms are usually very compartmentalized; "intermediate sector" traders who were trading the callable bonds would not have paid attention to the callable's yield spread to one-year coupons, while the short-end traders would not have followed the callable bonds, let alone spot a callable's attractive yield relative to coupons in the shorter maturity sector. On the other hand, portfolio managers who identified this type of opportunity might not be able to act because they were limited to investing in securities with *maturity less than five years,* callable or not!

The Trade.   [2.1] On February 4, an arbitrageur bought long $1 million face value of the callable UST 7 percent of 5/15/98 (Call date 5/15/93) at a price of 101.19 (yield to call = 6.006 percent), and sold short $1 million face value of the UST 7.625 percent of 5/15/93 at a price of 103.56 (yield to maturity = 4.686 percent). Except for a few missing data, the daily performance of this trade was followed for a 5-month period, between 2/4/92 and 6/29/92. The results are shown in Table 8.6a and Table 8.6b.

[2.2] Financing for the two components of this trade was obtained in the repo market. Because the Federal Reserve Bank cut the Fed funds rate from 4.00 percent to 3.75 percent on April 9, 1992, the performance table is separated into two parts. Table 8.6a covers the period from 4/9/92 to 6/29/92 and Table 8.6b covers the period 2/4/92 to 4/8/92. For simplicity's sake, the presented figures use a fixed repo rate of 3.95 percent (3.75 percent) for the callable (non-callable) issue in the first period, and a corresponding fixed rate of 4.20 percent (4.00 percent) in the second period.

[2.3] For each trading day, each issue's closing price, yield (to call or maturity), costs of carry (under fixed price assumption) since last trading day, and price change from last trading day are all shown in Table 8.6. Also included are (1) the yield spread between the two issues, (2) the daily P&L change, (3) the accumulated P&L since February 4, 1992, and (4) the yield-to-maturity of the current 5-year note.

[2.4] The yield spread traded at 132 basis points on February 4, 1992, when the then 5-year note yielded 6.454 percent. It traded up to a spread of 187 basis points on April 1, when the 5-year note yielded 6.83 percent, very close to the coupon rate of the callable issue. This spread actually widened further to 192 basis point on April 9, when the 5-year note's yield came back down to 6.575 percent after the Fed eased monetary policy. From then on, the spread continuously decreased to a level of 107 basis points on June 29, when the then 5-year note yielded 6.29 percent.

[2.5] In hindsight, the best time to put this trade on was April 9, or *when the yield spread was relatively wide, and the then 5-year note's yield was far lower than 7.00 percent.* This makes sense because if the callable issue is more likely to be called, then its yield spread to the non-callable issue should be lower.

Table 8.6a   Performance Table, 4/9/92–6/29/92

| | 7% of 5/15/98 (call date 5/15/93) | | | | 7.625% of 5/15/93 | |
Date	Closing Price	Yield to Call (%)	Carry Cost @3.95%RP	Daily Price Change	Closing Price	Yield to Mat. (%)
29-Jun-92	101.53	5.172	233.92	312.50	102.98	4.099
26-Jun-92	101.50	5.214	77.99	0.00	102.97	4.102
25-Jun-92	101.50	5.220	78.08	625.00	103.00	4.102
24-Jun-92	101.44	5.308	78.17	625.00	102.98	4.151
23-Jun-92	101.38	5.385	78.16	−312.50	102.88	4.285
22-Jun-92	101.41	5.354	312.83	−312.50	102.91	4.243
18-Jun-92	101.44	5.328	78.26	312.50	103.00	4.174
17-Jun-92	101.41	5.379	78.32	312.50	103.00	4.187
16-Jun-92	101.38	5.419	78.48	1,250.00	103.00	4.215
15-Jun-92	101.25	5.565	235.62	0.00	103.00	4.224
12-Jun-92	101.25	5.569	78.63	625.00	103.00	4.217
11-Jun-92	101.19	5.644	78.68	312.50	103.00	4.244
10-Jun-92	101.16	5.691	78.70	0.00	102.97	4.290
09-Jun-92	101.16	5.694	78.69	−312.50	103.00	4.283
08-Jun-92	101.19	5.664	236.26	0.00	103.00	4.292
05-Jun-92	101.19	5.668	78.81	312.50	103.00	4.285
04-Jun-92	101.16	5.706	78.83	0.00	102.97	4.328
03-Jun-92	101.16	5.717	78.92	625.00	102.97	4.356
02-Jun-92	101.09	5.789	78.91	−312.50	102.97	4.365
01-Jun-92	101.13	5.763	316.10	312.50	103.06	4.300
28-May-92	101.09	5.800	79.11	625.00	103.06	4.310
27-May-92	101.03	5.878	79.17	312.50	103.03	4.353
26-May-92	101.00	5.915	396.36	0.00	103.00	4.395
21-May-92	101.00	5.921	79.12	−1,562.50	103.09	4.332
20-May-92	101.16	5.769	79.07	−625.00	103.28	4.159
19-May-92	101.22	5.707	79.20	937.50	103.34	4.104
18-May-92	101.13	5.809	237.78	0.00	103.25	4.209
15-May-92	101.13	5.812	157.26	312.50	103.25	4.219
13-May-92	101.09	5.858	78.68	312.50	103.28	4.223
12-May-92	101.06	5.893	78.74	312.50	103.25	4.279
11-May-92	101.03	5.928	236.51	312.50	103.22	4.319
08-May-92	101.00	5.962	78.96	937.50	103.19	4.359
07-May-92	100.91	6.061	78.95	−312.50	103.13	4.414
06-May-92	100.94	6.036	79.04	625.00	103.25	4.314
05-May-92	100.88	6.102	79.16	937.50	103.22	4.369
04-May-92	100.78	6.199	237.78	312.50	103.16	4.423
01-May-92	100.75	6.232	158.88	1,250.00	103.16	4.431
29-Apr-92	100.63	6.365	79.46	0.00	103.13	4.508
28-Apr-92	100.63	6.360	79.52	312.50	103.13	4.516
27-Apr-92	100.59	6.399	238.64	−312.50	103.13	4.508
24-Apr-92	100.63	6.369	79.60	312.50	103.19	4.455
23-Apr-92	100.59	6.405	159.36	312.50	103.16	4.516
21-Apr-92	100.56	6.437	79.73	312.50	103.13	4.553
20-Apr-92	100.53	6.469	318.73	−1,250.00	103.13	4.561
16-Apr-92	100.66	6.347	79.60	−937.50	103.22	4.479
15-Apr-92	100.75	6.257	79.55	−625.00	103.38	4.354
14-Apr-92	100.81	6.203	79.54	−312.50	103.44	4.327
13-Apr-92	100.84	6.175	239.02	625.00	103.44	4.320
10-Apr-92	100.78	6.237	79.69	0.00	103.41	4.371
09-Apr-92	100.78	6.239	79.89	1,562.50	103.47	4.321

Table 8.6a (continued)

7.625% of 5/15/93			Spread Analysis			

Carry Cost @3.75%RP	Daily Price Change	Yield Sprd (bp)	Daily P&L	5-Year Hedge's P&L	Accum. P&L	5-Year Yield
297.11	156.25	107	93.06	0.00	6,255.44	6.290
99.02	−312.50	111	291.47	0.00	6,162.38	6.334
99.06	156.25	112	447.77	0.00	5,870.91	6.299
99.20	1,093.75	116	−489.78	0.00	5,423.14	6.385
99.19	−312.50	110	−21.03	0.00	5,912.91	6.478
396.70	−937.50	111	541.13	0.00	5,933.94	6.423
99.20	0.00	115	291.57	0.00	5,392.81	6.364
99.22	0.00	119	291.60	0.00	5,101.24	6.413
99.24	0.00	120	1,129.24	0.00	4,809.64	6.432
297.92	0.00	134	−62.30	0.00	3,580.41	6.480
99.33	0.00	135	604.30	0.00	3,642.70	6.488
99.38	312.50	140	−20.70	0.00	3,038.40	6.547
99.37	−312.50	140	291.83	0.00	3,059.10	6.585
99.39	0.00	141	−333.20	0.00	2,767.26	6.589
298.37	0.00	137	−62.11	0.00	3,100.46	6.555
99.51	312.50	138	−20.70	0.00	3,162.57	6.548
99.53	0.00	138	−20.70	0.00	3,183.27	6.597
99.55	0.00	136	604.37	0.00	3,203.97	6.604
99.48	−937.50	142	604.43	0.00	2,599.61	6.619
398.25	0.00	146	230.34	0.00	1,995.18	6.690
99.62	312.50	149	292.00	0.00	1,764.84	6.650
99.67	312.50	153	−20.50	0.00	1,472.84	6.726
498.41	−937.50	152	835.45	0.00	1,493.35	6.763
99.51	−1,875.00	159	292.11	0.00	657.89	6.722
99.47	−625.00	161	−20.39	0.00	365.78	6.536
99.58	937.50	160	−20.39	0.00	386.17	6.458
298.95	0.00	160	−61.16	0.00	406.56	6.581
198.20	−312.50	159	584.05	0.00	467.72	6.500
99.16	312.50	164	−20.47	0.00	−116.33	6.627
99.21	312.50	161	−20.47	0.00	−95.86	6.649
297.93	312.50	161	−61.41	0.00	−75.39	6.694
99.40	625.00	160	292.07	0.00	−13.98	6.720
99.29	−1,250.00	165	917.16	0.00	−306.04	6.788
99.34	312.50	172	292.20	0.00	−1,223.21	6.751
99.43	625.00	173	292.23	0.00	−1,515.40	6.807
298.48	0.00	178	251.80	0.00	−1,807.64	6.811
199.14	312.50	180	897.24	0.00	−2,059.43	6.818
99.59	0.00	186	−20.13	0.00	−2,956.67	6.882
99.62	0.00	184	292.40	0.00	−2,936.54	6.865
298.85	−625.00	189	252.29	0.00	−3,228.94	6.888
99.67	312.50	191	−20.07	0.00	−3,481.23	6.847
199.49	312.50	189	−40.14	0.00	−3,461.16	6.900
99.77	0.00	188	292.47	0.00	−3,421.03	6.870
399.04	−937.50	191	−392.81	0.00	−3,713.49	6.874
99.62	−1,562.50	187	604.98	0.00	−3,320.68	6.745
99.57	−625.00	190	−20.02	0.00	−3,925.67	6.648
99.60	0.00	188	−332.56	0.00	−3,905.64	6.589
299.09	312.50	186	252.43	0.00	−3,573.09	6.563
99.65	−625.00	187	605.04	0.00	−3,825.52	6.612
99.97	2,812.50	192	−1,270.08	0.00	−4,430.56	6.575

Table 8.6b   Performance Table, 2/4/92–4/8/92

| | 7% of 5/15/98 (call date 5/15/93) | | | | 7.625% of 5/15/93 | |
Date	Closing Price	Yield to Call (%)	Carry Cost @4.20%RP	Daily Price Change	Closing Price	Yield to Mat. (%)
08-Apr-92	100.63	6.392	72.76	312.50	103.19	4.589
07-Apr-92	100.59	6.423	72.86	625.00	103.16	4.639
06-Apr-92	100.53	6.484	218.89	312.50	103.13	4.661
03-Apr-92	100.50	6.515	73.20	1,875.00	103.13	4.682
02-Apr-92	100.31	6.692	73.19	−312.50	102.94	4.846
01-Apr-92	100.34	6.665	73.32	937.50	103.03	4.794
31-Mar-92	100.25	6.754	73.34	0.00	102.91	4.900
30-Mar-92	100.25	6.755	220.34	312.50	102.91	4.906
27-Mar-92	100.22	6.784	73.51	312.50	102.88	4.955
26-Mar-92	100.19	6.814	73.46	−625.00	102.84	4.975
25-Mar-92	100.25	6.757	73.48	0.00	102.88	4.979
24-Mar-92	100.25	6.757	73.65	1,250.00	102.78	5.055
23-Mar-92	100.13	6.873	221.15	0.00	102.66	5.173
20-Mar-92	100.13	6.873	73.59	−1,250.00	102.69	5.164
19-Mar-92	100.25	6.758	73.25	−3,125.00	102.72	5.128
18-Mar-92	100.56	6.475	73.27	0.00	102.72	5.158
17-Mar-92	100.56	6.476	73.40	937.50	102.72	5.150
16-Mar-92	100.47	6.562	220.42	0.00	102.63	5.238
13-Mar-92	100.47	6.563	73.31	−1,562.50	102.66	5.230
12-Mar-92	100.63	6.423	73.19	−1,250.00	102.75	5.139
11-Mar-92	100.75	6.316	73.07	−1,250.00	102.91	5.020
10-Mar-92	100.88	6.206	73.09	0.00	102.97	4.985
09-Mar-92	100.88	6.208	219.80	937.50	103.03	4.936
06-Mar-92	100.78	6.292	73.29	0.00	102.97	4.983
05-Mar-92	100.78	6.294	73.20	−937.50	102.91	5.056
04-Mar-92	100.88	6.216	73.22	0.00	103.09	4.912
03-Mar-92	100.88	6.218	73.21	−312.50	103.09	4.905
02-Mar-92	100.91	6.192	219.29	−1,562.50	103.09	4.911
28-Feb-92	101.06	6.058	73.23	937.50	103.31	4.745
27-Feb-92	100.97	6.141	73.25	0.00	103.25	4.790
26-Feb-92	100.97	6.147	73.42	1,250.00	103.22	4.835
25-Feb-92	100.84	6.256	73.48	312.50	103.19	4.867
24-Feb-92	100.81	6.285	220.52	−312.50	103.13	4.938
21-Feb-92	100.84	6.259	806.11	−4,062.50	103.13	4.931
10-Feb-92	101.25	5.941	219.83	−625.00	103.81	4.448
07-Feb-92	101.31	5.892	73.34	312.50	103.81	4.467
06-Feb-92	101.28	5.920	73.40	312.50	103.63	4.624
05-Feb-92	101.25	5.952	73.49	625.00	103.63	4.642
04-Feb-92	101.19	6.006	—	—	103.56	4.686

[2.6] The historical performance shown in Table 8.6 is indicative of a trade that has some exposure to interest-rate directional risk. This trade obviously would have lost money if the yield of the 5-year note increased rapidly to levels way beyond 7 percent, because the likelihood that the callable issue would be called by the Treasury would have been greatly reduced in such a scenario.

Table 8.6b   (continued)

7.625% of 5/15/93			Spread Analysis			
Carry Cost @4.00%RP	Daily Price Change	Yield Sprd (bp)	Daily P&L	5-Year Hedge's P&L	Accum. P&L	5-Year Yield
92.65	312.50	180	−19.88	0.00	−3,160.48	6.751
92.71	312.50	178	292.65	0.00	−3,140.59	6.724
278.33	0.00	182	253.06	0.00	−3,433.24	6.732
93.01	1,875.00	183	−19.80	0.00	−3,686.30	6.758
92.93	−937.50	185	605.26	0.00	−3,666.50	6.856
93.09	1,250.00	187	−332.27	0.00	−4,271.76	6.830
93.11	0.00	185	−19.77	0.00	−3,939.49	6.920
279.65	312.50	185	−59.31	0.00	−3,919.72	6.935
93.28	312.50	183	−19.77	0.00	−3,860.42	6.973
93.26	−312.50	184	−332.31	0.00	−3,840.65	6.984
93.39	937.50	178	−957.41	0.00	−3,508.34	6.958
93.55	1,250.00	170	−19.91	0.00	−2,550.93	6.988
280.77	−312.50	170	252.88	0.00	−2,531.02	7.088
93.58	−312.50	171	−957.49	0.00	−2,783.90	7.103
93.60	0.00	163	−3,145.35	0.00	−1,826.41	7.018
93.62	0.00	132	−20.35	0.00	1,318.94	7.045
93.75	937.50	133	−20.35	0.00	1,339.29	7.045
281.36	−312.50	132	251.55	0.00	1,359.64	7.118
93.71	−937.50	133	−645.39	0.00	1,108.09	7.121
93.56	−1,562.50	128	292.13	0.00	1,753.48	7.003
93.51	−625.00	130	−645.45	0.00	1,461.35	6.862
93.46	−625.00	122	604.62	0.00	2,106.79	6.780
280.81	625.00	127	251.48	0.00	1,502.17	6.765
93.70	625.00	131	−645.41	0.00	1,250.69	6.840
93.51	−1,875.00	124	917.19	0.00	1,896.10	6.866
93.54	0.00	130	−20.31	0.00	978.91	6.754
93.56	0.00	131	−332.85	0.00	999.22	6.757
280.16	−2,187.50	128	564.13	0.00	1,332.07	6.724
93.48	625.00	131	292.25	0.00	767.94	6.579
93.54	312.50	135	−332.79	0.00	475.69	6.672
93.60	312.50	131	917.32	0.00	808.48	6.664
93.69	625.00	139	−332.71	0.00	−108.84	6.751
281.28	0.00	135	−373.25	0.00	223.87	6.789
1,025.77	−6,875.00	133	2,592.84	0.00	597.12	6.751
279.97	0.00	149	−685.13	0.00	−1,995.71	6.368
93.55	1,875.00	142	−1,582.72	0.00	−1,310.58	6.372
93.58	0.00	130	292.32	0.00	272.14	6.349
93.67	625.00	131	−20.18	0.00	−20.18	6.406
—	—	132	—	—	—	6.454

The Hedged Trade.   [3.1] One way to hedge away the interest-rate risk would be to buy a one-year put, with expiration date 5/15/93, on a generic 5-year note with a strike yield of 7.00 percent. Alternatively, the trader could use dynamic hedging techniques (see Wong, 1991) to synthetically create such a hedge. The daily performance of this trade, hedged by a synthetic put on the 5-year note, is shown in Table 8.7a and Table 8.7b.

Table 8.7a Performance Table, 4/9/92–6/29/92

	7% of 5/15/98 (call date 5/15/93)				7.625% of 5/15/93	
Date	Closing Price	Yield to Call (%)	Carry Cost @3.95%RP	Daily Price Change	Closing Price	Yield to Mat. (%)
29-Jun-92	101.53	5.172	233.92	312.50	102.98	4.099
26-Jun-92	101.50	5.214	77.99	0.00	102.97	4.102
25-Jun-92	101.50	5.220	78.08	625.00	103.00	4.102
24-Jun-92	101.44	5.308	78.17	625.00	102.98	4.151
23-Jun-92	101.38	5.385	78.16	−312.50	102.88	4.285
22-Jun-92	101.41	5.354	312.83	−312.50	102.91	4.243
18-Jun-92	101.44	5.328	78.26	312.50	103.00	4.174
17-Jun-92	101.41	5.379	78.32	312.50	103.00	4.187
16-Jun-92	101.38	5.419	78.48	1,250.00	103.00	4.215
15-Jun-92	101.25	5.565	235.62	0.00	103.00	4.224
12-Jun-92	101.25	5.569	78.63	625.00	103.00	4.217
11-Jun-92	101.19	5.644	78.68	312.50	103.00	4.244
10-Jun-92	101.16	5.691	78.70	0.00	102.97	4.290
09-Jun-92	101.16	5.694	78.69	−312.50	103.00	4.283
08-Jun-92	101.19	5.664	236.26	0.00	103.00	4.292
05-Jun-92	101.19	5.668	78.81	312.50	103.00	4.285
04-Jun-92	101.16	5.706	78.83	0.00	102.97	4.328
03-Jun-92	101.16	5.717	78.92	625.00	102.97	4.356
02-Jun-92	101.09	5.789	78.91	−312.50	102.97	4.365
01-Jun-92	101.13	5.763	316.10	312.50	103.06	4.300
28-May-92	101.09	5.800	79.11	625.00	103.06	4.310
27-May-92	101.03	5.878	79.17	312.50	103.03	4.353
26-May-92	101.00	5.915	396.36	0.00	103.00	4.395
21-May-92	101.00	5.921	79.12	−1,562.50	103.09	4.332
20-May-92	101.16	5.769	79.07	−625.00	103.28	4.159
19-May-92	101.22	5.707	79.20	937.50	103.34	4.104
18-May-92	101.13	5.809	237.78	0.00	103.25	4.209
15-May-92	101.13	5.812	157.26	312.50	103.25	4.219
13-May-92	101.09	5.858	78.68	312.50	103.28	4.223
12-May-92	101.06	5.893	78.74	312.50	103.25	4.279
11-May-92	101.03	5.928	236.51	312.50	103.22	4.319
08-May-92	101.00	5.962	78.96	937.50	103.19	4.359
07-May-92	100.91	6.061	78.95	−312.50	103.13	4.414
06-May-92	100.94	6.036	79.04	625.00	103.25	4.314
05-May-92	100.88	6.102	79.16	937.50	103.22	4.369
04-May-92	100.78	6.199	237.78	312.50	103.16	4.423
01-May-92	100.75	6.232	158.88	1,250.00	103.16	4.431
29-Apr-92	100.63	6.365	79.46	0.00	103.13	4.508
28-Apr-92	100.63	6.360	79.52	312.50	103.13	4.516
27-Apr-92	100.59	6.399	238.64	−312.50	103.13	4.508
24-Apr-92	100.63	6.369	79.60	312.50	103.19	4.455
23-Apr-92	100.59	6.405	159.36	312.50	103.16	4.516
21-Apr-92	100.56	6.437	79.73	312.50	103.13	4.553
20-Apr-92	100.53	6.469	318.73	−1,250.00	103.13	4.561
16-Apr-92	100.66	6.347	79.60	−937.50	103.22	4.479
15-Apr-92	100.75	6.257	79.55	−625.00	103.38	4.354
14-Apr-92	100.81	6.203	79.54	−312.50	103.44	4.327
13-Apr-92	100.84	6.175	239.02	625.00	103.44	4.320
10-Apr-92	100.78	6.237	79.69	0.00	103.41	4.371
09-Apr-92	100.78	6.239	79.89	1,562.50	103.47	4.321

Table 8.7a (continued)

7.625% of 5/15/93		Spread Analysis				
Carry Cost @3.75%RP	Daily Price Change	Yield Sprd (bp)	Daily P&L	5-Year Hedge's P&L	Accum. P&L	5-Year Yield
297.11	156.25	107	93.06	−50.00	4,753.98	6.290
99.02	−312.50	111	291.47	52.50	4,710.92	6.334
99.06	156.25	112	447.77	−132.71	4,366.95	6.299
99.20	1,093.75	116	−489.78	−393.75	4,051.89	6.385
99.19	−312.50	110	−21.03	380.00	4,935.41	6.478
396.70	−937.50	111	541.13	252.29	4,576.44	6.423
99.20	0.00	115	291.57	−142.50	3,783.02	6.364
99.22	0.00	119	291.60	−101.87	3,633.95	6.413
99.24	0.00	120	1,229.24	−303.33	3,444.23	6.432
297.92	0.00	134	−62.30	−143.75	2,518.32	6.480
99.33	0.00	135	604.30	−495.83	2,724.37	6.488
99.38	312.50	140	−20.70	−371.25	2,615.90	6.547
99.37	−312.50	140	291.83	0.00	3,007.85	6.585
99.39	0.00	141	−333.20	282.50	2,716.01	6.589
298.37	0.00	137	−62.11	63.54	2,766.71	6.555
99.51	312.50	138	−20.70	−434.58	2,765.28	6.548
99.53	0.00	138	−20.70	−72.29	3,220.56	6.597
99.55	0.00	136	604.37	−147.50	3,313.56	6.604
99.48	−937.50	142	604.43	−768.75	2,856.69	6.619
398.25	0.00	146	230.34	183.33	3,021.01	6.690
99.62	312.50	149	292.00	−916.67	2,607.34	6.650
99.67	312.50	153	−20.50	−595.00	3,232.01	6.726
498.41	−937.50	152	835.45	534.37	3,847.51	6.763
99.51	−1,875.00	159	292.11	2,458.33	2,477.69	6.722
99.47	−625.00	161	−20.39	655.42	−272.76	6.536
99.58	937.50	160	−20.39	−736.67	−907.79	6.458
298.95	0.00	160	−61.16	−68.96	−150.73	6.581
198.20	−312.50	159	584.05	−416.67	−20.61	6.500
99.16	312.50	164	−20.47	−314.17	−188.00	6.627
99.21	312.50	161	−20.47	−581.88	146.64	6.649
297.93	312.50	161	−61.41	−370.00	748.98	6.694
99.40	625.00	160	292.07	−881.25	1,180.40	6.720
99.29	−1,250.00	165	917.16	560.42	1,769.58	6.788
99.34	312.50	172	292.20	−939.38	292.00	6.751
99.43	625.00	173	292.23	−116.04	939.18	6.807
298.48	0.00	178	251.80	−116.88	762.99	6.811
199.14	312.50	180	897.24	−1,301.67	628.07	6.818
99.59	0.00	186	−20.13	131.67	1,032.50	6.882
99.62	0.00	184	292.40	−512.50	920.96	6.865
298.85	−625.00	189	252.29	1,196.25	1,141.06	6.888
99.67	312.50	191	−20.07	−1,368.12	−307.48	6.847
199.49	312.50	189	−40.14	406.25	1,080.71	6.900
99.77	0.00	188	292.47	−516.67	714.60	6.870
399.04	−937.50	191	−392.81	2,340.00	938.80	6.874
99.62	−1,562.50	187	604.98	1,237.50	−1,008.39	6.745
99.57	−625.00	190	−20.02	497.50	−2,850.87	6.648
99.60	0.00	188	−332.56	141.25	−3,328.35	6.589
299.09	312.50	186	252.43	−260.83	−3,137.04	6.563
99.65	−625.00	187	605.04	301.67	−3,128.64	6.612
99.97	2,812.50	192	−1,270.08	−1,489.58	−4,035.35	6.575

235

Table 8.7b   Performance Table, 2/4/92–4/8/92

	7% of 5/15/98 (call date 5/15/93)				7.625% of 5/15/93	
Date	Closing Price	Yield to Call (%)	Carry Cost @4.20%RP	Daily Price Change	Closing Price	Yield to Mat. (%)
08-Apr-92	100.63	6.392	72.76	312.50	103.19	4.589
07-Apr-92	100.59	6.423	72.86	625.00	103.16	4.639
06-Apr-92	100.53	6.484	218.89	312.50	103.13	4.661
03-Apr-92	100.50	6.515	73.20	1,875.00	103.13	4.682
02-Apr-92	100.31	6.692	73.19	−312.50	102.94	4.846
01-Apr-92	100.34	6.665	73.32	937.50	103.03	4.794
31-Mar-92	100.25	6.754	73.34	0.00	102.91	4.900
30-Mar-92	100.25	6.755	220.34	312.50	102.91	4.906
27-Mar-92	100.22	6.784	73.51	312.50	102.88	4.955
26-Mar-92	100.19	6.814	73.46	−625.00	102.84	4.975
25-Mar-92	100.25	6.757	73.48	0.00	102.88	4.979
24-Mar-92	100.25	6.757	73.65	1,250.00	102.78	5.055
23-Mar-92	100.13	6.873	221.15	0.00	102.66	5.173
20-Mar-92	100.13	6.873	73.59	−1,250.00	102.69	5.164
19-Mar-92	100.25	6.758	73.25	−3,125.00	102.72	5.128
18-Mar-92	100.56	6.475	73.27	0.00	102.72	5.158
17-Mar-92	100.56	6.476	73.40	937.50	102.72	5.150
16-Mar-92	100.47	6.562	220.42	0.00	102.63	5.238
13-Mar-92	100.47	6.563	73.31	−1,562.50	102.66	5.230
12-Mar-92	100.63	6.423	73.19	−1,250.00	102.75	5.139
11-Mar-92	100.75	6.316	73.07	−1,250.00	102.91	5.020
10-Mar-92	100.88	6.206	73.09	0.00	102.97	4.985
09-Mar-92	100.88	6.208	219.80	937.50	103.03	4.936
06-Mar-92	100.78	6.292	73.29	0.00	102.97	4.983
05-Mar-92	100.78	6.294	73.20	−937.50	102.91	5.056
04-Mar-92	100.88	6.216	73.22	0.00	103.09	4.912
03-Mar-92	100.88	6.218	73.21	−312.50	103.09	4.905
02-Mar-92	100.91	6.192	219.29	−1,562.50	103.09	4.911
28-Feb-92	101.06	6.058	73.23	937.50	103.31	4.745
27-Feb-92	100.97	6.141	73.25	0.00	103.25	4.790
26-Feb-92	100.97	6.147	73.42	1,250.00	103.22	4.835
25-Feb-92	100.84	6.256	73.48	312.50	103.19	4.867
24-Feb-92	100.81	6.285	220.52	−312.50	103.13	4.938
21-Feb-92	100.84	6.259	806.11	−4,062.50	103.13	4.931
10-Feb-92	101.25	5.941	219.83	−625.00	103.81	4.448
07-Feb-92	101.31	5.892	73.34	312.50	103.81	4.467
06-Feb-92	101.28	5.920	73.40	312.50	103.63	4.624
05-Feb-92	101.25	5.952	73.49	625.00	103.63	4.642
04-Feb-92	101.19	6.006	—	—	103.56	4.686

[3.2] From the results shown in Table 8.6 and Table 8.7, it is clear that hedging was useful in dampening the trade's P&L volatility. In hindsight, since we really did not need the hedge, the put protection ate up a sizable piece of the profit.

[3.3] For leveraged traders who could trade $1 million one-year-maturity issues with a capital of $10,000, this trade would have earned a return of over 40 percent in less than 5 months! Of course, there were periods when the

Table 8.7b   (continued)

7.625% of 5/15/93			Spread Analysis			
Carry Cost @4.00%RP	Daily Price Change	Yield Sprd (bp)	Daily P&L	5-Year Hedge's P&L	Accum. P&L	5-Year Yield
92.65	312.50	180	−19.88	313.13	−1,275.68	6.751
92.71	312.50	178	292.65	−197.50	−1,568.92	6.724
278.33	0.00	182	253.06	−502.08	−1,664.08	6.732
93.01	1,875.00	183	−19.80	−1,481.67	−1,415.05	6.758
92.93	−937.50	185	605.26	378.75	86.42	6.856
93.09	1,250.00	187	−332.27	−1,812.50	−897.59	6.830
93.11	0.00	185	−19.77	−139.58	1,247.17	6.920
279.65	312.50	185	−59.31	−856.25	1,406.53	6.935
93.28	312.50	183	−19.77	−451.87	2,322.08	6.973
93.26	−312.50	184	−332.31	611.67	2,793.73	6.984
93.39	937.50	178	−957.41	−590.37	2,514.37	6.958
93.55	1,250.00	170	−19.91	−2,460.00	4,061.78	6.988
280.77	−312.50	170	252.88	−174.58	6,541.69	7.088
93.58	−312.50	171	−957.49	1,421.67	6,463.39	7.103
93.60	0.00	163	−3,145.35	−800.00	5,999.21	7.018
93.62	0.00	132	−20.35	0.00	9,944.56	7.045
93.75	937.50	133	−20.35	−1,656.25	9,964.91	7.045
281.36	−312.50	132	251.55	−361.67	11,641.51	7.118
93.71	−937.50	133	−645.39	2,721.88	11,751.63	7.121
93.56	−1,562.50	128	292.13	2,980.63	9,675.15	7.003
93.51	−625.00	130	−645.45	1,402.50	6,402.39	6.862
93.46	−625.00	122	604.62	331.25	5,645.33	6.780
280.81	625.00	127	251.48	−1,287.50	4,709.46	6.765
93.70	625.00	131	−645.41	−614.58	5,745.48	6.840
93.51	−1,875.00	124	917.19	1,668.33	7,005.47	6.866
93.54	0.00	130	−20.31	−105.00	4,419.95	6.754
93.56	0.00	131	−332.85	316.88	4,545.26	6.757
280.16	−2,187.50	128	564.13	1,678.75	4,561.24	6.724
93.48	625.00	131	292.25	−822.50	2,318.36	6.579
93.54	312.50	135	−332.79	87.92	2,848.61	6.672
93.60	312.50	131	917.32	−1,293.75	3,093.48	6.664
93.69	625.00	139	−332.71	−835.00	3,469.91	6.751
281.28	0.00	135	−373.25	673.75	4,637.62	6.789
1,025.77	−6,875.00	133	2,592.84	4,070.63	4,337.12	6.751
279.97	0.00	149	−685.13	−24.58	−2,326.34	6.368
93.55	1,875.00	142	−1,582.72	−25.42	−1,616.62	6.372
93.58	0.00	130	292.32	−20.62	−8.49	6.349
93.67	625.00	131	−20.18	−260.00	−280.18	6.406
—	—	132	—	—	—	6.454

trade's marked-to-market P&L looked ugly, and inexperienced traders might have taken or been asked to take the trade off, possibly at the worst possible moment. Experience and strong management support come in handy when most traders start second-guessing their own analyses. On the other hand, it pays to remember that *the market will always find a way to humble even the best traders*.

REFERENCES

Tang, E.M., (1988). *The Effect of Delivery Options on Interest Rate Futures and Option Contracts,* San Francisco: Portfolio Management Technology.

Wong, M. Anthony, (1991). *Trading and Investing in Bond Options,* New York: John Wiley & Sons.

9
Critical Success Factors
of an Arbitrage Trading Unit

Fixed-income arbitrage trading must begin with significant trading capital and reasonably high leverage on the committed capital. A successful team is often equipped with a diverse set of bread-and-butter trades, to be executed by experienced traders, and must also be armed with the research capabilities necessary to spot new profit opportunities created by market innovations and regulatory changes. Patience and discipline are of utmost importance in securities trading, and arbitrage trading is no exception. Well-defined entry and exit points, stop-loss provisions, and risk-concentration avoidance must be religiously followed. The importance of a superb infrastructure, including an efficient back office and a well-informed repo trading desk, can never be overstated. Since arbitrage trading profits from razor-thin margins, any lowering of transaction costs such as financing rates and futures commission fees contributes to the bottom line. The ultimate success, however, depends on teamwork, including strong management support, excellent strategies, and top-notch execution. In addition, even the best arbitrage team can use a little bit of luck.

TRADING CAPITAL/CREDIT LINE AND LEVERAGE

The Importance of Leverage

The investment return generated by arbitrage trading is critically dependent on the amount of leverage the traders are allowed to use in their trading portfolios. Consider a relative-value trade in which a $100 million long in 13-month coupons is hedged by a $100 million short in 1-year bills. Suppose that the trade generated a $40,000 profit in three weeks. The actual investment return generated would depend on the amount of capital needed to execute the trade:

If $1 million capital were needed, the return would be 4 percent in three weeks; if $2 million capital were needed, the return would be a much lower 2 percent in three weeks.

Financial and Professional Credibility

Proprietary traders working for the primary dealers get the highest leverage because of the firms' financial credibility and the traders' track record as leveraged traders. Banks, which are not primary dealers, are also allowed significant leverage on their trading capital, largely because of their financial strength. For individual traders, private funds, and even sizable investment pools, the process of getting higher leverage is an iterative one; generally speaking, the amount of leverage goes up with increasing years of financial stability and superior track record. Nondealer-based leveraged traders with a capital commitment of $5 to $10 million and a decent track record can expect to get a 10-to-1 leverage in 30-year-bond equivalents in fixed-income securities trading.

Trading Environment.   Arbitrage trading can be conducted either as a proprietary unit within a primary dealer, or through a private leveraged investment firm (hedge fund). In addition to the benefit of getting a higher leverage than nondealers, the advantages of being a primary dealer team include (1) access to interdealer broker screens, which is important for trading off-the-run issues, (2) direct participation in Treasury auctions and in bill and coupon pass transactions, and (3) better infrastructure, including repo operations, clearing facilities, and counterparty-credit control. On the other hand, nondealers often enjoy higher liquidity and better information access than many small primary dealers, because the major primary dealers provide their customers (but not their small dealer competitors) with research, analysis, and detailed market flow information. Some of the smallest dealers often have to offer incredible prices, thereby providing tremendous liquidity to their trading customers, in order to maintain their already low market shares. On balance, however, primary dealers provide a much better environment for arbitrage trading.

TRADING STRATEGIES AND RISK MANAGEMENT

Bread-and-Butter Trades

To generate significant above-market investment returns on the committed capital via leveraged trading, the trading team must deploy a diverse set of market-tested strategies. Diversity is important because opportunities provided by a small set of trades may not occur frequently enough to generate sufficient profits, and risk concentration presents a major control problem if a single trade accounts for more than 25 percent of the committed capital. Having a set of market-tested bread-and-butter trades is important because the trading revenues can pay the bills and build credibility and confidence; besides, it is by no means easy to find new profitable and executable strategies, especially when traders are hard pressed to find one.

In fixed-income arbitrage, a typical set of bread-and-butter trades might include:

1. Short-Maturity Arbitrage
   1.1. Basis Trades: Cash versus futures strategies in Treasury bills and coupons
   1.2. Rolling Yield Curve: Local yield-curve plays using relative-value analysis
   1.3. Bill-to-Coupon: Profiting from mispriced yield spreads between T-bills and coupons
   1.4. Coupon-to-LIBOR: Betting on relative credit spreads, including the TED spread

2. Intermediate and Long-End Arbitrage
   2.1. Basis Trades: Cash versus futures strategies as relative volatility trades
   2.2. Yield-Curve Butterflies: Betting on yield-curve movements
   2.3. Callable Bond Arbitrage: Callable versus noncallable bonds, plus options
   2.4. Cross Market Trades: Treasuries versus mortgages versus swaps
   2.5. Foreign Markets: JGBs, *Bunds*, and OATs

3. Special Situations
   3.1. Illiquid Derivatives: Profiting from mispriced mortgage derivatives, for example
   3.2. Closed-end Funds: Relative-value trades between a fund and its securities holdings

Research Capabilities and Technology

Continuous upgrading and improvement in arbitrage trading requires strong research capability and state-of-the-art technology. The important role of quantitative analysis and computer technology in fixed-income securities trading, especially in arbitrage trading, has been described and illustrated. This section describes an information-based decision support system that would be useful to arbitrage traders. This support tool should have the following capabilities: collecting, massaging, and analyzing price data and presenting the resulting analytics in a way that enables the traders to spot relative value–based profit opportunities quickly; providing timely information with regard to P&L levels and risk parameters; alerting traders to new developments in the market place; and revealing the market sentiments of other major participants.

The overall objective of such a system is to facilitate the trader's decision-making process and the management's risk control. It must have three subsystems to achieve this objective: a decision support system, a risk management system, and a news and technical indicator service.

Decision Support System.   Such a system should have the capability to retain and organize historical data, perform a variety of fixed-income analytics, perform statistical analysis of financial data, and conduct scenario analysis. Although each trading strategy requires different data and analysis, there are some generic elements that can form the backbone of the system and can be used in the evaluation of almost all strategies.

1. A theoretical zero-coupon yield curve derived from the empirical yield curve
2. An implied forward yield curve derived from the empirical yield curve
3. A strip yield curve of the Eurodollar contracts and the associated implied forward rates
4. A forward rate curve inferred from the swap market
5. An implied repo rate calculator
6. A cost-of-carry calculator
7. A system for evaluating embedded options
8. Options pricing models and algorithms
9. Models for evaluating mortgage-backed securities
10. A collection of credit spread indicators

Risk Management System.   The function of such a system is to identify the risk associated with all open positions. First, the system must generate a reconciled position report, including both itemized and aggregate positions in securities. Second, it should be able to reveal the realized and unrealized profit of any trade and each trade's exposure to different scenarios of credit spread, volatility levels, interest rates, and the position's cost-of-carry under different assumptions about repo and reverse repo rates.

News and Technical Indicator Service.   It is important for arbitrage traders to keep abreast of any development in the market that may effect structural changes in the market or the economy. If a trade is executed without considering any such new development, the potential loss can be damaging. Traders, therefore, must subscribe to one or more of the many information services that provide up-to-the-minute market quotes and news updates. While most arbitrage traders do not use technical analysis, it is still helpful for them to know the current behavioral tendencies of the technical traders. Hence, access to some kind of charting service is also recommended.

Discipline, Discipline, Discipline

Patience and discipline in execution are of utmost importance in securities trading, and arbitrage trading is no exception. No proprietary trader ever lost any money because he or she did not do a trade; there may be an opportunity cost, but this is more than counter-balanced, in the long run, by the risk forgone. Just like speculative traders, arbitrageurs should religiously use well-defined entry and exit points and stop-loss provisions. Because the biggest trap in arbitrage trading is a squeeze play, either in credit spread or in financing cost, spreading risk by having no single position accounting for more than 25 percent of trading capital is one of the most useful disciplines.

SUPERB INFRASTRUCTURE

Efficient Back-Office Operations

Committing capital and knowing how to put the money to work is an important first step in proprietary trading. Arbitrage trading, as a business venture, involves many complicated and tightly regulated operations including counterparty agreements, trade executions, clearing and settlement of trades, and repo arrangements. Without an efficient back office, traders get frustrated with the mundane tasks and may fail to focus on what they do best. In particular, a streamlined, in-house repo trading desk adds tremendous value to any proprietary trading unit.

Importance of Having Repo Capabilities

There are four important reasons for having in-house repo capabilities:

1. To ensure that trading positions are financed at the best possible rate.
2. To provide technical information about certain issues, especially tight issues.
3. To follow and interpret the Federal Reserve's activities and their implications for monetary policy.
4. To alert the trader to early signals of a short squeeze.

In light of the multiple objectives of a repo operation and the time-consuming nature of repo trading, a well-established repo trader is essential to the success of arbitrage trading. Such a repo trader should have previous experience in the repo market and extensive connections with other repo traders as well as with portfolio managers; successful repo trading is less a function of analyzing the fundamental value of an issue than of knowing the activities of other repo traders and retail accounts that are frequently involved in squeezing issues. The trader should also be knowledgeable about the Fed fund market because this rate is the perceived underlying driving force of the cost of money and the main indicator of the Federal Reserve's monetary policy.

Cost Control

Suppose that an arbitrage unit employs $10 million trading capital and is getting a 10-to-1 leverage in 30-year bond equivalents. The maximum position on the team's balance sheet would be the $4,000 million 3-month T-bill equivalents ($1 million face value 30-year bond's VBP is about $1,000, and $1 million face value 3-month Treasury bill's VBP is about $25) on each side of the balance sheet.

If the team's relative value trades generated a total profit of five basis points on the maximum position size in a 3-month period, then the team would have a profit of $500,000 ($4,000 million × $25 per million per basis point × 5 basis points), or would have earned a 5 percent investment return in three months. Given such a leverage, therefore, identifying relative-value trades that would make an annual total profit of 20 basis points on the maximum position size would bring a 20 percent return on the investment capital. While this may, at first glance, appear to be an easily attainable goal, consistently achieving such a feat in practice requires perpetual hard work and incredible discipline. One reason is that leverage magnifies losses just as it would magnify gains, and no arbitrage team can survive even a few major losing trades in a year; consequently, untested "casual trades" should be avoided because they are not profitable in the long run, and worse, they are distracting and often represent an unnecessary source of anxiety and frustration. Another reason is that all relative-value trades have high transaction costs.

Every relative-value trade involves at least two components (legs), one long position and one short position. In many options trades, including conversions and reverse conversions, there is a third component, and there are four legs in a butterfly spread trade. Arbitrage trading's transaction costs are at least 2–3 times those of outright, speculative trading. Any lowering of transaction costs such as financing (repo and reverse repo) rates and futures commission fees, therefore, is a direct contribution to the team's bottom line.

Access to Global Capital Markets

In its early stages, fixed-income arbitrage trading in the United States provided plenty of opportunities and handsome low-risk profits to the pioneering relative-value traders. Basis trading in the early 1980s, OTC options and mortgage-backed pass-through securities arbitrage in the mid-1980s, and the recent opportunities in long-dated options and mortgage derivatives are prime examples. Low-risk profit opportunities in the U.S. markets are undoubtedly difficult to find in the 1990s, and relative-value traders have to work much harder and take higher risks to generate profits similar to those of yesteryear. Attractive above-market returns, however, can still be obtained by diligent and conscientious traders with ready access to cash and derivative markets.

Many arbitrageurs would argue, "Why compete with the best on Wall Street in a mostly efficient market, when there are better profit opportunities elsewhere?" For example, basis trading in the French, German, and Japanese bond markets proved fruitful to many enterprising traders while these markets were growing rapidly in the late 1980s. More recently, mispriced options in these emerging markets provided some solid opportunities for relative-value traders. However, with U.S.-trained arbitrageurs rushing in to exploit such opportunities, inefficiencies in the evolving market tend to disappear quickly. Because facilities for securities lending and borrowing (repo markets) are generally not well developed in the emerging markets, traders must also recognize that transaction costs are much higher in these markets and squeeze plays are regular events, not exceptions. It is therefore difficult to be consistently successful in the developing markets without the assistance of experienced traders who are familiar with the local market practice and have good working relationships with the major participants.

With the emergence and further development of bond markets in Europe (Italy and Spain, for example), Latin America (Mexico and Argentina, in particular), and Asia (most notably Taiwan), arbitrage trading will slowly but surely spread to these new grounds. To exploit new profit opportunities, proprietary trading units must have ready access to these emerging markets, and therefore must (1) have a proper legal structure, (2) establish a good working relationship with reputable local dealers and clearing firms, and (3) acquire a thorough understanding of local tax, accounting, and securities laws and regulations.

MANAGEMENT SUPPORT AND TEAM EFFORT

The ultimate success of an arbitrage unit depends on excellent teamwork (including strong management support), effective strategies, top-notch execution, and efficient back-office operations.

All successful arbitrage teams have strong leaders with excellent people skills. A trading manager's responsibilities include the following:

1. *Raise Capital and Get Leverage*
   The initial hurdle for any trading team is obtaining sufficient capital and significant leverage, and this is the first test of management's resolve.
2. *Determine Scope of Activities and Build Infrastructure*
   Management must first decide on the team's size and the markets that the team will focus on. Building an appropriate infrastructure establishes management's strong commitment.
3. *Define Risk Tolerance and Set Return Targets*
   Risk tolerance for each trade, each trader, and each month or quarter must be clearly defined. Attainable profitability targets should be set and updated periodically.

4. *Recruit and Motivate a Focused Team*
This is one of management's greatest challenges. Recruiting mistakes waste a lot of time and money. Experience is crucial in relative-value trading because there is not much room for second-guessing. Because of the high transaction costs involved, top-notch execution adds significant value to the bottom line. Experienced strategists and execution specialists form a potent combination for any arbitrage team. Even with sizable capital and leverage, superior infrastructure, and well-defined risk and reward parameters, however, it is difficult to attract consistent producers because proven winners are already making money in familiar environments. Management's experience in judging trading talent is critical in recruiting, although luck and timing are often contributing factors. Keeping the team focused and motivated also requires strong interpersonal skills.

5. *Maintain Consistency and Enforce Discipline*
Success in arbitrage trading is critically dependent on management support. A consistent management that strictly enforces well-defined risk tolerance guidelines is needed to avoid any significant adverse P&L volatility. Stringent cost control measures and generous profit-sharing schemes are well-accepted management practice in the arbitrage trading business.

A LITTLE BIT OF LUCK

Timing is everything. It is especially so in securities trading. Strange things happen in the securities business, and worse yet, they often happen when they are least expected. Arbitrageurs, for example, lost a lot of money in 1986 because of the unprecedented UST $9\frac{1}{4}$ percent bond squeeze, and again in 1991 because of the infamous two-year note squeeze. Several arbitrage units that started trading only months before either of these events lost money and credibility so early in their existence that they never recovered. To avoid bad timing, even the best arbitrage team needs a little bit of luck. It is good to be smart; it is a blessing to be lucky!

REFERENCES

Bookstaber, R. M. (1987). *Options Pricing and Investment Strategies*, Chicago: Probus Publishing Company.

Tang, E. M. (1988). *The Effect of Delivery Options on Interest Rate Futures and Option Contracts*, San Francisco: Portfolio Management Technology.

Wong, M. Anthony. (1991). *Trading and Investing in Bond Options*, New York: John Wiley & Sons.

INDEX

247